MW00760255

FIRST EDITION
   Library of Congress Cataloging-in-Publication Data
   Austin, Miles J. (Miles Jonathan), 1933-
   How Was I Supposed to Know that God Has Created a Perfect World/Universe?/by Miles J. Ausin.—1st ed.
   p. cm.
   1. Philosophy, Christian. 2. History—Religious aspects—Christianity. 3. Christian life. 4. Spirituality. 5. Austin, Miles J. (Miles Jonathan), 1933 - I. Title.
   BR 100.A97 2009
   230.01 - dc 22   2009036521
   ISBN: 978-1-56492-366-5
   © 2009 Miles, Jonathan

How Was I Supposed to Know That God Has Created a Perfect World/Universe?

The Tranquility Experienced Living in This Medium of Existence

by

Dr. Miles Austin

DORRANCE PUBLISHING CO., INC.
PITTSBURGH, PENNSYLVANIA 15222

Dorrance Publishing Co., Inc.
701 Smithfield Street
Pittsburgh, PA 15222
Visit our website at *www.dorrancebookstore.com*

ISBN: 978-1-4349-1052-3
eISBN: 978-1-4349-5912-6

How Was I Supposed to Know That God Has Created A Perfect World/Universe?

by

Dr. Miles J. Austin

Contents

Introduction...ix

Acknowledgments...xiii

Brief Chapter Descriptions xv

Foreword..xix

Chapter One...1
My People Are Destroyed for Lack of Knowledge.
Hosea 4:6

Chapter Two 14
A Rite of Passage Is Necessary to Change the Course
that One's Life Has Taken By Nature from the Mother's
Womb Towards the Truth of God Understood in His
Perfect Universe

Chapter Three..23
The Significance of the Developing Personality in a Child

Chapter Four 49
Every Human Being Yearns for Peace and Happiness
During His, or Her Lifetime. However, the Devil Is in
the Details Experienced as Psychic Stress, Physical and
Mental Pressure

Chapter Five 87
Every Life Experiences a "Turning Point"

Chapter Six 101
    Jesus Christ, God's Gift for the Execution of His Will in
    Bringing into Existence His Perfect Universe

Chapter Seven 139
    Jesus Christ Is the Manifestation of God's Intentions for
    a Perfect World/Universe, or Our Judgment and
    Destruction

Chapter Eight 159
    Jesus Christ Is the Embodiment of the Perfection of the
    Law Given to Moses Necessary for the Perfection of His
    World the Provisions for Our Salvation

Chapter Nine 174
    Whatever God Is Doing in this World to Build Up His
    Kingdom, Jesus Christ Is the Cornerstone, Nothing, and
    No Other Way Can Be Used to Alter this Architectural
    Blueprint: Key, the Law of Moses, the Decalogue

Chapter Ten 189
    The Life of Jesus Christ Has Everything to Do with the
    Perfection with which God Intends to Rule the Universe

Chapter Eleven 208
    When God Delivered the Hebrew People from Pharaoh
    in Egypt, They Were the Chosen People for the Same
    Deliverance of the Other Oppressed People in God's
    Universe, (II Corinthians 5:17)

Chapter Twelve 226
    Experiencing a Miracle in the Process of Seeking Peace
    and Rest

Chapter Thirteen 232
    The Defense of a Truth that to Many Is Just An
    Assumption

Chapter Fourteen 246
    Several Excerpts from Books and Their Authors

Chapter Fifteen 253
    The Basic Significance of the Main Components of the
    Grant Applications

Introduction

In our world that is headed into the "invisible shadows of the universal dim unknown," we as human beings seem most ready to seek the answers to issues about both life and death only when we are forced to do so. My conclusion in the form of a hypothesis is derived from:

1. My experience as a former director of Disaster Relief for the American National Red Cross. I was always amazed at the unselfish sacrifice shown by neighbors who never spoke before to each other before disaster struck. During and after Hurricane Katrina, nothing of this magnitude had occurred in America since 9/11. Although our government failed us, the generosity of humankind was evident from the heart of most Americans. The point I make here is that when we experience death happening next to us, we respond as though it could happen to us. We take no time to contemplate any other factor than that of a life about to be lost. Nothing else matters.

2. For approximately twenty years, I served as the spiritual leader of a congregation of Christian believers. This responsibility involves (a) Dedication to young children; (b) Service of Baptism, usually to new converts to Christianity; (c) Acting as the celebrant at the Holy Communion service where the blood and broken body of Jesus Christ is made understandable as He invites us to commune with Him continuously through His Holy Spirit; this is understood as our rite of Passover from death into eternal life, the Kingdom of God that is with us presently as we live in flesh and blood;

(d) Officiating at weddings; (e) Ordination of new ministers, new deacons, and deaconesses who are elevated to higher Christian service, Church School superintendents, auxiliary presidents, ministers of music, and president of the Missionary Society whose primary service is to the sick, and those who request other needs from the community. The point I make here is that after being very close to these very special people over a long period of time, I have serious doubts that they took these rites and rituals, symbolic of a deeper understanding and meaning of Jesus Christ, for their lives to heart.

3. A book that was very popular fifty years ago, entitled *On Death and Dying* by a medical physician, Dr. Elizabeth Kublar Ross, must be mentioned here. I mention the five stages a dying person experiences, as she studied them in a hospice, or in a terminally ill condition at the hospital: (1) Anger, (2) Isolation, (3) Argument with God, (4) Bargaining and finding no way out, and (5) Accepting their fate before the bar of divine justice, God. The point here is that this situation and condition could, and should have been settled by the opportunity to join in the communion with God, spiritually, through the broken body, and spilled blood of Jesus Christ, represented in the Lord's Supper, or Passover Supper mentioned immediately above.

4. The lessons of death go where it is scary, go where you don't want to. The proceeding statements lead into a front page article in *The Star Ledger* of Newark, New Jersey, the leading newspaper in New Jersey, September 19, 2008. It describes a course taught by Professor Norma Bowe of Kean University entitled, "Death in Perspective." The picture shows students lined up to feel the softness inside a coffin at the McCracken Funeral Home in Union during a field trip. The class has a three-year waiting list to get in. On this trip, Rebecca Schmidt, a biology major, leans in towards a corpse, captivated by the disfigured ball of metal lodged behind the left ear of the deceased. She breathes through her mask sprayed with perfume, which does little to block the smell of death. For the last decade, Bowe has led her classes of thirty students into the refrigerated tombs of bodies stacked bunk bed style in the morgue, and into hospice bedrooms, glowing with television screens, occupied by the sickly "and soon to die." The question here is how many of these people, either in the morgue or in the hospice, seriously considered the opportunity extended to be able to face life triumphantly, in the knowledge of their salvation spiritually, and eternally, as Jesus Christ was raised from

the dead, and has guaranteed those who believe in Him that same eternal life.

I will leave a few Scriptures here, hopefully to illustrate the gravity of my conclusions.

- Psalms 51:5: 1}"Behold, I was shaped in iniquity, and in sin did my mother conceive me."
- Ephesians 2:8: "For by grace we are saved through faith, and that not of ourselves, it is the gift of God."
- Romans 1:16: "For I am not ashamed of the Gospel of Christ: for it is the power of God unto Salvation to everyone that believeth."
- Luke 9:26: "For whosoever shall be ashamed of me and of my words, of him shall the Son of man be ashamed, when He shall come in His own Glory, and in His Fathers, and of the holy angels."
- Matthew 22:36: "Master, which is the great commandment in the law? Jesus said unto him, Thou shalt love the Lord thy God with all thy heart, and with all thy soul, and with all thy mind. This is the first and great commandment. And the second is like unto it. Thou shalt love thy neighbor as thyself. On these two commandments hang all the Law and the Prophets."
- Roman 10:4: "For Christ is the end of the Law to everyone that believeth."
- John 10:10: "The thief cometh not, but for to steal, and to kill, and to destroy: I am come that you may have life, and that they might have it more abundantly."

Because of the grace and forgiveness grounded in God's perfect world/universe and laws, no human being has to serve out his or her sentence of death from these violations. The Scriptures above are ample escape from the death mentioned here for anyone who calls upon the name of the Lord with a broken spirit, a humble, and a contrite heart.

Acknowledgments

In concluding the work begun a few years ago, I acknowledge the assistance from so many along the way. Lynne Hedenburg has not just been a professional in putting the manuscript together, she has been a friend. My wife Mary's assistance as I used her computer and her knowledge of the software at home was essential. The board of trustees was always available for meetings during this process; Reverend James Turpin, Dr. Norman Van Houten, and Mrs. Viola Thomas Hughes were especially helpful. Judy Goodson, at the Adult Reference Desk at the main library in Edison was essential with her quick locating and printing of critical research that was necessary.

Critical to arriving at this point is my close spiritual relationships as a member of the Stelton Baptist Church in Edison, New Jersey. After becoming a member ten years ago, I am still humbled to be connected with such a friendly and relaxed worshipping atmosphere in a Christian church founded before our nation, in 1689, and celebrates 320 years of worshipping our awesome God this year. Along with the warm and friendly membership, I mention particularly Reverend Kathleen Tice, the pastor, and David Tice, the minister of music, and their leadership of the Adult Bible Class, including Phyllis L. Hailes, Ada Dice, Jim Purcell, Jacklyn Corley, Mary Hallman, Wayne Baungardner, Thomas and Kelly Eng, Dania Velez, and Charles Holt.

My wife, Mary, and I express our indebtedness to each and every member of Stelton that has been a blessing to us during our stay in Edison, New Jersey.

Brief Chapter Descriptions

Description of the Chapters to Inform the Reader of Points of Interest

Chapter One - Every person who has been responsible for earning a living will agree with the need to strive for balance, emotionally, mentally, and spiritually.

Chapter Two - If you have children, please look into (1) the phenomenon of juvenile delinquency, (2) a unique counseling model, and (3) the need for some form of *rite of passage*.

Chapter Three - Failure, or flawed value judgments can begin early in life. If there is a fear that your child may get into trouble, please read this chapter thoroughly to head him or her off at the pass.

Chapter Four - Putting the first three chapters into perspective involves a brief study of the three *Citadels of Authority* as I have chosen to call them. They are: (1) the church, (2) the state, and (3) the community's citizens—you and I. Unless we acknowledge the serious responsibility of each, and agree to work together across the lines of self-interest, we all suffer. A challenge here is to consider the churches, mosques, temples, and other religious orders of our community in our global, multicultural world, as necessary to be involved in setting the agenda for peace, justice, and freedom for all. "Democracy," as a philosophy involving "terms of engagement" globally, has not been the answer when the bases of conflicts have underlying motives of unfair distribution of wealth and power.

Chapter Five - Consider this: the laws of God given to Moses 3,500 years ago, through the *Decalogue*, or as we refer to it, *the Ten*

Commandments, are the same laws you and I are subject to when we break the law in the United States of America.

Chapter Six - It took me sixty years to get my life together. I was licensed to preach the Gospel of Jesus Christ in 1960. I knew during the golden years of the Black Revolution that God had a precise locus of power for the freedom of all human beings regardless of color, income, geography, sex, religious denomination, or whether they were married of the same sex. From 1992 through 2007, fifteen years were applied to focus on that shaft of light where the Truth of God for man was sought and found.

Chapter Seven - This chapter explains the events in search of "Truth" mentioned in Chapter Six.

Chapter Eight - This chapter challenges the authenticity of 90 percent of Americans who say they believe in God.

Chapter Nine - This chapter explains how God, sending His son, Jesus Christ, has rescinded the judgment of death on mankind after *the fall* in Genesis 2 and 3. In other words, the world in which you and I live has been judged to an eternal death because of sin, or our violations of the laws of God. Those sins, violations, have been annulled because the life of Jesus Christ allows us to live by grace. As Ephesians say, "By grace we are saved through faith, and that not of our selves it is the gift of God. Should we fail to acknowledge our condition and ask for forgiveness with a broken spirit, and repent of our sins, or our violations of the Law, we remain under the eternal judgment of death.

Chapter Ten - With all the statements mentioned in this book, there is a danger of any human being in God's creation "sleeping through this change, this revolution" that Jesus revealed in opening the seven seals in the book of Revelations. The key, or the difference, in our lives resulting from the "Revolution" is the significance of Jesus' body and his blood. "Take eat, this is my body" is meant literally, or rather spiritually, not as a metaphor.

Chapter Eleven - When God delivered the Hebrew people from the evil Pharaoh in Egypt thirty five hundred years ago, they were the chosen People of God. This election was based on the purpose for which they were saved, and that is always to and for His Glory. This, God's Glory, is for all human beings of His perfect creation. Corinthians 5:17: "God was in Christ, reconciling the world to Himself." Here, following on from this premise, a discussion is held involving a scenario towards relieving structures of oppression for all humanity in God's Perfect World/Universe.

Chapter Twelve - This chapter involves the actual implementation of a program by the Life for Christ Foundation. This program will involve bringing together the Three Citadels of authority, the Church, the State, and the Citizens of the community for solving the problem faced by the young black boy at the Florida School for Boys in Okeechobee, Florida.

Chapter Thirteen - Critical observations about people's attempt to find answers to the perfection in God's World/Universe, resulting from a lack of spirituality, the failure of the Christian Church in asserting its credibility before the state, and the need to impose the Church's opposition to the theory of evolution when we consider mankind to have been created by an omnipotent, omniscient, and omnipresent God. Jean Paul Sartre, in this chapter, talks about man's limitations and inability to understand where he came from, resulting in the conditions he experiences, including his admission of his helplessness in solving the problems he faces with the disorder in the perfect world/universe.

Chapter Fourteen - A survey of contemporary ideas, and conclusion from other thinkers corroborating the need for an answer to the question asked in this book.

Chapter Fifteen - The basic significance of the grant application.

Foreword

As I begin to chronicle the steps leading to the answer to "How Was I Supposed to Know that God has Created a Perfect World/Universe?" I would begin by pointing out two groups of people comprising a nation by origin, who, after being oppressed by a foreign nation, God exercised his power to deliver the oppressed by intervening, against their oppressor, on their behalf. It should be noted here that they called upon the name of God for their deliverance. It must also be made clear here that God is unalterably opposed to oppression of human beings one against another, however the configuration of the context. So, it is correct to say that God does intervene when the laws of His Kingdom are violated as in one person violates the relation he or she should possess between themselves and their God. Jesus, in His prayer for us, in a few words but over-arching as to the inevitable presence of God in His Kingdom: His word says "Forgive us our trespasses, as we forgive those who trespass against us," (Mark 11:25-26). The key to this understanding is seen in the perfection of the Kingdom of God in every way, whether in nature, or between human beings. The eighth Psalm: "When I consider the heavens, and the works of Thy hand, what is man that Thou hast made him a little lower than the angels, and hath crowned him with glory and honor."

A key factor in our time after Jesus' meaning for us as our Savior, is the Spirit given at Pentecost for power, direction, and for leading us into all truth, (John 16:13). I would like to compare the deliverance of the children of Israel (Hebrews at the time) from

Egyptian bondage with mighty signs and wonders, including the crossing of the Red Sea on dry land to Black people in America, from slavery during the early years of the American Republic. In the case of American history involving slavery, as I have not researched the beliefs of the Abolitionists, however, even if they were not all Christians, they must have believed in the equality established by the founders of the nation: "We hold these truths to be self-evident that all men are created equal, endowed by their Creator with certain inalienable rights, that among these are life, liberty, and the pursuit of happiness."

It is important to realize here that if the behavioral principles and values deeply imbedded in the establishment of the Kingdom of God inaugurated by Jesus Christ two thousand years ago were adhered to, there could not have been two world wars. The criminal justice system would not have occupied an inordinate degree being the center of our attention today, both in its cost to the taxpayers and its devastating impact on human lives and families. There might not be as close a relationship between war and those committing crimes against others that fills the penitentiaries of our land as one might think; nevertheless, if seen in the violation of the laws established by God, through the life of Jesus Christ establishing His Perfect World/Universe, the bottom line is the same. It is the functional behavior of the human being without the Spirit of God available to him or her, as will be seen in Chapter Three, and more specifically in Chapter Eleven.

The imperative is seen in the followers of Jesus Christ as being an alternate people, or a separate nation from the one seen by the world, a counter culture.

The subject for the book and its answer to "How Was I Supposed to Know that God has Created a Perfect World/Universe?" screams out for some resolution, even if by some stroke of absolute authoritative judgment the question would be stricken from the record as having never existed, or as not having any redeeming purpose or value to humanity, or civilized society.

What has made the question real to me is that my values of the world are understood as a friendly place and my existence in it as not being threatened. I sought the answer in either the positive or the negative conclusion. This book is to confirm the positive, if you will brave the task of seeking the plausibility explained herein.

Just after graduating from Florida A&M University, and having been interviewed at a job fair months earlier, I went to work for the Florida School for Boys in Okeechobee, Florida, as a teacher. At the end of the first year, a young man appeared to me as a perfect candidate to be released back to a public school in his neighborhood. The hope was to confirm our assessment, both academically and psychologically, that he would be a perfect candidate to graduate from high school and continue towards developing acceptable citizenship responsibilities. Approaching the school administration for permission to start the chain of referrals, I was turned down with the understanding that I was to have no contact with him, or have anything to do with his case, after he was released from custody.

It should be observed here, based on the perfect world/universe that God has created and who judges based on His establishment of His Kingdom, which is to be recognized as existing in the hearts of human beings, especially those called out by him as disciples of Jesus Christ, this was an overt form of oppression (Matthew 25:31-46). There was no room for forgiveness, a basic tenet of the principles to be followed by those existing to experience the peace, freedom, and salvation possible when the laws of the perfect world/universe of God's creation are adhered to.

I could, and perhaps I should, assign dereliction to those who say they follow Jesus Christ as disciples and daily violate with overt behavior, defying any real association of their existence anywhere near the Spirit of the presence and Kingdom of God. However, there are those who cling to moral values, whether Christian, Moslem, Jewish, or another religion. The charge here is that of one being an oppressor if he or she does not set hands and heart to free anyone who is oppressed by another human being. This can be done in many ways not enumerated here, but would free the conscience of that human being from this terrible charge of the willful neglect of ethical and human values, hopefully grounded in their belief system for daily living.

During the summer of 1978, the state assemblyman from the Westfield Legislative District visited the Bethel Baptist Church as a courtesy leading towards the coming elections. The church bulletin on that occasion noted an upcoming meeting had been scheduled involving the dismissal of the pastor, myself. A disruption of conflicting concerns was obvious at this announcement, because of the question involving my pastorate possibly being terminated, including the financial support for my family. A week or so later, I called upon the assemblyman, informing him of my prior applications and interviews at East Jersey State Prison seeking employment, the prison being in the assemblyman's legislative district. Shortly thereafter, I received a phone call from the assemblyman that the commissioner of the department had confirmed the availability of the position I had applied and interviewed for.

Briefly moving along, the summation of a letter written to the assemblyman reads as follows: "This letter comes to express my deep sense of appreciation for your invaluable assistance in securing the position of social worker at the Rahway State Prison. I will begin work there on July 3, 1978. I am excited about the challenge of assisting the state in this very important area of family welfare."

The following statement was made approximately fifteen years after incorporating the Life for Christ Foundation in the wake of the challenge to me as I ministered to a Baptist Congregation of baptized believers who confessed to being followers of Jesus Christ.

During the fall of 1992, the State of New Jersey experienced a serious budget shortfall. All departments were commanded to make immediate adjustments in positions, laying off those staff with less seniority in each position. I transferred to Bayside State Prison in Leesburg, New Jersey, of Maurice River Township as a social work supervisor III, corrections, in this process.

I would be guilty of failing to see the Divine Providence of this transfer if I only explained what would have occurred in the mind of the casual observer resulting from this transfer. Questionable living arrangements existed for a new employee moving into a geographical area that would be classified as country. I lived with one of my female staff members with arrangements considered by my wife. Within three weeks, I was given a five-bedroom house on the spacious grounds for staff across the Ancora Psychiatric Hospital in Hammonton, New Jersey, at the invitation of the Department of Staffing for families by the State of New Jersey.

Because of preparations to attend a Baptist congregation beforehand, I traveled approximately forty miles both to my office and to the Baptist Church in Woodbine, New Jersey. I worked very closely with three pastors during my six-year stay, leading to retirement in 1998. I humbly refer here to the citations given to me for my revered assistance of the First Baptist Church during this time.

During what was a physical, or material deliverance for my life as I transferred to the southernmost part of our state, I experienced a spiritual conversion in the victory over my human weaknesses. During my stay in Woodbridge, New Jersey, after resigning from the Bethel Baptist Church suddenly, and with the continuing pressure from the congregation in 1989, I underwent the most stressful pressure, financial and otherwise, that I had ever experienced before. My faith in God was tested. Therefore, after exerting strength over the

Tempter in Woodbridge, New Jersey, I was given relief not only from the physical and material stress, but for space and serenity to grow and develop for the task I was to perform in South Jersey during that six-year sojourn.

I have mentioned very important providential, or divine, experiences while in South Jersey, which were physical, material, and spiritual. I accept readily that these experiences were to ease my approach to the work of the Life for Christ Foundation. It was in Vineland, New Jersey, that an attorney volunteered to take the case of the foundation to the Internal Revenue for the 501 (c) (3) Tax Exempt privileges.

There are three factors that set the stage for this next movement in the direction for the answer to "How Was I Supposed to Know that God has Created a Perfect World/Universe?"

1. The young black boy in Florida's lack of support, leading to oppression.
2. The flawed response to the Gospel of Jesus Christ at the Bethel Baptist Church.
3. The experience in Woodbridge and South Jersey.

In this Epiphany experience, I saw how, at sixty years of age, earning three degrees of learning, having the Doctor of Ministry degree from a leading theological School Seminary, I was like Paul on the Damascus road, having to learn all over the way God's world operates rather than the one made by the hands of man. The key to this spiritual experience was that I had to practice being spiritual. The experience I had in Woodbridge, New Jersey, where I read the Scripture "with fear and trembling," (Philippians 2:12), "He that hath begun a good work will perform it until the day of Jesus Christ," (Philippians 1:6), "The Law and the prophets were until John, since then the Kingdom of God is preached and men press into it," (Luke 16:16), "For the preaching of the Gospel is to them that perish foolishness, but to us which are saved it is the power of God," (1 Corinthians 1:18): "For I am not ashamed of the Gospel of Christ, for it is the power of God unto Salvation," (Romans 1-16), "By *grace* we are saved through faith and this not of ourselves it is the gift of God," (Ephesians 2:8).

As I observed the desire of hardened criminals to seek a way to heal themselves, I mentioned the words of Jesus Christ to those who, like me, thought that because of my good health, winning looks, I would gain the favor of many in authority that could boost my career endeavors. I thought that if I worked with all my heart, soul, and mind for Jesus Christ, everything would work itself out. The problem is I did not know I was a sick man according to the laws God chose to govern His world. Where there is no sickness, there can be no healing. Where there is no fault, there can be no correction. Those who are well need no physician (Jesus Christ in Luke 9:12). "How Was I Supposed to Know that God has Created a Perfect World/Universe?"

Chapter One

My People Are Destroyed For
Lack Of Knowledge (Hosea 4:6)

SEIZE THE DAY, FOR SO SOON, IT WILL BE LATER THAN YOU THINK.

IN THE FINAL ANALYSIS, GETTING ONE'S LIFE TO-GETHER WILL RESULT IN EITHER ETERNAL LIFE OR ETERNAL DEATH. Ecclesiastes 1:1 and 14: "Remember now thy creator in the days of thy youth while the evil days come not, nor the years draw nigh, when thou shall say, I have no pleasure in them. For God shall bring every work into judgment, whether it be good, or whether it be evil."

THE PROBLEM: Because of the lack of spiritual enabling, one depends on an employer, employment, someone or something, rather than developing strength through "self enabling" against all odds, even physical death.

THE TRAGEDY OF BRINGING OUR LIVES TOGETHER WITHOUT THE POWER AND SPIRIT OF GOD

I left the employment of a wonderful organization in order to attempt the goal of bringing an answer to the claim of oppression of a young boy in Florida. The attempt was to free him up to see how he might ultimately accept the call to true citizenship, assisting others as he had been assisted, who possibly needed him as he had needed others.

Leaving employment that allowed me financial security required a sacrifice on my part. I had to make a choice involving the time I had left in my life, my health that I understood would not be good always, and the question of how much time I had left to do what I think should have been done to help the young man in Florida, thereby, believe it or not, save my own life. "The wages of sin is death, but the gift of God is eternal life," (Romans 6:23). Even as I left under pressure of being fired, I had no desire to stay; as a matter of fact, I received *a* possible opportunity of a job from a member of the administration. My response was that there was not enough money in the world to deter me from my objective immediately ahead.

THIS TASK INVOLVED LOOKING AT THE WORLD AS IT SHOULD BE RATHER THAN HOW IT IS.

The familiar jargon is "It is what it is"; I say it is more than what it appears to be.

THE TRAGEDY OF BRINGING OUR LIVES TOGETHER WITHOUT THE POWER AND SPIRIT OF GOD

A: THE LAWS OF THE BIBLE: GOD'S WORD

The *fall* of man is presented clearly in a lecture dated December 30, 2003 in Chapter Three, using hypothetical references to matters involving those who are incarcerated after having been judged to have violated the laws of God and were sentenced by a human judge, or a judge of the criminal justice system for these violations. Man's failure, even as we speak, to have dominion of God's World/Universe, because of the *fall*, results in God's Love and *grace*, as opposed to our proper and admitted sentence of justice and judgment of death. This will be referred to as "the deferment of the sentence of our death," but not being exonerated of the charge that, in our own mind and spirit, is still outstanding, resulting in or separation from God. Hebrews 9:27 says, "It is appointed unto man once to die, but there must be a judgment at the last death that we experience." In other words, as Jesus has promised, John 11:25-26 et. al., "Jesus said unto her, I am the resurrection and the life, he that believeth in me though he were dead, yet shall he live, and he that liveth and believeth in me shall never die." Romans 10:4 states: "For Christ is the end of the law for everyone that believeth." I Corinthians 15:22: "Everyone dies because all of us are related to Adam, the first man. But all who are related to Christ, the other man, will be given new life. But there is an order to this resurrection: Christ was raised first; then when Christ comes back, all His people will be raised. After that, the end will come, when

He will turn the Kingdom over to the Father, having put down all enemies of every kind. Christ must reign until He humbles all His enemies beneath His feet. And the last enemy to be destroyed is death" (Verses from the Life Application Bible).

B: BASED ON THE LAWS OF GOD, MAKING A LIVING CAN BE A GOOD WAY TO LOSE ONE'S LIFE:

If I had not struggled beyond the paradigm of the life that I experienced making a living in the workplace, I would have become cynical, angry, and vindictive towards those I always found in my workplace. The subject of this chapter puts the Sermon on the Mount by Jesus Christ entirely inescapable to the life of his followers. For the casual observer, this sermon dictates that a follower of Jesus must live everyday as though he or she is experiencing the actual Spirit presence of the Kingdom of God. In other words, a follower of Jesus Christ must be prepared to "turn the other cheek" when attacked, and love those who hate a disciple.

C: THE EMPLOYMENT THAT ONE SEEKS SHOULD BE THE RESULT OF A SEARCH FOR THE MEANING OF "LIFE" RATHER THAN JUST TO MAKE A LIVING. THE ENDS SHOULD JUSTIFY THE MEANS.

My extended approach at the doctorate level of theological education involved and still involves the connecting of God the Father, and the following dispensation of the Son, Jesus Christ, and the third dispensation of the Holy Spirit. This third dispensation of the Spirit of God involves human beings, every human being, "pressing into this Presence of God, also referred to as His Kingdom, which is omnipresent and eternal. Also, these three dispensations are directed towards saving mankind and his world, that whether man knows it or not, belong to God.

D: OBSTACLES "BY NATURE," GET IN THE WAY OF MAKING A "LIFE" RATHER THAN A LIVING: THE CHALLENGE IS EITHER TO OVERCOME THE OBSTACLES, OR FAIL IN LIFE, TO DIE.
THIS CHALLENGE IS TO MS. CAROL LIN.

I could not have found a clearer reference to my research for the solution to the young boy in Florida not being able to get help in reintegration into his community from prison. The frustration of Ms. Carol Lin, involving care for the son of Mr. and Mrs. Christopher

Reeves, who died within a year of each other, is described in detail in the eleventh chapter.

I consider the case involving Ms. Lin to have providential applications from God for my presentation of the steps of my journey towards authentic Christian discipleship.

E: THIS INVOLVES CONTENT DIRECTLY RELATED TO THE DOCTRINE AND ACADEMIC RESEARCH AND STUDY FOR MY DISSERTATION PRESENTED TO DREW UNIVERSITY, "TO INCREASE THE CONGREGATION'S UNDERSTANDING OF CHRISTIAN DISCIPLESHIP."

The essential need for the True Church of God through Jesus Christ, and the Holy Spirit which authenticates the Kingdom of Heaven in our world and time, is a counter culture to the dominant non-believing culture. This counter culture would, in fact and truth, be the body of Jesus Christ in the world. There is a juxtaposition between church and state, and the three citadels of authority: church, state, and people (Vox Populi-Voice of the People). The need for this counter culture is to point out the systemic flaw in man's nature resulting from the *fall* outlined in Genesis 2 and 3, and to make clear the deceptions in man's earthly planning involving race, geography, economics, sex, or any other factor in the homo sapiens nomenclature.

PART A
THE LAWS OF THE BIBLE - GOD'S WORD

These universal laws establish judgment, justice, peace, love, joy, forgiveness, grace, truth, salvation, and eternal life. They touch and regulate all facets of humanity. These laws are obeyed only as man's primary concern is obedience by first becoming aware of his need first to see himself as God sees him. And this posture is understood as repentance. Whenever man becomes repentant, he can then obey the laws and words of God—THE ONLY WAY THIS CAN BE ACCOMPLISHED IS TO ACKNOWLEDGE GOD'S GIFT FOR THIS PURPOSE, HIS SON, AND OUR SAVIOR, JESUS CHRIST.

The poem by J. A. Alexander: It seems cogent to state verse two:
There is a line, by us unseen,
which crosses every path,
which marks the boundary between
God's mercy, and his wrath.

Considering the fact that the above is critical to the establishment of God's Kingdom on Earth, it is important here to see and understand what God considers essential after the above. Matthew 25:31-46 give the most extensively detailed description of man's interpersonal responsibilities in living in the World/Universe Created by God.

On these responsibilities by man hinges the Law and the Prophets as stated by Jesus in Matthew 22:36-40: "Master, which is the great commandment in the law? Jesus said unto him, Thou shalt love the Lord thy God with all thy heart, and with all thy soul, and with all thy mind. this is the first and great commandment. And the second is like unto it, thou shalt love thy neighbor as thyself. On these two commandments hang all the law and the prophets."

Obedience to the Law, as stated above, resulting in justice, peace, truth, and so on, is possible because of what the Spirit of God made possible through Jesus as Savior, as stated above. Jesus Christ is our example or model for our Salvation (John 16:6-13), "But because I have said these things unto you, sorrow hath filled your heart. Nevertheless I tell you the truth; it is expedient for you that I go away; for if I go not away, the Comforter will not come unto you; but if I depart, I will send him unto you. And when he is come, he will convince the world of its sin, and of God's righteousness, and of the coming judgment. The world's sin is unbelief in me. Righteousness is available because I go to the Father, and you will see me no more. Judgment will come because the prince of this world has already been judged. Oh, there is so much more I want to tell you, but you can't bear it now. When the spirit of truth comes, he will guide you into all truth."

Romans 10 verses 1 through 4 are very significant for understanding the laws of God. But I mention verse ten here: "For Christ has accomplished the whole purpose of the law. All who believe in him are made right with God" (Life Application Bible).

I think belief here in the above verse 4 of Romans 10 can be mistaken in the realm of salvation from sin, or the violation of the laws of God. Obedience to the laws of God can only be achieved if a human being understands how Jesus Christ acted when he was in flesh and blood. Before I state the next two verses from Paul, it is clear that we must act in this world as though we have been sentenced to the death that Satan has in store for us if we violate the laws of God:

(1) Philippians 2:5, "Your attitude should be the same that Christ Jesus had"; verse 8, "And in human form he obediently humbled himself even further by dying a

criminal's death on the cross"; verse 9, "Because of this, God raised him up to the heights of heaven and gave him a name that is above every name."

(2) Philippians 3:7-11, "I once thought all these things were so very important, but now I consider them worthless because of what Christ has done. Yes, everything else is worthless when compared with the priceless gain on knowing Christ Jesus my Lord. I have discarded everything else, counting it all as garbage, so that I may have Christ and become one with him. I no longer count on my own goodness or my ability to obey God's law, but I trust Christ to save me. For God's way of making us right with himself depends on faith. As a result, I can really know Christ and experience the mighty power that raised him from the dead. I can learn what it means to suffer with him, sharing in his death, so that, somehow, I can experience the resurrection of the dead!" (Life Application Bible).

As stated in the first paragraph, obey God and keep His laws that are given to us by Him to accomplish the demands of Jesus in Matthew 25:31-46; otherwise, we do not have the same mind and attitude that was in Christ Jesus.

THE GOSPEL, THE GOOD NEWS: the Spirit of God that we experience by calling upon Him in prayer is God listening and our experiencing Him as Paul says above. The Law and prophets were until John "since that time the Kingdom of God is preached, and every man presseth into it" (Luke 16:16: KJV). In other words, if we pray to God with the above considerations in mind, we are pressing into the Kingdom of God. Then, it can also be concluded that if are we not praying as explained here, we are not pressing into the Kingdom of God.

1. God has not given us the spirit of fear, but of power, love, and of a sound mind.
2. Greater is He that is in you, than he that is in the world.
3. By *grace* we are saved through faith, and this not of ourselves, it is the gift of God.
4. Philippians 1:6: "Being confident of this very thing, that he which hath begun a good work in you will perform it until the day of Jesus Christ."
5. Philippians 2:12: "Wherefore, my beloved, as ye have always obeyed, not as in my presence only, but now much more in

my absence, work out your own salvation with fear and trembling" (KJV).

6. Hebrews 11:6: "But without faith it's impossible to please Him; for he that cometh to God must believe that He is, and that He is a rewarder of them that diligently seek Him."

PART B
EXPERIENCING THE CONTRADICTION OF THE LAWS OF GOD, WHILE PREPARING, THROUGH PUBLIC EDUCATION, TO "MAKE A LIVING"

A JOB, A CAREER, A LIVELIHOOD IS THE NORMAL PSYCHOLOGICAL ENTRENCHMENT FOR SURVIVAL AND NORM SETTING BEHAVIOR IN A CULTURE.

Although religion is not necessarily a survival pursuit as it should be, this is what most likely allow human beings to develop a paradigm of cognitive reality. Psychologists, not theologians, would agree that each person, based on perception of what is real about life, creates his or her own idea of how he or she should act in order to survive. In Chapter Eleven, reference is made to insights relating to Ms. Carol Lin's obsession in light of society's and the universe's seeming lack of control and oversight by anyone in authority and power.

As I mentioned there, her concern was with the young son of Mr. and Mrs. Christopher Reeves being left alone as both parents are deceased almost within a year of each other. My reason for this chapter is the very same concern Ms. Lin has, and which I had, leading to "How Was I Supposed to Know?" My concern was the young boy in Florida who was not allowed to get help for his return home from prison. Along with that are all those people I preached to about an Almighty God, in Washington DC, while attending Howard University, the top Black University in the world, in the greatest nation in the world, during the civil rights movement, and the defining moments of our great republic.

There are four statements to be referred to as we move forward that will be helpful in this chapter. I mention them here to preface "Obstacles to Success, or the Acceptance of Failure." I resigned a rather interesting and challenging position as youth director of the Princeton, New Jersey, YMCA in 1967. This is the first statement in that regard:

(1) "I will chance to coin a phrase that I think has a deep sense of truth. The fact that a person is paid a lot of money for a particular job does not mean that the accomplishment of that

7

job brings happiness to the one who performs it, or to society as a whole."

(2) The second case of disappointment in trying to make a living I experienced as project director of the Essex County Neighborhood Youth Corps, sponsored by the Essex County Youth and Economic Rehabilitation Commission in 1968. The political flurries of backstabbing and false accusations among the "players" in this experience were nightmarish, and emotionally and mentally suffocating. A person from the East Orange Political Action Program came to my office and informed me that he was sent there by the Commission to take my position. I was fired, and although I appealed through one of the best law firms in East Orange, it was all politics. Someone else experienced hardships surviving due to the lack of employment, and had better political connections than I did.

"Although my association in that job was in line with the assertion that I seemed destined in my career to be involved with both church and state, I felt at that time that there was just too much politics in Essex County for me. Where there is too much politics, it is hard to measure success based on any system of management by objectives."

(3) The third occasion involving motivation toward success, or resignation in failure, came while I was the pastor of the Bethel Baptist Church from 1974 to 1989. On October 13, 1977, I began to receive correspondence from strong organized elements of my church, both officers and members. Another letter of the same note was received on November 11, and on November 17, I received a letter from Attorney Stanley Lewis of Plainfield, New Jersey, to the effect that he represented the Bethel Baptist Church vs. Reverend Miles J. Austin. On December 16, 1977, I received a letter from Attorney Walter Cohn whom I had known and worked with for years that on yesterday, as it were, December 15, Superior Court Judge Harold Ackerman signed a Show Cause involving the matter.

"At this point, I would like to risk an oversimplification by making the following statement: "Because of the stark contradictions within the Christian Church, the 'Body of Christ' the Life for Christ Foundation, Inc. became relevant, if not essential."

(4) The fourth experience in this chapter on the dichotomy between working for a living and living for a work that brings "life" is as follows: Beginning August of 2000, I began a four-and-a-half year employment with the Community Education Centers of America at Talbot Hall in Kearney, New Jersey. Sometime around the middle of December 2005, I was challenged because I did not work quickly enough and efficiently enough preparing diagnostic case files. Although I do not believe that was the real reason for the challenge, I resigned anyway. My reason was that I had been putting off this decision in light of putting all my time into the Life for Christ Foundation. This following fourth statement sets me in line to come full circle with my original concerns in ministry, particularly as this relates to the Christian Church not being prepared to assist the young black boy return to a stable life in his community.

How Was I Supposed to Know? includes not only the full circle for me, but also for Ms. Carol Lin, considering that she has a long way to go. The following statement was made to a top executive of the corporation who obviously thought I was upset, or worse, was stressed from losing my livelihood, or so he thought.

(5) "From now on, I will be working for God only. Mr. Clancy does not have enough money to deter me from this decision. If he gave me a blank check, I'd have to turn him down, because I'm not turning God down. As a matter of fact, there is not enough money in the world to prevent me from moving on."

The problems I have put forward here that involves the process of working to take care of oneself can be left as problems if they are not overlaid with a purpose for living that goes beyond money, paying bills, and modeling other person's lives. I would chance to conclude that had Ms. Lin developed a paradigm for her life that was existential, or was daily considered as being more important than anything else in her life, she would have thought of a way to find out more about young Mr. Reeves's situation, and how she could help. Instead of lighting a candle, she appeared to curse the darkness. I could have done that down in Florida by remaining there and perhaps make a good living. For that young boy I speak of down there, I would have been cursing the situation instead searching for the solution, which I always knew was hid with God, in Jesus Christ, now revealed.

Actually, I could feel the stress and complexity of Ms. Lin in her assessment of young Mr. Reeves's situation. That stress, pressure, and in fact oppression, can be multiplied a million times over depending on the human beings who fail to see the perfection of God's Creation.

PART C
SEARCHING FOR THE ANSWER TO LIFE IN THE PROCESS OF MAKING A LIVING THROUGH PUBLIC EMPLOYMENT

There are two reasons why this chapter is central to *How Was I Supposed to Know?*

First, it ought to be made clear that holding just any job can lead to confusion, stress, mental illness, and possibly death. Enough said. Nevertheless, when we add the "reality" of the people we work with who possibly never had an idea of what is real and what is not, the first statement stands to reason.

The second reason is as follows: We would not be able to complete the circle of "How Was I Supposed to Know?" if we left out the important, if not essential, nature of the need to have a job. What we really need is the lifestyle based on priorities of a "reality" based on Truth as to what our journey in life is really all about.

This is where we speak of the cognitive awareness of the quality of life. I Timothy 4:8 states, "For bodily exercise profiteth little: but Godliness is profitable unto all things, having promise of the life that now is, and of that which is to come." Chapter 6:7-10: "For we brought nothing into this world, and it is certain we can carry nothing out. And having food and raiment let us be therewith content. But they that will be rich fall into temptation and a snare, and into many foolish and hurtful lusts, which drown men in destruction and perdition. For the love of money is the root of all evil: which while some coveted after, they have erred from the faith, and pierced themselves through with many sorrows."

At this point, it would be relevant to look at the four statements above in Part B, excerpted from a document of record relating to former positions of employment:

- I deliberated quietly before making up my mind to spend the four years following military service getting an education. The times seemed to demand it.
- I chose to work with juveniles who were adjudicated delinquent.

- The times again dictated that I extend my education at divinity school.
- I felt the need to get involved in the community in order to be a part of the solution that the times made obvious.
- I felt the need to be a part of a community organization that had as its mission the Christianizing of society.
- I attempted to move up within such an organization and was blocked by contradictions, four of which are mentioned in Part B.
- Although I never interpreted the involvement of the organized Christian Church as intricately applying its power to the "Problems of the Time," I knew that God had ordained the answer, and that Jesus Christ had brought the Kingdom of God into reality with power and glory. My continued theological education led me beyond the civil rights movement toward the power that Jesus Christ meant to apply to "the Problems of Our Time."
- Jesus warns us about the future crisis: St. Luke 12:54-59 have it: "Then Jesus turned to the crowd and said, 'When you see clouds beginning to form in the west, you say here comes a shower.' and you are right. When the south wind blows, you say, 'Today will be a scorcher.' and it is. You hypocrites! You know how to interpret the appearances of the earth and the sky, but you can't interpret these present times. Why can't you decide for yourself what is right? If you are on your way to court and you meet your accuser, try to settle the matter before it reaches the judge, or you may be sentenced and handed over to an officer and thrown into jail. and if that happens, you won't be free again until you have paid the last penny."
- My extended approach at the doctorate level of theological education involved, and still involves, the connecting of God to Jesus Christ, and Jesus Christ to the Spirit of God for human beings. THIS INVOLVEMENT ON MY PART CONSTITUTES MY INTERPRETATION AND EX-PECTATION OF THE CHRISTIAN CHURCH, THE ACTUAL BODY OF GOD, THROUGH JESUS CHRIST APPLIED TO "THE PROBLEMS OF THE TIME."

The above statement leads to PART D, entitled "Obstacles that, by 'nature', get in the way, leads to a challenge, either to succeed, or to fail." The option should be to light a candle with one's life, rather than to curse the darkness. John 3:16: "God so loved the world, that he gave his only begotten Son, that whosoever believeth in him should not perish, but have everlasting life." Verse 19: "And this is the condemnation, that light is come into the world, and men loved darkness rather than light, because their deeds were evil."

PART D
OBSTACLES THAT, BY NATURE, GET IN THE WAY OF OBEY-ING THE LAWS OF GOD, THEY LEAD TO A CHALLENGE; SUCCEED OR FAIL, EVEN IN THE CHRISTIAN CHURCH!

You may light a candle, or you can curse the darkness. "This is the condemnation, that light has come into the world, yet men loved darkness rather than light, because their deeds are evil," (John 3:19 KJV).

If Ms. Lin, the *CNN* news anchor we've highlighted throughout these chapters, could have had insight into the Church with a capital "C," she would have been able to see how young Mr. Reeves would have no problem thriving, rather than surviving, after his truncated misfortunes. To make a point here, as well as point out her "problem," it was all about "death." Death as an age-old problem is the reason I point it out here, along with Ms. Lin's obsession with it.

In the Gospel of John, the eleventh chapter and the twenty-fifth verse, Jesus clears up Ms. Lin's mind, but she has to believe in Jesus Christ. In the fourth chapter, death and man's response to it is the major theme.

The introduction here will be brief due to the itemized issues in this chapter speaking volumes without editorial opinions. I make two very, very significant points as I close this chapter:

(1) I could not have sought a more clear reference to my search in Florida with the young man leaving prison and not being able to get help from the church, than this situation involving Ms. Lin. Therefore, I must attribute this gift as having come from God, and having ordered my steps and the stages of my journey.

(2) The only way Ms. Lin will be able to access this information for herself will be through faith. I could say by joining a church, being baptized, having hands laid upon her, and continuing in prayer, even having the experience of the Spirit of God. This happens all the time. Ms. Lin has to understand what Jesus said and meant, "The Law and the Prophets were until John, since then the Kingdom of God is preached and men press into it." Ms. Lin, or anyone else who wants to

obey Jesus Christ as His disciple, must be willing to keep pressing into the presence of God until it becomes second nature—no, first nature. She must be born again of the Spirit of God.

There is no conclusion to conviction war for a disciple of Jesus Christ. He who has begun a good work in you will continue to perform it until the Day of Jesus Christ.

Chapter Two

A RITE OF PASSAGE IS NECESSARY TO CHANGE THE COURSE THAT ONE'S LIFE HAS TAKEN BY NATURE, FROM THE MOTHER'S WOMB TOWARDS THE TRUTH OF GOD UNDERSTOOD IN HIS PERFECT UNIVERSE

THIS CHANGE IS NECESSARY FROM A PHYSICAL TO A SPIRITUAL EXISTENCE NECESSARY TO PASS FROM DEATH INTO AN ETERNAL EXISTENCE WITH GOD IN HIS PERFECT UNIVERSE.

TRAIN UP A CHILD IN THE WAY HE SHOULD GO: AND WHEN HE IS OLD, HE WILL NOT DEPART FROM IT (Proverbs 22:6).

THE PROBLEM: Because of the lack of spiritual enabling, the human body has never been released, set free, still bound to dependence on the needs that have been supplied externally from birth.

A RITE OF PASSAGE:

A *rite of passage* is a ceremony to facilitate or mark a person's change of status on a significant occasion, as at the onset of puberty or upon entry into a select group. It is any act or event marking a passage from one stage of life to another.

Although life involves a journey ending in death, there are several stages requiring physiological maturation and aptitude, along with physical growth. Along with these series of intervals that are logical in the passing of time are the pains of growth, where societal norms and individual responsibility are required.

The pain can be interpreted when the individual's violation of these normative behaviors is called to his, or her attention, hopefully beginning at a very early age, and before negative value judgments have been learned. The second chapter in the book shows the need for the parent or guardian to instill in the growing child the ability to make good choices in his, or her behavior, drawing on the laws of God as hinted at in Proverbs 22:6, stated at the beginning of this chapter. The third chapter will outline some of the results of failing to "train up the child in the way he should go."

Because of the learning curve in adolescence with an acceptable level of maturity coming at approximately twenty-five years of age, without early training, there is a high risk of failure. The adolescent must develop self-initiative and responsibility as he or she takes on life, such as a job, losing a job, marriage or sexual dating, having children, and having experienced the death of close relationships.

Although a *rite of passage* is best expressed in a ritual, the event can be trivialized if the meaning is not clear and is based on the true meaning of life as seen in the laws God has created as the fabric of the universe for happiness, and individual peace and freedom. This statement in no way leads to the person going through the *rite of passage* to be expected to join a church or religious body. What it should mean is that the laws we mention can change what they thought to be freedom into years of incarceration as a result of not acknowledging that secular society is based directly on the laws of God in the *Decalogue*, or the *Ten Commandments*. When one is brought to justice, his or her sentence is from violation of the laws of God in his or her relationship with another human being. In this case, criminal justice is an adjunct of the Divine laws of God as expressed more generally throughout the Bible, the Koran, and where other religious orders are the basis for their laws; refer to the laws given to Moses by God.

We all know the serious consequences when a boy or girl is left to formalize his or her own *rite of passage*. We see this in teen pregnancies, youth gangs, My Space internet exposure, corruption in government by politicians having contributed the greater part of their adult lives to serving their communities, yet failing to acknowledge the damage done to those in need they were sworn to serve, respect, and honor.

Much is being discussed at this time around culturally specific "Rites of Passage" involving the Black community. Most parents never envisioned their daughter pregnant at sixteen years old, or their fifteen-year-old son in prison for ten, twenty years for disrespecting the property or the person of another human being, many times the victim a member of their own family or community.

The basic tenet and Mission of the Life for Christ Foundation is to bridge a gap between teenagers who are arrested, and for all customary practices, could be headed for a lifetime of criminal activity and offenses. Our goal is that they be returned to their community where the problem began and where it can be corrected. There is, at this time, several generations of black young men incarcerated, when they should never have left their communities in the first place.

We agree with Dr. Bill Cosby, the legendary comedian and contributor to these efforts in our community and nation, and President Barack Obama, that too many of our children have their *rite of passage* after they have made errors in the direction in their young lives. My favorite call in this area is the "new philosophical vision" and "preventive strategy" in treating ex-offenders of the criminal justice system. In the not-too-distant past, social workers were told they could have no contact with an ex-offender after he or she was released from custody, or parole, or otherwise. Realizing the ominous betrayal of trust of the citizens who put up taxpayer money to correct behavior, the result was to let them flounder where they were before they came into the system, and surely, they will return to us much worse than when we discharged them.

The old morality of "Boys Town" has been exchanged for a National Criminal Justice System Industrial Complex. One recent commissioner of the Department of Corrections in the State of New Jersey was reprimanded, and eventually fired for referring to the system of corrections in New Jersey as having a "plantation mentality philosophy."

Any successful *rite of passage* should be based on the child being involved in the faith of the parents, or the mores and folkways of respect for other human beings on a worldwide respect and acceptance of a human rights philosophy. We live in a global multicultural community with the three citadels of authority, the state, the church, and the community working together to effectuate the general, as well as the specific implementation of the U.S. Bill of

Rights upon which this nation was established and should, and must, continue to honor and trust.

There are three words that must be understood before we continue the discussion on the significance of a *rite of passage*:

(1) Perceive: Using the senses, of which there are five, to understand or to become aware of, as in forming a conclusion.
(2) Conceive: to form an opinion or purpose. Origination: beginning a design in the mind, a plan.
(3) Idea: Any concept existing in the "mind" as a result of mental understanding, awareness, or activity, a plan of action or intention.

A man who has a "religion" has made a conception that rests in his "mind." He has concluded that he is in need of something more than what he presently has already. The man who has no need to be reminded of his incompleteness, even as he is confused and "angry" and dissatisfied with his present existence or condition, is an infidel and a "brute" (a non-human crude person).

Dr. Sigmund Freud regards religion as a neurotic need of man. And in so doing, he levels at our society a false value put on its relevance and importance. He continues: "There is a tendency to reject natural religion as it is stated, and practiced as a ritual. Science is enough - for truth's sake, for the conduct of life, for society's welfare." I would disagree with Dr. Sigmund Freud here by applying religion to the ritual, and practice of members of alcoholic and narcotic anonymous. The NA and AA societies are so closely related to the teachings of the word of God that they meet in the basement of many churches throughout the local community and around the world. One jewel of a quip from a member of AA and NA: "Many members of churches are there because they don't want to go to hell. We come to meetings because we've been to hell, and don't want to go back."

In these terms, Dr. Sigmund Freud states, "As opposed to 'Abnormal Psychology,' as man's mind is confused and angry, the religion of the ordinary man is justified and the only religion that ought to bear the name."

Detriech Bonhoeffer would agree with Dr. Sigmund Freud on this point: "It is the religion of the philosophers and the theologians which Dr. Sigmund Freud questions. He criticizes the philosophers for trying 'to preserve the God of religion by substituting for Him an impersonal, shadowy, abstract principle"; and he, Bonhoeffer, challenges the grounds on which he thinks the theologians hold it to be "an impertinence on the part of science to make religions a subject for investigations." They deny that science has any competence whatsoever "to sit in judgment on religion." Dr. Sigmund Freud declares, "but inquire on what grounds religion bases its claim to an exceptional position among human concerns, the answer we receive, if indeed we are honored with an answer at all, is that religion cannot be measured by human standards, since it is of divine origin, and has been revealed to us by a spirit which the human mind cannot grasp.

"It might surely be thought," he continues, "nothing could be more easily refuted than this argument; it is an obvious begging of the question." The point which is being called into question is whether there is a divine spirit and a revelation; and it surely cannot be a conclusive reply to say that the question cannot be asked because the deity cannot be called into question.

To support the proof that the Spirit of God (the divine Spirit of divine origin) has been inaugurated through the birth, life, ministry, death, resurrection, and continuing presence of Jesus Christ in the world through His followers, is to say that one's physical lifestyle can experience a paradigm shift to existentially experience and exist in another psychological realm of reality. Historians, scientists, philosophers, physiologists, psychologists, psychiatrists, theologians, teachers, physicians, social workers, and senior counselors, have all agreed on the following:

Intelligence cooperates with instincts to solve the problems of adjustment to our environment. Abnormal psychology studies and seeks solutions to expressions of anger and frustration. Medicating your perception will not alter what you need, that is, another "conception" of the "problem."

Thomas Aquinas, a religious philosopher says: Instinct (response to the environment) and reason (mental powers concerned with forming conclusions) are the exclusive means which God provides for the ends of animal and human life. This statement tends to interpret animal behavior in all its details as predetermined by elaborate instinctive endowments. In the case of animals, the goal is to satisfy instinct without regard to reason.

As a result, animals, or nonhuman behavior, even when voluntary rather than purely the action of physiological reflexes, is said not to be free, or an expression of free choice, if it brings suffering or anger as a result of not having used reason during the time the response was made to the instinct or impulse. For as "will" dictates, behavior is "voluntary" if it involves some knowledge or consciousness of upcoming consequences of the objects to which the response is directed (Pavlovian psychology).

Instinctive behavior, such as an animal's flight from danger, or its pursuit of food, or to mate/sex, involves sense perception (vs. conception) of the objects of these actions and desires, as well as feelings and emotions about them.

Even though it is "voluntary," in the sense in which Aquinas used the word, instinctive behavior is, according to him, the exact opposite of free will. If an incarcerated felon thinks that what he did, resulting in his incarceration, was to show that he was a man over his affairs, and just the opposite resulted in him losing all the definitions of a free, strong "man or human being," the loss of self-esteem, he has failed at any interpretation of what "free will" results in.

Such freedom of choice, Aquinas holds, depends on reason's ability to contemplate alternatives, one of which is the human "will" for freedom bound by natural necessity. Every instinctive act in an animal with memory must cease to be "blind" after being once repeated, and must be accompanied with foresight of its "end" just so far as that end may have fallen under the animal's cognizance (the ability to have prevented a repetition).

In his consideration of "the intellectual contrast between brute and man," James places "the most elementary single difference between the human mind and that of brutes" in the "deficiency on the brute's part to associate ideas (any conception existing in the mind) by similarity.

THE MATURATION OF THE MENTAL PROCESSES IN THE HUMAN BEING

The First Phase: The mental processes of the infant are active although he is a totally unfocused organism. Unless there is congenital malfunction of the brain, the infant records stimuli or impulses through the five senses: hear, taste, feel, smell, and "see," without either being able to interpret or respond to it. The baby reacts if it is either too hot or too cold. It reacts if it is hungry, or is neglected with its basic needs, such as changing the diaper when it becomes uncomfortable. In other words, we could say the five senses are scrambled.

The Second Phase: Within three months, the child's five senses begin to focus. I would like to give an example here to amplify the significance of what psychologists call the greatest learning possibility in the child's lifetime. Fifty percent of the child's lifetime of learning takes place within the first year of its life. During the second year, the child learns 75 percent of what it will learn in its lifetime, leaving only 25 percent for the rest of its life (Cline 1979). To flip this script, whatever the child learns by the time it is two years of age will, without a doubt, define the mental fabric of its life. The insight here is to consider the choice the child made in reaching for the coo-coo clock as opposed to everything else in the playpen.

The Third Phase: This phase is very significant as it relates to parenting, and role modeling for the child. The child has learned a lot in those first two years. What the child needs now is putting the knowledge to good use, as opposed to making decisions without rational judgment. The example for insight here is the "crossing the busy intersection syndrome." If the parent does not explain to the child in ways the child understands judgment as well as decisions about crossing a busy intersection, danger means nothing. Or, as a matter of fact, to the child, danger could mean having fun. A child is not sufficiently intuitive or able to use deductive reasoning in order to understand death.

Instructing children to cross only on green, is not enough, even with a trained crossing guard. At this age, six to eleven, because of the tremendous impact on the child's actions of peer pressure, obedience, and trust in the parent or guardian is better than instructing the child on good judgment. The danger for the child is that experience is always the best, and sometimes, the fatal teacher. Even if you told the child that crossing at a dangerous intersection without due caution could cause death, they are not, by reason, mental powers necessary to form a conclusion, able to internalize the gravity of a serious accident. The loss of blood can result in the vital signs of the body dropping to zero, causing life to cease.

Another example involving the deficiency of reasoning in a child of six to eleven years of age, one that older persons can relate to, is the effect of the death of a loved one in the mind of the child. A child this age is not able to immediately consider the gravity of never being able to see that person alive again.

Failing to apply reason to the gravity of the loss could result in the child asking where is Uncle Bud two weeks from the funeral, after having viewed him in the casket at the wake, or funeral, and possibly seeing him lowered into the ground at the cemetery.

There are two reasons why adolescence is such an important phase of the maturation of the human being: (1) Unless there is a *rite of passage*, by parents or guardians, of the necessity of the child adopting societal norms and cultural identifications to accept his or her responsibility in a particular society. The child will join a gang, or accept those norms from the street. *Rite of passage* will be explained later under this general heading, and (2) Because of the laws of our nation involving equal protection of the law, and due process, technically, a child under eighteen years of age should not be tried in a court of law in this country. Unless it can be attested to that he or she understood the psychological limitations obscuring the consequences of his or her behavior prior to the commission of a crime, for which he or she would be punished. The title of the book, *How Was I Supposed to Know?* validates this premise, as well as the selection of the "first offender" for assistance with the counseling modality, "Release to the Captives." A theological, legal discussion entitled, "The Focal Point of Our Efforts" concludes this general presentation on "Juvenile Delinquency vs. a Rite of Passage."

The Fourth Phase: Although this explains adolescence, it focuses on the later stages. We should agree here that in most cultures, a boy and a girl become adults when they can think like one. This is where *rite of passage* explains our concern for this age group. In the Jewish faith, there is *bar mitzva*h for a boy who reaches his thirteenth birthday and attains the age to religious duty and responsibility. This is the stage of mental maturity when the twelve to seventeen-year-olds begin acting on the dictates of acquired knowledge. They make judgments with what we call in counseling therapy as the ABCs. When stimulated by their environment, an action is called for. Their belief system kicks in to consider alternative responses within a split second, and choose the one that will result in the best set of consequences. The key here is that water can never rise higher than its source. Homo sapiens, man born of a woman, cannot receive knowledge from their Creator, unless the five senses, given by another human being, are applied in diligently seeking Him. If the child is not trained up in the way he should go so that when he is old he will remember his way, all the knowledge he or she acquires will be directed towards a confused lifestyle—eventually dying physically, never receiving the knowledge of their spiritual heritage from their Creator.

An example at this stage in mental maturity would be a boy or girl utilizing the attributes of their physical body to achieve immediate gratification, or some other apparent goal. We speak here of sex, money, other gifts such as cars, jewelry, travel, jobs—in other words, supposed forms of security that might have strings attached. All human beings seek role models. Small children, playing with each other, seek role models without an intending payoff in mind. In late adolescence, role models are sought to achieve whatever that role model has done with his, or her life, most of the times, illegally.

The Fifth Phase: The stage of mental maturity, including eighteen to twenty-five years of age, can involve "Life coming at you fast" as the commercial calls it. The young adult is in a danger zone because life's decisions at this level become final, for better or worse. Steven R. Covey speaks of *The Seven Habits of Highly Effective People*. The deciding habit is being proactive. With as best knowledge at your disposal, act in the present, with your future in mind. Because of the heightened sense of expected gratification, the five senses are capable of going out of control.

The Sixth Phase: The adult persona must be able to face critical decisions in life, based upon a world system of Truth. If this is not done, any attempt to make any "sense" during your lifetime will be meaningless.

The maturation of the mental processes of the human being involves the following:

1. The ability to control anger and settle differences without violence. Maturity is patience. It is the willingness to pass up immediate pleasure in favor of a long-term gain.
2. Maturity is perseverance, the ability to sweat out a project or a situation in spite of heavy opposition and discouraging setbacks.
3. Maturity means dependability, keeping one's word and coming through in a crisis. The immature are masters of the alibi. They are the confused and conflicted. Their lives are a maze of broken promises, former friends, unfinished business, and good intentions that somehow never materialize.
4. Maturity is the art of living in peace with what we cannot change, the courage to change what should be changed, and the wisdom to know the difference.

Chapter Three

THE SIGNIFICANCE
OF THE DEVELOPING
PERSONALITY IN A CHILD

PHASE I

The basic premise in the book, *How Was I Supposed to Know?* is as follows:

1. It is generally accepted that a human being born into the world at some point asks, "Who am I?" "Where did I come from?" and "Where am I going?" As we mature as human beings, using reason, mental powers concerned with forming conclusions, one will more than likely ask questions like, "Why is there so much suffering, evil, and death in the world?" The next question is, "Who, or what organized authority is to supply the answers and the power to bring about solutions to these universal conditions?"

2. This was the crux of my thinking as I began to study and become active in preaching. This was the crux of Ms. Carol Lin's of *CNN's* thinking upon the death of young Mr. Christopher Reeves. This thinking can rhetorically be accepted as the fact of the late Reverend Jerry Falwell of the Christian Coalition, including those of the Christian Evangelical Movement leading to man's efforts to solve the problems with moral means, as we see in the political area, without God's Spirit in the third dispensation of His purpose and Will. Isaiah 54:17: "No weapon formed

against thee shall prosper; and every tongue that shall rise against thee in judgment thou shalt condemn." Zechariah 4:6: "Then he answered and spake unto me, saying, this is the word of the Lord unto Zerubbabel, saying, Not by might, not by power, but by my Spirit saith the Lord of hosts."

3.   This thinking precipitated the very strong motivation on my part to attend Drew University. Of course, the critical moment was the scenario at the Calvary Baptist Church in 1973, when Mrs. Leona Allen asked that provocative question after I spoke on Brotherhood Sunday involving Black history, modeling my sermon after the work of Dr. Martin Luther King Jr. "Reverend, I didn't understand a word you said."

4.   In the Introduction on page one, I state that I feel I am genetically wired to seek justice between all human beings in all situations or circumstances.

5.   I mention Deitrich Bonhoeffer's statement to the extent that "cheap grace" is the violation of God's will to bring divine justice to the world through the Christian Church. Chapter Eight - Truth: The Guiding Principle.

6.   In Chapter Five, the "Focal Point of Contact" document, a philosophical interpretation of divine justice is engaged in by Dr. Martin Luther King Jr. and Rhienhold Neibuhr. Their conclusion is that divine law, justice, and peace are inextricably intertwined, and has nothing to do with democracy. We went to the Middle East to establish democracy. When Hamas, the radical militant Palestinian Group used the democratic process to gain power, we concluded that it was not the democratic process we intended. And if there is more than one interpretation of democracy, who is to rule on the authoritative version?

PHASE II

The X factor, or the Point of Contact of Effort of the Life for Christ Foundation is the Kingdom of God. We mention three citadels of "Authority" in place: the Church, the state, and the community (Vox Populi). If the Church does not stand up for the community, acknowledging that the community is dependent on humanity's search for meaning, explained in Phase I, it must come from the state, which is sworn not to have stipulated in its administration of the law the name of the God we are sworn to uphold as our Authority.

The fact, at present, is that the state, or the government, in any strict interpretation of Church and state law, acts as the Christian Church's proctor, or monitor. We in the Christian Church don't seem aware that we should spend our money to further the Kingdom of God as instituted based on exemplifying the body of Jesus Christ, which is the only definition of discipleship. Instead, the money we take in on any given Sunday morning, with the exception of maintaining the operation of the Church, the concerns of the members needs, and those of the surrounding neighborhood, are spent in something altogether of no consequence to Christian ministry as interpreted just above.

Within a few weeks of an offering of $50,000 taken in and deposited in a bank, it will find its way to Wall Street, bounced around and finding its way into the bidding process of the military industrial complex, or for technological weapons of mass destruction. The word of God spoken that Sunday morning and the incentive from it winds up destroying a village of innocent human beings thousands of miles from that church, with no concern on the part of members of what has just taken place.

This is the provocative impact of my questions in Washington, D.C. during the civil rights movement in the 1960s, and now Ms. Carol Lin's concern for human beings seemingly left out of the equation by all three of the citadels of authority, the Church, the state or government, and the community which, in all cases, are helpless, of course, unless there is a violent uprising seen presently by "gangs" of young men left out of the equation mentioned just above.

Most important here is the mistaken assumption by the late Reverend Jerry Falwell, and the Evangelical Christian Movement, that getting involved in government will bring about the Kingdom of God through the Christian Church as it is today. THE LAW MUST BE USED TO MAKE JUDGMENTS AND CONVICTIONS. GOD HAS GIVEN US THE PERFECT LAW AND HE WILL EXECUTE THE PERFECT JUDGMENT. Jesus Christ is the perfect example of the judgment God will use to either save us, or is without any joy in our death.

THE WATCHMAN'S MESSAGE Ezekiel 33:10-11: "Son of man, give the people of Israel this message: You are saying, 'Our sins are heavy upon us; we are wasting away! How can we survive?' As surely as I live, says the Sovereign Lord, I take no pleasure in the death of wicked people. I only want them to turn from their wicked ways so they can live. Turn, turn from your wickedness, Oh people of Israel! Why should you die?!" Romans 10:4: "For Christ has accomplished the whole purpose of the law. All who believe in him are made right with God" How was I Supposed to Know? I was supposed to search. John 5:39: "You search the Scriptures because you think they give you eternal life? But the Scriptures point to me! Yet you refuse to come to me so that I can give you this eternal life."

The conclusion of the entire book might be summed up with the need for a counter culture that would closely represent the unity of God's Spirit in the world. Jesus Christ embodied that Truth, and left His Spirit, the Spirit of God at Pentecost, to be secured by the Christian Church, representing His risen redeeming body for the salvation of God's world.

We, in the LIFE FOR CHRIST FOUNDATION see the Israelites and Black people in slavery in America as counter cultures. God's incarnation in Jesus Christ symbolizes his concern for all human suffering, individual, as well as collective as mentioned above. Their cases are what we needed now to save our specie, the human race. This is the example of the intelligent design seen in the saving incarnation of God in Jesus Christ, and is mentioned in this writing most judgmentally as referred to by Jesus Christ in Matthew 25:31-46.

"GOD WAS IN CHRIST, RECONCILING THE WORLD TO HIMSELF," (II Corinthians 5:19).

PHASE III

This is the actual Life for Christ Foundation Operation, and movement philosophy in the grant proposal.

THE TITLE OF THE COUNSELING MODALITY FOR THE Life for Christ Foundation IS ENTITLED: "RELEASE TO THE CAPTIVES."

I am heavily indebted to Dr. Thomas S. Szasz, the author of *The Myth of Mental Illness*. My conclusion is that God has created a perfect universe, and that any human being finding a problem with it is suffering from confusion, a form of mental illness.

Dr. Szasz's conclusion is that when a person's behavior does not fit the norm, that bothers others, he or she is considered to be mentally ill. His conclusion, further, is that if the mind is sick, why treat the body? Psychiatrists prescribe a myriad of drugs for the mentally ill. They are, in fact, treating the physical body, which actually has nothing to do with their problem that originated in the mind. A psychiatrist who prescribes medication to help the individual cope in the presence of others, or after being disoriented to the three spheres of cognitive reality, has not gotten to the problem. The problem is failing to accept the laws that God's perfect universe is established upon.

The most significant contribution this book should make is to explain in clear and relevant details the mistake made after, let's say, the massacre at Virginia Tech University on April 16, 2007, by a student, Mr. Cho. After he was thrown out of the class taught by Professor Nikki Giovanni, she referred him to the head of her department, English, for further assistance or referrals. The head of the English Department at Virginia Tech University was perhaps the least person capable of changing Mr. Cho's mind, and thereby his flawed perception of a perfect universe.

But more importantly, let us look at why Mr. Cho was flawed in his perceptions. He mentioned those who had Mercedes automobiles, fine clothes, in other indexes of wealth, while his brothers and sister were treated like dirt. He also mentioned others who he called martyrs such as Dillon and Klebold, the persons who massacred students at Columbine High School in Colorado. But it is even more revealing, and relevant, that he mentioned Jesus Christ in this same light, being a martyr.

What I consider here in this context to be most troubling in the publishing of the truth, is that many persons thought there was no hint of truth in what Mr. Cho said even if what he did was reprehensible. In other words, should we conclude that there should be no effort put forward to explain anything that Mr. Cho did or said as having any redeeming value, that is, to treat the mental illness with the Truth, and perhaps save other lives? THIS OBFUSCATION OF THE TRUTH BEGS FOR AN ANSWER TO THE QUESTION: "HOW WAS I SUPPOSEDTO KNOW?" AND IT BEGS FOR THE TRUTH IN BOTH THE SCRIPTURES FROM THE WORD OF GOD, AND THE IMMINENT SENTENCE OF DEATH TO THE VIOLATORS WHO REJECT THE INTELLIGENT DESIGN OF JESUS CHRIST AS SAVIOR AND LORD WHO HAS USHERED IN THE PERFECT UNIVERSE, AS IT WAS BEFORE THE FALL, THE KINGDOM OF OUR GOD.

THE OVERRIDING THESIS: "HOW WAS I SUPPOSED TO KNOW?"

Proverbs 22:6: "Train up a child in the way he should go: and when he is old, he will not depart from it."

Hosea 4:6-7: "My people are destroyed for lack of knowledge: because thou hast rejected knowledge, I will also reject thee, that thou shalt be no priest to me: seeing thou hast forgotten the law of thy God, I will also forget thy children. (7) As they were increased, so they sinned against me: therefore will I change their glory into shame."

Matthew 17:5: "While he yet spake, behold, a bright cloud overshadowed them; and behold a voice out of the cloud, which said, this is my beloved Son, in whom I am well pleased; hear ye him."

John 14:3-6: "And as I go and prepare a place for you, I will come again, and receive you unto myself; that where I am, there you may be also. And whither I go ye know, and the way ye know. Thomas saith unto him, Lord, we know not whither thou goest, and how can we know the way? Jesus saith unto him, I am the way, the truth, and the life: no man cometh to the Father, but by me."

Human beings (Homo sapiens) cannot correctly, by reason (mental powers concerned with forming a conclusion) determine who they are simply by being the offspring of the combination, sexually, of a male and a female Homo sapiens. Minute cell structures of elements of the earth, although miraculously combined comprising a human being, will not automatically give rise to understanding of God's perfectly created universe.

The rejection of the intelligent design of Jesus Christ, given by God His Father, provided in order to deliver on His original promise to Abraham, and after the warnings in the *Ten Commandments*, results in the sentence and judgment of death.

There are two guidelines for understanding the subject title "How Was I Supposed to Know?"

(1) And after Moses and Aaron went in, and told Pharaoh, Thus saith the Lord God of Israel, LET MY PEOPLE GO, THAT THEY MAY HOLD A FEAST UNTO ME IN THE WILDERNESS. Exodus 5:1 the following Scriptures reiterate God's command by way of Moses and Aaron to the Pharaoh: LET MY PEOPLE GO, THAT THEY MAY SERVE ME. Exodus 8:1, 8:20, 9:1, 9:13, and 10:3.

(2) St. Luke 4:17-19: "And there was delivered unto him the book of the prophet Esaias. And when he had opened the book, he found the place where it was written (18), the Spirit of the Lord is upon me, because he hath anointed me to preach the gospel to the poor, he hath sent me to heal the broken hearted, to preach deliverance to the captives, and recovering of sight to the blind, to set at liberty them that are bruised" (19) to preach the acceptable year of the Lord."

WHO A.M. I? WHERE DID I COME FROM? AND WHERE A.M. I GOING? WHY DO PEOPLE CHANGE THEIR NAME?

Without a *rite of passage* recommended in Chapter Two, it is hard to avoid the temptation to become someone else in time of trouble or stress. Self deception is used to escape the individual responsibility of the truth, so he or she chooses to take the name of another person, an alias. This shifts the blame for lacking in acknowledging guilt in transgression of GOD'S LAW.

THE PROBLEM: Because of the lack of spiritual enabling, one refuses to internalize the guilt when convicted of one's faults. There are forms of conviction: (1) Conviction by a judge in a court of law, and (2) Mental, and spiritual relating to having broken the laws of God. In both cases, the authority is from God, the *Ten Commandments*.

"And so dear brothers and sisters, I plead with you to give your bodies to God. Let them be a living and holy sacrifice—the kind he will accept. When you think of what he has done for you, is this too much to ask? Don't copy the behavior and customs of the world, but let God transform you into a new person by changing the way you think. Then you will know what God wants you to do, and you will know how good and pleasing and perfect his will really is," (Romans 12:1-2, *Life Application Study Bible*).

TALBOT HALL/SERENITY UNIT
PSYCHOLOGICAL ASSESSMENT AND BEHAVIORAL THERAPY
MOCK PRESENTATION TO BEGIN ANY OF THE EIGHT-WEEK COMPONENTS OF THE CURRICULUM

- For an overall explanation of the Talbot Hall experience, it is essential that the resident understand why he is here. That reason being to assess where your mind is, based, and I repeat, where your mind is based on your past behavior as stated on your rap sheet of actual convictions adjudicated before a Superior Court judge after being indicted, sentenced before a jury selected by your defense counsel, he or she having exercised peremptory challenges against anyone who might be inclined to be prejudiced in examining the evidence brought against you. Any one of those jurors finding the evidence to be irreconcilable beyond a reasonable doubt, based upon your defense attorney's presentation, you would be free to walk, as a result of a hung jury.

The assessment team psychologically assesses where your mind is in comparison to your past behavior, determines in what areas, risk for using substances, risk for problem solving that also leads to criminal behavior, calculates the likelihood of you continuing to behave in the future as you have in the past. So in fact, consider this: They are only comparing how you think now with how you thought in the past; if you disagree with what they came up with, you must be able to refute what the record says about your past. In other words, if you have been arrested for some violation of the criminal justice system five times in the past, don't say that someone, or the classification department, has a bad image of you as a person.

Self awareness is fundamental to psychological insight. This is the faculty that much of psychotherapy means to strengthen.

I'd like to explain the significance of that statement. A week or so ago, as I was in the senior counselor's office; Mr. Brooks, one of our senior counselors, was interviewing for some reason, Resident Blackson, I believe for his continuum of treatment profile. Obviously, after a question put to Resident Blackson about his future possibility of having difficulty, he made the following statement, "There is nothing out there that will be able to stop me this time."

What caught my attention was Resident Blackson's confidence that he would have nothing stop him when released back into the community. So I asked the question almost without hesitation, "Do you know what is out there that might stop you?" and he answered quickly, "No." I continued, "If you do not know what might stop you, how do you know that you won't be stopped?" He had no response.

So I continue as though Resident Blackson is present with us now. "If you do not know all you would need to know about yourself to guarantee your behavior under almost any given set of circumstance, how can you predict so precisely your response to that unknown situation?"

Because Resident Blackson cannot imagine what might stop him from committing a similar act that violates the laws of the criminal justice system, he is "at risk" for what the LSI and the assessment evaluation has to say about him. In other words, Resident Blackson will "feel" the same way he did when a situation/circumstance caused him to respond the way he did then, unless he can explain why there would be a difference; and if there is a difference, it would have shown up on his psychological assessment, removing him from the "at risk" assessment he was given.

Behavior exhibited in the precognitive state of awareness, triggered by the amygdala and causing anxiety and impulsive reactions, is stifled and controlled by the thalamus of the prefrontal lobes, controlling feelings in order to deal more effectively with the situation at hand, or when a reappraisal calls for a completely different response.

This progression, which allows for discernment in emotional response, is the standard arrangement, with the significant exception of emotional emergencies, when an emotion triggers within moments, the prefrontal lobes perform what amounts to a risk/benefit ratio of a myriad possible reactions, and bet that one of them is best. The neocortical response is slower in brain time than the hijack mechanism because it involves more circuitry. It can also be more judicious and considerate, since more thought precedes feeling.

There are five steps to absolute truth and wisdom: 1) the only way to keep from depression and anger from not getting your way resulting in cognitive distortion, neurosis, psychosis, etc. is to be able to keep the "law," the truth of the universal creation by its creator. Unless you subscribe or call upon a higher power, you have no influence over your body (Twelve Steps).

Your body demands its power from the physical and material world. In order to have influence over your body, you must be able to discipline its desires, but you cannot because you and your body are made of the same stuff. Your body disputes the principles that allow you to reject stimuli that cause you to have cravings and urges to feel differently from the way that you must based on the laws that govern the universe (exemplified in the *Ten Commandments*).

You are "at risk" unless you have at your constant disposal the power over your body, thereby allowing you to cognitively restructure any impulse or stimuli regulating your behavior or response.

Freedom and peace is to be able to exert the correct influence against any impulse or stimuli, including physical death. Then you have kept the law and its truth.

A person can be "at risk" for many things. Every human being is at risk of dying unless when faced with the death of their physical body They have come into the knowledge and belief and faith of "life" as determined by the laws that govern the universe and is constantly controlled by the creator, the higher power.

The key here is to have the "self" made aware of what death is and be ready to question any challenge to your existence in the face of the judgment of ultimate reality.

Resident Blackson does not know the flawed nature of his existence as it is presently, or he would not have made such a statement. He thinks he has influence over his behavior because he knows what he did wrong to come to jail, and he in fact and truth does not want to do that again, but if he truly understood his condition and his lack of influence over his body, he would not have told that "lie."

What he did wrong and is now thinking about negatively, is an afterthought. The key to solving his problem is not retraceable in his mind while he now speaks because it was not in his mind when he did what he did. What happened to him had more influence over him than he did of himself. The only way Resident Blackson could have had control over his response then or now is to have power over himself that did not come from within himself. And proof that Resident Blackson has not changed is the fact that he is not ready to accept the truth that he was wrong then. Listen, unless he has a reason (powers concerned with forming conclusions) to act differently, understanding his past errors, where would the power come from for him to be stronger or wiser now, than he was then?

Wanting to change is not good enough. There are twelve steps in remaining "sober" or "free" in peace. You cannot do the twelve steps by starting with number twelve, or number four. They would not be steps. You can't climb steps by going from the bottom halfway in one movement. That's why they say recovery is not an event but a journey. The journey of a thousand miles begins with what? The first step.

Resident Blackson must be able to problem solve by preventing the stress and confusion in his mind (powers concerned with forming conclusions) that went prior to his offense for which he is now incarcerated. Otherwise, he will always have the afterthought that "Nothing will stop me the next time."

DEVELOPMENT OF PERSONALITY
COMMUNITY EDUCATION CENTERS
Tully House II
SUBJECT: RELEASE AND REINTEGRATION
MONDAY, SEPTEMBER 20, 2004
DR. AUSTIN, LECTURER

This lecture is to prove to you that you had to act as an imposter in order to maintain any sense of self-esteem, weak and shaky as it was, and still is. Those five "at risk" factors in your early childhood were, in most cases, without nurturing and loving intimate positive attachments. Because your "self," the person that you became, was developed on false and inadequate values necessary to give you a strong sense of self-esteem. When your flawed sense of self was challenged, or you had a need to show character, you had to find a suitable model that you "thought" would protect you in these moments of embarrassment and emotional injury.

You literally took a "self" from someone else that seemed to fit your needs in what you came to understand as a value-less, hostile, cruel, and unjust world. I want to show you two things here: (1) The "weight" on your subconscious mind of negative memories called "baggage," which is heavy and you are grieving from it. The bad results that it has caused you will not go away voluntarily, and you have done nothing by the way of building a strong positive belief system to remove it. As a result, you have not been the person you should have been in those responses, which we have said put you "at risk" then and still keeps you "at risk." As it is said, if you have a problem (of which there are four parts), you are headed for trouble as sure as you live and don't change, (2) Because children have not developed a negative opinion of the world, their ego is always on neutral. They do not have an ego to defend when insulted, embarrassed, or are "put down." This is why they carry no grief-ridden "baggage." They may argue and fight with a playmate in the morning, but by noon they are hugging and rolling on the ground in laughter.

Because children are "nobodies," no "selves," they act as impersonators. It does not matter who they become, they have fun with their characters. When our ego is flawed and based on negative "baggage" from past grievances, insults, and anger, we choose to impersonate people like Bogart, Big Willie, Scarface, Willie Sutton in order to protect ourselves from insults and emotional injuries. Children might imitate Scarface and Bogart, but they also imitate Muhammad or Jesus Christ.

Based on the "self" or "belief system," you need to protect your flawed "self" or "belief system"; you would never choose Muhammad or Jesus Christ to impersonate. Their belief systems, which are based on the strength that gives the ego values and purpose to "stand firm" when desired or to have influence over what happens to them, would leave you vulnerable to insults, emotional injuries, and "put downs." You might say Muhammad or Jesus Christ was always getting insulted from low self esteem.

The basic demands in the perfect universe, "Life on Life's Terms," of Jesus and Muhammad allow them to face insurmountable odds, including death of the physical body. Freedom is making the right choice of responses in life regardless of what might appear to be the negative outcome.

DEVELOPMENT OF THE HUMAN PERSONALITY II
TALBOT HALL/SERENITY UNIT - WEEK EIGHT
A.M. - THE SEVEN HABITS OF HIGHLY EFFECTIVE PEOPLE
P.M. - THE FIST HABIT
MONDAY, APRIL 12, 2004
DR. AUSTIN, THERAPIST

Following on from last week, "problem solving," the seven habits in my mind, mean that something of "value" is being repeated in order to reproduce effectiveness. We also discussed the crux of confusion. To "think" you are solving a problem, and repeating what results in negative consequences. When what you want is not making your "self" any better, in terms of being able to repeat in your mind what it is that you want/need, you have taken your "mind," "thoughts" off the important need/want and focused on what happens to your "self." You have been distracted from your "self" and become concerned about something other than your "self," which is the only way, or the result necessary to get you what your "self" want/need. Listen, if you do not replenish the insight, energy of your "self," you are killing the goose before he 1}can lay the golden egg. If you don't see your "self" as the goose, you will never see the golden egg. If it does not come from "you," you will never get it, the want/need.

If, as we see here, your body, not your "self," continues to override your sense of hear, taste, see, smell, and feel, to what you want/need, what habits would you have to practice or repeat to prevent this from happening again, based on "you" being the goose?

Based upon the above, Dr. Szasz, the psychiatrist who has said there is no such thing as mental illness, makes the statement, "I hold that psychiatric interventions are directed at moral, not medical, problems." We conclude with Dr. Szasz as we confirm in the spirituality gained from following the Twelve Steps of Alcohol and Narcotic Anonymous. Mental illness, which, by the way, cannot be voluntarily detected and treated, is confirmed in the first two steps of the twelve referred here in AA and NA, Alcohol and Narcotic Anonymous programs.

As we confirmed last week on problem solving, there are four parts to a problem: 1) the way it is, that is, the way the world has been created by an All-Wise, All-Powerful Creator, 2) the way you would like it to be, 3) the difference between one and two, and 4) the way you your "self" "feel" about it. If you do nothing about the way you feel after disagreeing with number one, you are or will eventually become mentally ill.

Abnormal psychological symptoms are nothing but "symptoms of relapse" or failure to reinforce want/need, as we have explained them above. Relapse occurs when thoughts in the subconscious mind are recalled into our present thinking process to be considered for an immediate response to stimuli from our environment that never occurred before in that exact way.

This is what Dr. Sigmund Freud has to say about the ultimate importance of what I have said above: "Mental life is made up the conscious, the preconscious, and the subconscious may have never been at the conscious level, the preconscious is that part of our mind which, in "appropriate" circumstances, either through an effort of the will, or stimulated by associated ideas, can be brought up into the consciousness, and the conscious level which is the smallest of the three levels and contains thought and ideas of which we are "aware at any given time." The content of the conscious mind is extremely transitory or fleeting and is constantly changing.

Let me show you how inappropriate and self-destructive it is to respond to symptoms of relapse by using any remedy other than a correct paradigm of the perfect universe and your "self" as it responds to that perfection. Your response to stimuli received, whatever stimuli are, produces a symptom in your mind/body that you consider to be unwanted. Using drugs or psychoactive chemicals, made up of the same "stuff" your physical body is made of, is an attempt to come up with an answer to what is happening to you, that you did not understand before taking the chemical. What do you hope to receive from the chemical's effect on those tissues that it anesthetizes, or dulls into a stupor that would strengthen your "self" to that particular or those particular symptoms of relapse that will always repeat the negative result you received before?

If you are here today and don't have a clue as to how your "self" allowed you to be here, you are mentally ill. You can't see the four parts of the problem, only what you want/need, which comes after number one. If you could see the difference in number three, which is the difference between one and two, you might be ready to see and understand why you feel the way you do. You will always feel that you are the victim and is resentful and angry at someone or something else other than your "self." What you need to correct your feelings, number four, is to get it in line with number one, the way it, the universe, is. This is referred to in treatment as "Living Life on Life's terms." There is no more constructive way than this.

DEVELOPMENT OF THE HUMAN PERSONALITY III
BO ROBINSON THERAPEUTIC TREATMENT CENTER
TRENTON, NEW JERSEY
JANUARY 13, 2004
TOPICS FOR DISCUSSION

I do not intend to remind you of what you did, rather to explain that you had a different choice. I do not plan to accuse, blame, or insult you, rather to make this a healing experience.

If I spoke of change, it would be basic to all human beings, rather than to those who have committed crimes against society. You already have a problem of being singled out for your flaws in thinking.

If I took a universal approach to change and universal problem solving, it would have to do with basic behavioral psychology. The discussion has long been that heredity deals the cards and environment plays them.

That being the case, as most psychologists agree, if you do not have control over your genetic contributions from your parents, you have no control at all. Human beings of all walks of life—doctors, lawyers, mathematicians, scientists, bankers, teachers, who medicate their body (heredity) in order to answer problems that are based on stimuli or impulses from outside, or from the "environment," usually by swinging a mood of depression, or mental confusion, find that they have no control over themselves (genetically). People who practice living by the first two steps of NA and AA need only to be reminded of the first two steps to realize that humility is a sign of power over the imagination of stress, and the need to swing a mood of depression from fear and uncertainty conclude (1) I have come to realize that my life is unmanageable and, (2) I have no control over it.

If we say the environment means the outside "world," we must give a more definitive explanation of the "Outside World." I believe you have the same curriculum for therapeutic treatment here as we do at Talbot Hall. If this is so, I call your attention to several cognitive typologies that bring unity between our two facilities. That there are four parts to a problem and the only way to get an answer to problem solving is to accept the first one without compromise: (1) the way it is, (2) the way you want it, (3) the difference, and (4) the way you feel about it.

Then there is 10/90 or it is not what happens to "you"; it's how you respond, which confirms it's not heredity when something happens to you; it's what you have come to understand about how to respond. Failing in this, we become depressed and/or confused in stressful or trying situations. Then there is "Living Life on Life's terms," based upon the universal acknowledgment of a set of laws, judgments, and government, as human beings who practice the twelve steps have resigned themselves to acknowledge. The obedience of God's laws allows them to order their lives in such a plan that saves the physical body, as well as their soul. Then they can understand the deception of medicating their physical body to change the way they "feel" (four parts of a problem). And finally, there is "Attitude," which means that the stressed person, or oppressed person, should meet all the requirements set up by the Creator of the universe (the first part of a problem) with its laws and perfect government. At this point, they will probably, like those who practice the twelve steps, become humble by the truth of their circumstances, notwithstanding what they inherited from their parents.

The "change" then that we apply in treatment to improve one's cognitive awareness has to do with their admitting who they are based on the truth of their incarceration. The values we encourage you to adopt has to do with shifting your view of the "world" based upon your DNA, to conform to the way the universe is controlled by the Creator, the "way it is."

I like to use some abnormal psychological conditions that explain why human beings become stressed, depressed, and need to change, since they, undergoing psychiatric treatment for personality disorders and not sure who they were, did not like the person they appeared themselves to be.

Before I go any further, and since I rather recently retired from the New Jersey Department of Corrections, I remember vividly at East Jersey State Prison, as social work supervisor, sitting with the classification committee. The director of psychology department, as he presented case by case those inmates eligible for reduced custody, but requiring a positive psychological evaluation as a requisite, gave as his assessment of a particular candidate. "The inmate is or is not" orientated in all three spheres of cognitive awareness, which means he is not sure he knows who he is, or where he is, and what is going on at present. Another psychological assessment was as follows: "He has socialized to the norms of a deviant subculture."

Now, after everything I've said here today, if I introduced a crux in your life, would you admit to this condition? A crux is "a central point of pivotal or unresolved difficulty."

There are five "at risk" factors in your paradigm of the world that could put you at risk to continue to break the laws that govern a perfect universe: (1) a dysfunctional family, (2) leaving school, a positive character building structure, (3) joining others who have also rejected a positive character building structure, (4) using drugs and alcohol to neutralize the failure resulting from not conforming to that of normal human beings, that your own family for the most part adheres to, and (5) turning your "war," your "feelings," your paradigm, your flawed world against those who are keeping these laws and generating peace and well-being throughout the community.

I have observed how residents will steal anything from a senior counselor or anyone working in the facility—a pencil, a pen, a pointer, money, clothes that they know they won't fit into. You actually feel that "we" have done this to you and you have been held hostage and have every right to get what you can from us any way you can. You are "at risk" to break the laws that govern the universe and we have taken your freedom away from you again and again and again.

If you hate being at Bo Robinson because you thought you were going straight to a Halfway House, you almost always have gotten that attitude from someone else who did not want to be here. About two weeks ago, I printed up information for my case load. One resident said the print was too small and he could not read it. And if there had been sexually explicit messages, or photos, it would not have mattered how small the print was. As in Pavlovian psychology, you rejected what was good because you expected something bad, or faulty. Your values or what you want to become is mired in your "at risk" past, your genetic, school, family, drug/alcohol, and community past.

Less than a week ago, I was present with Ms. Reid, who is here with me today, counseling one of her residents. He was upset, clearly rejecting all the structure brought to bear on his negative behavior. Mr. Logan or Mr. Salaam, who directs the alumni program for the community education centers, was formerly a resident at Talbot Hall, and later became a senior counselor, explained to the resident Mrs. Reid was counseling, how Mr. Hooper, the chief of security at Talbot Hall had picked on him and his negative behavior. Eventually, Mr. Logan got it right.

I said to him, based on what I have said to you here today, he is sick, and Mr. Logan, who was sick like him, is now well. He could not see it, and you won't either unless you practice a "religious" ritual that allows you to access and process cognitive awareness of a perfect set of truths and laws that govern a perfect universe governed by a Perfect Creator.

DEVELOPMENT OF THE HUMAN PERSONALITY IV
TALBOT HALL/SERENITY UNIT
MONDAY, FEBRUARY 9, 2004
WEEK 8: SEVEN HABITS OF HIGHLY EFFECTIVE PEOPLE
A.M.: INTRODUCTION/P.M.: BE PROACTIVE (1st HABIT)
DR. AUSTIN, THERAPIST

Proactive is the power, freedom, and ability to choose our own response to whatever happens to us, based on our values. Anytime you think the problem is out there, in that outer circle, that thought is the problem. You have just empowered what's out there to control you. You are in a self-fulfilling prophecy. Sure enough, you will find that the evidence will support your conviction, made before anything happens to you.

As I have said before, if you do not say, "I need to change positively today," for the next three months, you will not have the mental attitude to have prepared as though you knew something would happen to you that you did not like, so you prepared to be the person you wanted to be when it happened.

Now, listen to this: the key here is not what you say as much as it is you remembering your condition against what happens to you. This has nothing necessarily to do with something negative happening to you. Based on the likes and dislikes of every human, nobody likes to get up in the morning, in winter, with snow on the ground, the battery in your five year old Oldsmobile might not kick over, understanding that you have a good excuse not to get up, you need to change today, whatever day it is.

Now, one of the most exciting and understandable examples of what this first habit tells us is seen in a circle within a circle. The dark part of the circle is you, and the outer white part of the circle is what happens to you. Obviously here, it is very clear that if you are not prepared, mentally and spiritually, when something happens to you, it is your body that you have depended on to handle the situation from that outer circle. Your body has no power other than that which comes from the food you ate at your last meal. That food has no impact or power that goes to your mind or your ability to interpret whatever happens to you.

If your mind has not been affected by knowledge of what you ought to do when you are impacted or stimulated by events and situations from outside of your body and your mind, you have just been blind-sided. Did you watch the Pro-Bowl last night? You can have your career abruptly ended by failing to see two opposing players coming at you from opposite directions and one hits you high and the other hits you low. Who can tell me what that is called? A chop block. It's illegal, but it won't matter if you didn't get out of the way. In life, like football, if you don't prepare your mind to figure out what people coming in your direction have in mind, you, too, might have to watch the parade of life from behind bars.

Now, let me turn the corner and show you how imperative and necessary it is to prepare your mind, not your body, for upcoming events to keep out of the crux and getting monkey-jerked. You are a functional illiterate if you argue about what just happened to you with someone else, rather than determining, before you open your mouth, what you need to say and do to have what you want to happen take place.

As a matter of fact, now, I am going to explain the crux.

The fear of God, or the Creator, is the beginning of wisdom. Why? Because then, you learn to think or use deductive reasoning. Reason: the mental powers concerned with making conclusions. When you learn to think, if you do not consider the power and judgment and laws of the Creator, you are dead in the water out of the gate (my mother's womb). When I mention God, or the Creator, I am not trying to get any of you to join any religion, because a religion (repetitive involvement in a ritual, which is important when you find out what it is that you want to be repetitive in getting from your repetition). I am trying to get you to see why you need a source of spiritual power over your physical body, five senses, in order to "conceive" understand as opposed to "perceive" and interpret and explain to your "mind" what is happening at any given moment in your life, based on the "perception" from your five senses.

Spirituality is explained as the pervasive all presence of the Creator of the universe. Man, from his beginning, has come up with words like "laws", "truth", "government", "peace", "justice", "life", and "death" to explain what is necessary in the wisdom needed to respect the fear that those who "know" the Creator have for Him. Without the power over our body given by the Creator, man is left to his depression, oppression, imaginings, neurosis, psychosis, pathology, psychopathology, schizophrenia, anger, resentment, and eventually death, which is the ultimate form of mental illness. These are the sentences and judgments from the All Loving, All Forgiving, All Powerful, Creator who has created a perfect universe.

Let's look at the meaning of "conception": which means to understand with the "mind," and not from what appears to the body from impulses, hear, taste, feel, see, and touch. You must have truthful information in your mind about what is happening at any given moment or understandably you have no power to reject the perceptions and illusions and imaginings in the perfect world/universe.

It is logically with this leading that this is why when "imaginations" get out of control, hysteria, and spells set in, and sometimes lead to seizures. By the way, these are mental disorders, not epilepsy or other physical disorders. People go to see a psychoanalyst because what starts in the "mind," mental, is felt, perceived, five senses, by the body.

Let's continue to put this in perspective: If a person feels (five senses) that something is wrong because problems in his or her mind, mental, misconception, caused the problem, and you treat him or her with drugs, psychoactive chemicals, pharmaceuticals, Librium, Valium, Darvon, Prozac, etc., and don't treat the mind, or their conception of what is wrong, where the problem started, what is the use. Will knowledge of what's wrong with your body do you any good? If you say "Yes," that is probably why you know what you need to get your life together, but in fact, that knowledge will not do you any good. Since you don't know what will happen to you when you get what you want, why don't you get what you need, knowledge that will do you good, and you can have or lose a lot of what you want, but you will always have what you need.

Look at this: Knowledge that will do you good will never lead to stress, depression, neurosis, psychosis, schizophrenia, ideations of suicide. These all start in the mind, or come to rest there when you realize that you do not have what you need, "knowledge" that will do you "good." Try to have peace of mind.

Two things I remind you of: (1) don't blame your body, blame your mind, and (2) if you treat or medicate your body, you are trying to "feel" better rather than becoming better ("knowledge" that will do you good."). The bottom line is you do not have knowledge that will do you good if you cannot conceive it in your mind and possess power over what happens to you.

Let me leave you with an example: Suppose a man watching TV and because of what he sees, and feels, hears, concludes that he does not like the programming on a particular night, calls the repairman to correct the problem. The repairman would say, "Sir, what's wrong with you, I fix TV sets, not what comes out of them." If the mind, mental condition system, is running on bad information, only bad things will result.

DEVELOPMENT OF THE HUMAN PERSONALITY V
COMMUNITY EDUCATIONS CENTERS
Tully House II
RELEASE AND REINTEGRATION
MONDAY THROUGH FRIDAY, SEPTEMBER 6-10, 2004
DR. AUSTIN, LECTURER

The adopted therapeutic model of the community Education Centers is REBT, or Rational Emotive Behavioral Therapy.

You cannot be "rational," which means to exercise reason (mental powers concerned with forming conclusions), unless you can identify and control triggers or emotions. If you want to control emotions or triggers, you must construct or build a positive "belief system" based on a higher power.

What is a positive "belief system?" To have confidence in the truth and existence of something not immediately understandable as proof. When an event occurs, good or bad, automatically, your mind activates (1)thought, (2) will, (3) determination, and (4) initiative.

Your "belief system" automatically describes and explains where and why your life is headed in the direction it is going and surely, the arrival at your particular destination is certain.

If you can never seem to get where you want to go or find your "self" in places you never intended to be, and would like to leave, but cannot, like prison, it is because your thoughts that initiate actions are not rational. Or, if you cannot reach goals that appear easily obtainable in your mind, like not going back to prison, you can rest assured that is because of what you BELIEVE.

Remember that the frog got into hot water because someone put him in there and kept raising the heat levels. If you are here and don't want to be here, and feel frustrated and resentful, and if you feel that someone has put you into this hot water, you are in hot water because you schemed, connived, and conned your way deeper into a lie, and not the Truth. Your thoughts and actions were based upon your selfish beliefs without any basis in facts.

At age six or seven, you were required to begin participating in a group or community system where your individual beliefs and ways are shared with others experiencing the same problems and frustrations you were having. There are six "at risk" factors that contribute to this rejection of societal norms: (1) Rejection of family teachings/or being a member of a dysfunctional family, (2) Rejection of the discipline required in early school and middle school, and either being expelled, or leaving in disgust, (3) Joining others who have taken a similar path to problem solving, (4) Using psychoactive chemicals, drugs, and alcohol, to swing a mood of failure and rejection in normal "problem solving" in society, (5) Defending the mistakes made up to that point by rejecting and organizing against any person or system that calls your failure and lies about the injustice and unfairness of the system and society to your attention, and (6) The real "hot water" starts to be felt when you "feel" that you have lost so much defending your "lie" that you cannot invest in a change at this point, and in fact this is the worst of the lies.

KEY: NO TRIGGER IS ACCURATE FOR A CORRECT RESPONSE TO SITUATIONS WE MUST FACE IN LIFE.

So I repeat: You can never get where you want to go, or stay away from places you don't want to be, such as in prison, unless you can rationally—which means to have mental powers concerned with forming conclusions, based on sound judgment—control your emotions, which are based on "triggers" only.

A TRIGGER is an answer to a problem without reason. It is a conclusion that has no basis in fact. A response based on a situation from one's past experiences, having absolutely nothing in fact to do with the present stimuli, impulse, impact, you presently must respond to.

In other words, you are functioning, acting like an illiterate person to life when you respond to an event that happened ten or fifteen years ago, as though the event is happening right now. IT SHOULD BE CLEAR TO YOU BY NOW THAT THIS IS EXACTLY WHAT HAPPENS IN YOUR MIND AND BY YOUR BEHAVIOR, WHEN YOU RESPOND TO A "TRIGGER," WHEN SOMETHING HAPPENS THAT YOU DO NOT LIKE, OR THAT YOU DO LIKE, BUT IS NOT ADVANTAGEOUS TOWARDS A PRE-SELECTED GOAL OR PLAN IN LIFE, INVOLVING, THOUGHT, WILL, DETERMINATION, AND INITIATIVE.

The only suggestion here would be to develop, and daily reinforce the belief system based on mental and emotional controls to offset the negative impact of "triggers."

One of my residents at Talbot Hall had a low salt diet symbol on his ID card, which meant he could not eat from the "snack machines." He explained to me that his low salt diagnosis was inaccurate, and I believed him. Mr. Keith Hooper, who is the director of operations at Talbot Hall, would see him at the snack machines and threaten to write him up if he continued. At this particular time, they exchanged high pitched words filled with "emotions." Mr. Hooper called for Resident Bethea to come to his office. Mr. Hooper spoke in an accusing and authoritative manner. Mr. Bethea's low or impaired self-esteem was triggered from past treatment of him by others at other times.

Mr. Bethea, after several exchanges in loud voices, said, "Well, send me back to prison. You don't talk to me that way." I followed him to the "Chicken Wing" the "lock-up" holding cells at Talbot Hall. I explained to him that because of his past thoughts and the negative things that had happened to him, he allowed Mr. Hooper to bring up and focus on parts of his life that were not helpful to solving this particular solution to the "low salt" diagnosis. This was proof of the fact that he had allowed Mr. Hooper to have influence over him by allowing his past experiences to cause him to fail in present problem-solving. He related to me in a very different and positive manner.

He went back and apologized to Mr. Hooper after I convinced him that he was not really talking to Mr. Hooper, but those in his past that had caused him to feel the way he did, while communicating with Mr. Hooper. He understood that how he felt while listening to Mr. Hooper has absolutely nothing to do with the problem of "low salt." What he really needed to do was to take Mr. Hooper out of the equation for the solution, and get the nurse to change the symbol on his ID card.

KEY QUESTION: How will he ever reach a goal that is very important for the rest of his life if he allows whatever and however someone treats him to confuse the directions he takes towards his goals and blocks his ability to influence his efforts? The answer is ATTITUDE.

LFCF: THE ESSENTIAL PERSONALITY
THE CORRECT RELATIONSHIP BETWEEN A PERSON, A SELF, AND OTHERS, INTERPERSONAL RELATIONS, IS ESSENTIAL TO OBEDIENCE TO THE LAWS, TEN COMMANDMENTS NECESSARY TO PRESSING INTO THE KINGDOM OF GOD. MATTHEW 22:35-40 AND LUKE 16:15 AND16
TALBOT HALL/SERENITY UNIT
WEEK 2: INTERPERSONAL SKILLS
SESSION 3 AND 4 FAMILY ISSUES/COMMUNICATION
TUESDAY, DECEMBER 30, 2003
DR. AUSTIN, THERAPIST

The meaning to be imparted: Inter, equal, reciprocal, interstate and interpersonal.

Person: the actual self, or the individual personality of a human being. A person or thing referred to with respect to complete individuality. Your self, My self.

Words that will be discussed this week relating to the subject of Interpersonal Relations, and Communication and Family are as follows:

1. The following are feelings, communication skills, and styles of communication: (a) aggressive, (b) assertive, (c) passive, and (d) passive aggressive.
2. Emotional bank account: "Beware of the king baby," and "Everybody loves Raymond."
3. There are five factors that sum up the "at risk" condition: (a) Member of a dysfunctional family, (b) Having trouble in, and leaving school because of anti-social problems, (c) Joining a gang, or "street club" of like-minded failures, (d) Turning to mind-altering substances, alcohol, drugs, etc., to mask and swing moods of stress and pressure, (e) And the dead end comes when he or she retaliates against the very same people he or she has been offending all along, those who obeyed the rules of citizenship.

First, I'd like to begin by showing you an example of the emotional and mental effects of a paradigm of reality, or one's lifestyle. Then I'd like to shift the paradigm to show how it can make or break the "person" or his or her personality, who he or she thought he or she was before his or her belief about this or that was changed. It will be clear here that your paradigm also effects what we call the ABC of living: (A) the activating event, (B) what you "believe" took place, and (C) the consequences of your response. Whether you behaved or not outwardly, events change what we thought before they occurred (Dr. Sigmund Freud).

Steven R. Covey, best known for *Seven Habits of Highly Effective People*, gives us this example: A man and his four little children get on the subway in New York City. The children begin to rustle about, bumping into passengers, knocking newspapers from readers' hands and other outward signs of misdemeanor. One of the passengers, sensing the combined frustration of the situation, responded by approaching the father, "Sir, why don't you speak to your kids, they seem to be out of control" The father, in somewhat of an emotionally detached state, "Oh, I'm sorry, we just left Belleview Hospital. Their mother just died." What is the necessary factor in a paradigm shift? Information that was not available, but necessary, before a conclusion is reached about what just took place: This is the ABC of the situation, or paradigm.

Suppose I put your present paradigm of the world, the country we live in, into focus, and then shifted it from flawed, based on faulty information, to perfection by adding the Truth.

Here's the paradigm: You are arrested for selling drugs. In your mind, your belief system, you did nothing wrong if this transaction made it possible for you to live and take care of your family. By the same token, if the person didn't buy the drugs from you, they would have bought them from someone else. You needed money to change your "self," that part of you that was not whole or real as it related to your paradigm of the world, your belief system. Both of you needed to swing a mood from wants that were not being met.

In both cases, yours and the buyer of the mind-altering substances, the Law was being violated. Based on your paradigm of the world, perfect as they say it is, you saw nothing wrong with breaking it. You are taking care of your problems; at the same time, the other violator is taking care of his. There appears to be nothing wrong with either paradigms or world views. You have a right to get money to take care of your life and the other person has a right to feel good, even if buying the drugs left his or her children without the basic needs to survive. The key to their paradigm is satisfying the five senses.

Based upon your world view, paradigm, you have to arm yourself with a .357 magnum, just in case someone tries to upset your paradigm of the world. You say, any law that keeps you from surviving like anyone else is wrong; based on your paradigm, that law is wrong. That law is not on your side, it is not in your best interest.

Now, let's remember those five "at risk" factors leading up to your present conviction. You are before the judge, and in your mind, the world has caused you your present predicament. You take no responsibility for your dysfunctional family, leaving school, joining and "socializing to the norms of a deviant subculture," using and abusing others, and all of this is to support the way you "feel" about your "self." Now, you are before the judge because he, the judge, says you have broken laws that all citizens are duty-bound to obey. You are here at Talbot Hall, preparing to go back to the same paradigm of the world, unless there has been a correction to your world view.

We all know—those of us who struggled to make America the country she says she is—that the civil rights movement has brought about many changes in the law. Based upon what your judgment of conviction says, would you put the blame on America for having been treated like an animal, called a piece of dirt by certain correction officers? Put in lock-up for being mistaken for somebody else? Would you blame this Just and Loving Creator you hear us talk about? Would you say He has not made Himself known to you in your twenty-five years?

As we set the world, the perfect world/universe of the Creator up for you to see as information to possibly change your flawed paradigm, let's take you back before the judge with this new perfect information. Now, remember, when you were here before you felt that you had not known any justice all your life growing up in Paterson, New Jersey. Your father could not get a job that paid enough money to take care of your mother, sisters, and brothers, so he left your mother to survive as best she could. You mother, as you watched, buckled under the stress and pressure, doing house work, waiting on the Welfare Department to finish lengthy paperwork. She becomes sick and is in and out of the hospital, while you and your siblings, in an unbelievable fashion, has to take care of your "selves." Listen to what the judge said to you now, after shifting your paradigm with new correct information about your life in the perfect world/universe.

John Doe, you are here because you have been found guilty of N.J.S.P.L. 3762.3. John Doe, based on these perfect laws under which you are being sentenced, you did not have to do what you did to justify your life, and how to live it. You did not have to break these laws. Because you did, you upset the absolute perfection and balance between your "self" and the rest of the perfect order thereof.

The first inhabitants of the world/universe were perfect in every way. They were created by a perfect, all wise, all powerful, all loving Creator. They were perfect in every sense of the word. They needed only to be at peace and well being in that perfection. The one factor was the difference in their mind, their paradigm of that perfection. Because they were created to be free in a world of natural, material, and physical attractions that acted to deceive and distract their spirit and soul from that perfection, they were unable to maintain what was theirs by the perfect nature of their Creation by the Creator.

John Doe, this deception, distraction, which results in violating the law was attempted at correction by those *Ten Commandments* given to Moses, which served to outline the violations resulting from being overcome with the physical, material world, a false paradigm.

What I am doing here today, John Doe, is to give you another chance to correct your paradigm, which proved to be false by your acknowledged behavior mentioned in your judgment of conviction. John Doe, every "self" is subject to these same laws that have convicted you. Violate them and death, similar to what your life has been like, will surely come, day in and day out, year in year out, until your heart loses its energy in helping you to believe in a false paradigm. You will, at that time, become permanently detached and separated from your Creator from that stress and pressure that caused you to violate these perfect laws. Without the paradigm I offer you today, John Doe, you will search for "life" your "self," but you will not find it. Whenever you think you have attained it, have it right in your hands, it will turn to sand right before your eyes, or after you have closed them for the last time.

John Doe, unless you struggle with every ounce of your body's energy in order to regain the "self" and the relationship with your Creator, unbroken in essence and spirit, you can never escape the wicked imaginations of your fractured and broken mind and soul. In taking what belongs to our brothers and sisters, including their "life," the injury you inflict on them is felt by "you" in a way that you cannot escape the penalty of violating the very laws on which your own peace is accorded.

John Doe, this judgment is not unto death, not yet; the hope is that you will come to see what death really is, and then seek "life" union with your Creator, who sustains you in keeping the laws for which you are here today because of their violation. In hopes that this will come to pass, you will be transferred to the New Jersey State Department of Corrections, the Honorable Devon Brown being the commissioner. Dated December 30, 2003. May God have mercy on your soul.

Chapter Four

**EVERY HUMAN BEING YEARNS FOR
PEACE AND HAPPINESS DURING HIS OR
HER LIFETIME. HOWEVER, THE DEVIL IS
IN THE DETAILS EXPERIENCED
AS PSYCHIC STRESS, PHYSICAL,
AND MENTAL PRESSURE**

THE COURAGE TO BE

T**HE PROBLEM**: Because of the lack of spiritual enabling
gained in a *rite of passage* one does not know who he is, where he
came from, and where he is going.

Putting the first three chapters into perspective involves a brief
study of the three citadels of authority, as I have chosen to call them:
the Church, the state, and the citizens of our community, you, and I.
Unless we acknowledge the serious responsibility of each, and agree
to work together across lines of special interest, we shall all suffer. A
challenge there is to consider the churches, mosques, synagogues, and
other faiths in our community, in a global multicultural world. Again,
in a "world sense," we all suffer. It has been made clear that freedom,
peace, and justice are not necessarily guaranteed in a democracy.
International "Terms of Engagement" where the basis of conflicts is
understood, and experienced by getting to the underlying motives for
conflict between any configuration of individual, or collective
interests, always lead to the righteous suggestion of the unfair

distribution of wealth and power. These conditions undermine the democratic philosophy where only a majority, right or wrong, is necessary. This state of existence in God's universe undermines the "law" on which the Kingdom of God is established. This condition cannot survive without the impending correction by God in his omniscient judgment of perfection in His universe. "Righteous exalts a nation not democracy," (Proverbs 14:34).

AGAIN, FAILING TO KNOW THE WAY HE SHOULD GO, HE IS SUBJECT TO MAN'S VERSION OF GOD'S LAW AS OPPOSED TO THE TRUTH OF IT. THE CRIMINAL JUSTICE SYSTEM AND THE DEPARTMENTS OF CORRECTION ONLY EXACERBATE THE PROBLEM, RATHER THAN CORRECT IT. THE TRUTH OF GOD'S LAW SAYS "LET MY PEOPLE GO!"

Understanding the Problem and the Good News of Salvation

Throughout the book, we mention two examples of a counter culture. The two examples we refer to are familiar to all of us: (1) The culture designed by God to Save the Jewish (Hebrew) people, and in turn, they were chosen to save the world, (2) The Christian culture adopted from their slave masters designed by God to save the African slaves from their suffering, humiliation, and cruel death at the hands of their captors in early American history.

In this chapter, we plan to make what we are calling the "problem" as it results in the decreased influence the Christian Church is having as it represents the same type of counter culture that Jesus Christ intends for it to have as it represents His Body, the Christian Church, in our world.

An agreeable admission: The Bible is written, and intended to be understood, from the point where we discern the spiritual world or the Kingdom of God that has been revealed by Him in three distinct dispensations: God the Father, God the Son, and God the Holy Spirit. Jesus answered Pilate who represented the government of Rome and Caesar as he was on trial before Caesar for crimes against Rome. The result was the judgment of death, and Jesus' subsequent death by crucifixion. Nevertheless, the judgment Jesus makes overrides Caesar's with his judgment, which is from God. "My Kingdom is not of this world; if my Kingdom were of this world, then would my servants fight, that I should not be delivered to the Jews; but now is my Kingdom not from hence," (John 18:36 KJV).

An agreeable admission: Consider these statements of King David, and from Paul, the chief exponent of the New Testament, in discerning the Kingdom of God after receiving the Holy Spirit, the third dispensation of God's presence in the physical world, making it not only possible but essential for our salvation. In other words, we, as Christians, must be able to coexist by being able to go in and out of these two distinct worlds simultaneously; nevertheless, this is possible only by adhering to a prescribed set of conditions for this privilege to be granted. "Unseal my lips, Oh, Lord, that I may praise you. You would not be blessed with sacrifices, or I would bring them. If I brought you a burnt offering, you would not accept it. The sacrifices you want is a broken spirit. A broken repentant heart, Oh God, you will not despise," (Psalm 51:15-17), *Life Application-Study Bible*; and Paul: "Therefore I, a prisoner for serving the Lord, beg you to lead a life worthy of your calling, for you have been called by God. Be humble and gentle. Be patient with each other, making allowance for each other's faults because of your love. Always keep yourselves united in the Holy Spirit, and bind yourselves together with peace. We are all one body, we have the same spirit, and we have been called to the same glorious future. There is only one Lord, one faith, one baptism, and there is only one God and Father, who is over us all and in us all and living through us all." However, he has given each of us a special gift according to the generosity of Christ. That is why the Scriptures say, "When he ascended to the heights, he led a crowd of captives and gave gifts to his people. He is the one who gave these gifts to the church, the apostles, the prophets, the evangelists, and the pastors and teachers. Their responsibility is to equip God's people to do his work and build up the church, the body of Christ, until we come to such unity in our faith and knowledge of God's son that we will be mature and full grown in the Lord, measuring up to the full stature of Christ," (Ephesians 4:1-8 and verses 11-12, *Life Application-Study Bible*).

An opportunity to assess where I am in terms of serving God and accepting Jesus Christ, God's son as my Lord and Savior: I am humbly proud to have been given this opportunity to be an instrument for peace through Jesus Christ's broken body and his spilled blood, to the glory of Almighty God, and hoping prayerfully that the body of believers in Christ Jesus at the Stelton Baptist Church will be edified by my example as well as my preaching and precepts discussed and exchanged in Bible Study on Sunday mornings. Any future success of the Life for Christ Foundation is based on this statement of beliefs just immediately above.

Matriculating at Howard University Divinity School in Washington, D.C., preaching almost on a monthly basis as an assistant to the pastor of the Greater First Baptist Church in the nation's capital, I saw all those people out there before me, when I preached, mostly of African American descent, really wanting to know what my God would do to help them in their sad state of existence, struggling for freedom. This was at the height of the civil rights struggles of the early sixties, in the nation's capital, the greatest nation in the world. My thesis in order to graduate from Howard University was "The Implications of Black Nationalism for the Black Church." My humble conclusion was, in a sentence, the Christian Church, black and white together, has to become what Almighty God intended for it to be from the foundations of His world, not the one that man created, and is threatening to destroy.

In 1973, my desire in applying to Drew University in Madison, New Jersey, for the doctorate in ministry was only progressively different from the findings at Howard University. My dissertation for completion at Drew was "To Increase the Congregation's Understanding of Christian Discipleship." There are two steps to where my spiritual growth has brought me to this point: (1) It was impossible for me to obtain the knowledge I sought in Washington, D.C., just by learning from books and professors, even as they taught from the Scriptures, the Bible; and (2) A crisis in my life in the early 1990's, after ministering to a congregation for almost twenty years, I had to find out who God was for myself. This struggle in the early nineties was identical with the crisis Job experienced in his life. GOD IS A SPIRIT. WE CAN ONLY GET TO KNOW HIM THROUGH OUR SPIRIT, WHICH MUST BE LIKE HIS SPIRIT, Psalm 51:15-17. The phenomenon that I speak of having experienced in the early nineties led me to question my faith, because it did not seem to be working in that crisis. This crisis that was similar to that of Job's, is seen in the word "presseth into it," obviously meaning the Kingdom of God that Jesus mentions here: And he said unto them, "Ye are they which justify yourselves before men; but God knoweth your hearts; for that which is highly esteemed among men is abomination in the sight of God. The law and the prophets were until John, since that time the Kingdom of God is preached, and every man presseth into it. And it is easier for heaven and earth to pass, than one tittle of the law to fail," (Luke 16:15-17).

God's Intended Purpose of His Counter Culture

The two instances of a counter culture mentioned above, (1) Hebrews/Jewish people coming out of Egyptian slavery, and (2) African slaves in early American history. Let's explain the term "counter culture": (a) Counter: Marked by or tending toward or in an opposite direction or effect; (b) Culture: The act of developing the intellectual and moral faculties, especially by education. I'd like to put "education" in quotes for the many ways that end result is accomplished.

There are two points to be made here:

(1) During the two instances of involuntary servitude, slavery, God intervened on behalf of the oppressed community, and (2) It has been made clear in the Gospel that is preached, the Good News from God through Jesus Christ, that human beings without the Good News are oppressed, by sin as violators of God's immutable laws that govern the universe. The Good News, the Gospel, being preached is to show the oppressors of the world that God, through Jesus Christ and His Spirit, is still, and will be, eternally delivering from oppression and evil oppressors.

The Key to Understanding "THE" Problem is Spiritual Unity among Believers

I have chosen a brief quote from *The Purpose Driven Life* by the celebrated author, Rick Warren, entitled, "Practice God's Method for Conflict Resolution." In addition to the principles mentioned in the last chapter, Jesus gave the church a simple three-step process: "If a fellow believer hurts you, go and tell him - work it out between the two of you. If he listens, you've made a friend. If he won't listen, take one or two others along so that the presence of witnesses will keep things honest, and try again. If he still won't listen, tell the church," (Matthew 18:15-17).

During the conflict, it is tempting to complain to a third party rather than courageously speak the truth in love to the person you're upset with. This makes the matter worse.

Instead, you should go directly to the person involved. Private confrontation is always the first step, and you should take it as soon as possible. If there were the effects of the unity of the Spirit represented in a counter culture, this behavior would be clearly unacceptable because of the power for change in the unity of the Holy Spirit, represented in the body of Jesus Christ.

On his chapter in the "Statement of Purpose," mention is made *Unfinished Reformation*, a book authored by Charles Clayton Morrison. The conclusion of that entire book might be summed up with the need for a counter culture that would most closely represent the unity of God's Spirit in the world. Jesus Christ clarified that Truth, and left the Spirit of God at Pentecost to be maintained by the Christian Church, representing His risen body. That spiritual Unity was intended by God for Israel, during their 400 years of wandering in the Old Testament, and I firmly believe, by Black people in slavery in America for 400 years, beginning in 1496 to 1861. Although both of these counter cultures endured inhuman misery and suffering, they called upon God and it is recorded that their salvation was based upon God's deliverance. Both races of people in these cases represented a counter culture. Their cases are representative of what is needed now to save our specie, the human race. This is an example of intelligent design.

I reiterate the stand of the Life for Christ Foundation as being committed to edifying the body of Christ at all times and under all conditions where in contractual agreement with another entity, our understanding of the same is made absolutely clear. We stand ready and willing to apologize and ask for forgiveness in order to bring reconciliation where there has been misunderstanding and injury to the Holy Spirit of Jesus Christ in His Body in the world, the Christian Church, wherever and whenever these misunderstandings occur unintentionally.

FOR FURTHER INSIGHTS IN THE RELEVANCE HERE OF THE COUNTER CULTURE NECESSARY IN OUR WORLD, I WILL CONCLUDE WITH A HIGHLY THEO-LOGICAL PROJECTION FOR THE FUTURE OF OUR CIVI-LIZATION

Because of the terms used in the legal profession and in the criminal justice system, all relating to the *Ten Commandments*, we fail as a Christian Church collectively, if we allow children in our congregation and families, and community, to be taken into custody without accepting responsibility for: (1) religious education or lack thereof; (2) taking their hand as they are taken into custody rather than have them use the right to call a legal counselor, Miranda Ruling; (3) not understanding the overall community breakdown of family and child welfare systems and concerns.

Apocalypticism and Eschatology

These two terms may be defined as dualistic, and cosmic in ramification, or understanding. Eschatology is the belief in two opposing cosmic powers, God and Satan (or his equivalent); and in two distinct ages—the present, temporal and irretrievably evil under Satan, who now oppresses the righteous but whose power God will soon act to overthrow. Eschatology describes the future, perfect, and eternal age under God's own rule, when the righteous will be blessed forever. We live in this age, and explanations are found in chapter nine.

Apocalypticism, then, provides both an explanation of the evil that is so evident in this present age and a solution of the concrete problem of the righteous. In some way or other, Satan, who is evil, has gained control of this present age, and he is responsible for its wickedness and corruption and for the evils and oppression suffered by the righteous. However, with the overthrow of Satan by God and with the end of his age, all evil disappears; and the new age, ruled over by God, will be perfectly good and righteous (*The Interpreter's Dictionary of the Bible* - Volume 1 - Abingdon-Cokesbury Press, - 158). See chapters nine and ten.

THE THREE CITADELS OF AUTHORITY, THE CHURCH, THE STATE, AND THE COMMUNITY MUST ACCEPT RESPONSIBILITY FOR THE WELFARE OF THE "BODY POLITIC" VOX POPULI "THE VOICE OF THE PEOPLE" OUR COLLECTIVE PURPOSE MUST BE GROUNDED IN THE NATURE OF OUR VERY EXISTENCE AND SURVIVAL PURPOSE: FOR OUR EXISTENCE AND SURVIVAL

The purpose for any action or behavior should precede the desire to acquire knowledge and power for the accomplishment thereof. In other words, the ends must determine the means. We as a community cannot lock young people up in hopes of reducing tension in the community with the agreed upon necessity of rehabilitating them without strategic programs. Unless they, "the system," have the power to convince us, with "reason," that we have no authoritative power to accomplish the objectives we both agree on, they, "the system," will have to admit, with Godliness, that our purpose exceeds theirs, even as it, our purpose, is based on theirs. The point here is that their purpose has to be grounded in reason. It has to be thoroughly questioned, understood, and embraced. Their failure in obviously having not applied the necessary power and knowledge to "the problem" that we all are experiencing, and some of us are being paid to solve, requires open redress by the three citadels of authority, the state, the Church, and the people, the community, Vox Populi, the voice of the people.

I will broach the discussion of intelligent design here, only as we move to the overarching purpose of the materialization of the peace that God has ordained for our world, and has so magnificently, meticulously, patiently, and faithfully provided in the provisions for our salvation. The "reason" being that physically, and mentally applying the field of psychiatry, psychology, physiology, theology, and last but most important, spiritually, human beings, bipedal, Homo sapiens, primate, mammal, must depend on an intelligent design that is not autonomously generated or carried on without outside control.

The most salient example I could give as an explanation of my premise here would be the twelve steps of Alcohol and Narcotic Anonymous International Association. This group has demonstrated the generic condition of human beings addicted to psychoactive substances. These chemical substances injected into the body of a human being are all found in the periodic Table of Elements found in nature, based on earth science. They are arranged in a sophisticated molecular structure to bring about an apparent change in the mental or spiritual mood of human flesh and blood, without any real positive change to the person's condition in life, or their ability to arrive at the ultimate truth, and end to their physical existence. From this conclusion we know for sure that there will be destructive, negative consequences for our human species. Matthew 5:1-12 commands the way a human being is expected by God to react for a blessing rather than a curse when stressed with earthly trouble.

Isaiah 66:1: "This is what the Lord says: Heaven is my throne, and the earth is my footstool. Could you build me a temple as good as that? Could you build a dwelling place for me? My hands have made both heaven and earth, and they are mine. I, the Lord, have spoken! I will bless those who have humble and contrite hearts who tremble at my word. But those who choose their own ways, delighting in their sins, are cursed. Their offering will not be accepted. When such people sacrifice an ox, it is no more acceptable than a human sacrifice. When they sacrifice a lamb or bring an offering of incense, it is as if they had blessed an idol. I will send great troubles against them - all the things they feared. For when I called, they did not answer. When I spoke, they did not listen. They deliberately sinned - before my very eyes - and chose to do what they know I despise:"

September 18, 2005. This is the date I have chosen to identify the beginning of this part of chapter four as explained at the beginning involving "The Purpose for Man's Existence." This particular search began at the Stelton Baptist Church of which I am a member, printed in the bulletin was an acknowledgment that this date, after Easter, was the fifteenth Sunday after Pentecost, the moment in human history where God, the Creator of the universe, executed, or divinely provided human beings with the free gift of His Holy Spirit, the third revelation or dispensation thereof. I have chosen four Scriptures from both the Old and the New Testament to connect the dots, so to speak, moreover more theologically appropriate we refer here to the Scarlet Thread of our redemption. Who would dare ignore this? Intelligent design by God, the Creator of the universe:

(1) Genesis 49:10 "the scepter will not depart from Judah, nor the ruler's staff from his descendants, until the coming of the one to whom it belongs, the one whom all nations will obey." Why was Judah, known for selling Joseph into slavery and trying to defraud his daughter-in-law-so greatly blessed? God had chosen Judah to be the ancestor of Israel's line of kings (That is the meaning of "the scepter will not depart from Judah."). This may have been due to Judah's dramatic change of character (44:33,34). Judah's line would produce the promised Messiah, Jesus.

(2) Isaiah 61:1-2: "The Spirit of the Lord is upon me, because the Lord has appointed me to bring good news to the poor, He has sent me to comfort the brokenhearted and to announce that the captives will be released and prisoners will be freed. He has sent me to tell those who mourn that the time of the Lord's favor has come, and with it, the day of God's anger against their enemies.

(3) Jeremiah 31:31-34: "The day will come says the Lord, when I will make a new covenant with the people of Israel and Judah. This covenant will not be like the one I made with their ancestors when I took them by the hand and brought them out of the land of Egypt. They broke that covenant, thought I loved them as a husband loves his wife, says the Lord. But this is the new covenant that I will make with the people of Israel on that day, says the Lord. I will put my laws in their minds, and I will write them on their hearts. I will be their God, and they will be my people. And they will not need to teach their neighbors, nor will they need to teach their family, saying, you should know the Lord. For everyone, from the least to the greatest, will already know me, says the Lord. And I will forgive their wickedness and will never again remember their sins."

(4) Luke 4:16-20: "When he came to the village of Nazareth, where he had been brought up; and, as his custom was, he went into the synagogue on the Sabbath day, and stood up for to read. And there was delivered unto him the book of the prophet Esaias. And when he had opened the book, he found the place where it was written, 'The Spirit of the Lord is

upon me, because he hath anointed me to preach the gospel to the poor, he hath sent me to heal the broken hearted, to preach deliverance to the captives, and the recovering of sight to the blind, to set at liberty them that are bruised, to preach the acceptable year of the Lord.' And he closed the book, and he gave it again to the minister, and sat down. And the eyes of all them that were in the synagogue were fastened on him. And He began to say unto them, 'This Scripture is fulfilled in your ears.'"

Slavery has been the scourge of human beings since the *fall* in the Garden of Eden, and will always be so without God's freedom that came at Pentecost and is provided to those who will truly call upon God, the Creator of the universe, as Father and mean it, just as Jesus did, even unto death, thereby gaining Him the resurrection from the dead and eternal life in God's Presence, the Kingdom of God.

It must be made clear that our major premise in purpose for the Life for Christ Foundation is to establish the moral imperative as bringing to fruition of a counter culture to demonstrate that man cannot survive either individually, or collectively without the acknowledgement of the intervention of God, however we perceive Him (AA and NA—Twelve Steps). This Higher Power is an intelligent design for mankind. I will ask a question and allow each reader or listener to draw their own conclusion or reason for their answer: Has the Christian Church—the body of Jesus Christ in the World—provided as an intelligent design, a counter culture to demonstrate the Higher Power found by people who by trial and error in AA and NA, using Twelve Steps, have done? And was not this the original intent of God in choosing a people called Israel in the Old Testament?

I want to refer to the two distinct examples we are using in the book of counter cultures formed by God as they called upon Him in their distress and as they relate to our concern here in "Purpose." But before I do that, I want to recall remarks made in conversation during a recent controversy in the Christian Church over gays and lesbians, homosexuals becoming members, and sometimes rising to top leadership positions in the church. It should be made clear that homosexuality in the Christian Church or any separate local congregation, has to do with each person understanding, or lack of their understanding, of a Spirit-filled or controlled lifestyle. An example here is demonstrated in the Life of Jesus Christ, intelligently designed. This very same design Jesus applied as He walked us through the steps beyond death itself into Eternal Life. There are those who acknowledge this power of Jesus' lifestyle as they access the power of God, His Father, and have committed themselves to following the Twelve Steps of NA and AA and claim access to this Higher Power (God's Holy Spirit) in controlling and subjugating a physical lifestyle to the Power to live a Spirit-Mind controlled lifestyle, in a perfectly created and controlled universe. These are not "holy rollers" as some Christian Churches are called where members are physical and demonstrative during the worship service. These people in AA and NA understand mentally, and with deductive reasoning how strong belief in a Higher Power keeps them alive in the flesh over their body, living a sober lifestyle with peace of mind and soul.

COUNTER CULTURE

If the purpose of "that" Christian Church was to make crystal clear what living a Christian lifestyle was all about, homosexuality could never coexist in conversation, let alone become a controversy. If what we have said above existed in the Christian Church, a homosexual could become a member, but there would be no need to mention his or her sexual preference in the context of their soul's salvation. The two could only become a controversy if the topic of Soul Salvation has not been made the superior concern in the Christian teachings of that church. In order for this to happen as we are supposing here, the purpose that this church has set as its only concern would automatically eliminate any other purpose or concern. If the Church cannot have this influence on the homosexual, the homosexuals have every right to ask for clarification of the priority of one over the other. Their concern is valid in demanding redress from us, the Christian Church, for not accepting them as they are, just as God and Jesus Christ accepts them, just as they are. "Judgment begins at the house of God," (Peter 4:17). The judgment is against both for not being what, by the word of God, and the provisions made by Him, says they should be. Galatians 3:25-29: "But after that faith is come, we are no longer under a school master. For ye are all the children of God by faith in Christ Jesus. For as many of you have been baptized into Christ have put on Christ. There is neither Jew nor Greek, there is neither bond nor free, there is neither male nor female; for all are one in Christ Jesus. And if ye be Christ's, then are ye Abraham's seed, and heirs according to the promise."

OUR PURPOSE: "RELEASE TO THE CAPTIVES"

The following Truth involving the Christian Church gives it a mandate, which no other institution in the universe can claim: The Kingdom of God has been made available as a provision for those who would seek salvation from hell, a place, physically, mentally, and spiritually, where mankind does not have this knowledge, and therefore is not able to perceive, discern the two distinct worlds that we who are spiritual, are able to coexist within, and experience. My people are being destroyed because they don't know me. It is all your fault, you priest, for you yourselves refuse to know me. Now, I refuse to recognize you as my priests. Since you have forgotten the laws of your God, I will forget to bless your children (Hosea 4:6 Life Application - Study Bible).

The *fall* of mankind from his original spiritual relationship with God, the Creator of the world that we are presently inhabiting is found in Genesis 2 and 3.

Followed immediately after insights into treating the human condition from the *fall*, it is a natural progression to concentrate on "treating man's human condition." For this treatment, we focus on God's provisions for obtaining peace in his, God's perfectly designed creation. There can be no peace, rather only death (Genesis 2 & 3) unless we come into the "knowledge" (Hosea 4:6) of God's LAW. There are two references used here to focus light and understanding on the need we have for God's perfect "LAWS" given to Moses at Mount Sinai for this knowledge needed for our peace and salvation. The *Ten Commandments* that God gave to Moses after deliverance from Egyptian slavery are the same laws our first offenders are being subjected to before a judge of the criminal justice system. In our friend of the court brief mentioned above, we state that the purpose for which we stand is the same as that of our nation's, that is, on the laws of the Constitution of the United States of America. The Pledge of Allegiance goes as follows: "I pledge allegiance to the flag of the United States of America, and to the Republic for which it stands, one nation, under God, indivisible, with liberty and justice for all."

I am not sure at this time in our nation's history what "indivisible" means to our Constitution and republic. Based on the discussion we make above involving the *Ten Commandments* as the basis of all the laws that govern the nation, the intense discussions today involving separation of church and state, and considering the word "indivisible" in the Pledge of Allegiance, something has come about, over hundreds of years, to cause the very foundation on which our nation stands to be questioned, if not done away with altogether

(Former President Jimmy Carter has at this writing, on the bookstands his response to the moral decline in America, relating to the concerns we present here.).

THE ELEMENTS OF JUSTICE/JUDGMENT: DIVINE VERSUS STATE

Mentioned in this chapter are several terms involving justice and judgment administered under both divine as well as state laws. Some of these terms are as follows: guilt, innocence, perpetrator or violator, culprit, fault, culpability, probable cause, due process of the law, and equal protection of the law.

ARREST - CONVICTION

The Miranda Ruling states, "A law-enforcement officer must warn a person taken into custody that he or she has the right to remain silent and is entitled to legal counsel." All of us are familiar with a scenario of this kind involving a first offender. That is the State's version of administering Justice, by the way, of the same laws that are administered by divine justice. Who should be called to administer divine justice when a first offender is arrested, or should we not expect him or her to be made to understand the law that they have violated, in fact and truth? Would it not be true then, that an entirely different set of parameters should be set in place to bring the perpetrator or violator to justice, divine justice that we refer to here in Life for Christ Foundation? Or at least, let them know what law they have violated and are about to be punished for? We repeat here that these laws are indivisible for both republics, one visible and the other invisible. Let's shift our paradigm to another way of looking at the world or worlds. Let's ask the question at this point, are we not, or shouldn't we understand that there are two different worlds, one physical and material, and the other mental and invisible and spiritual?

Let's take the legal term:
(1) Arrest, which, understood in two different worlds, would have two different meanings, necessary to be understood in each world differently: (1) The physical world: to bring to a stop; to take or keep in custody by the authority of the law (Merriam Webster Dictionary 1967); (2) Spiritual world: if, in the understanding of the Gospel of Luke, we could construct the steps leading to discipleship for a new member coming into the church, it would begin with proclamation or preaching, hearing the word of God, and in this experience

one's spiritual condition, relating to the degree they understand their having broken the laws of God would become clear to them. His or her attention is focused on their having violated a law.

(2) Conviction: (1) Physical world: conviction; the act or process of convicting of a crime, especially in a court of law; the state of being convinced of an error or compelled to admit the truth; a convict, a felon. (2) The spiritual world: repentance; it means becoming a different person: "Unless he or she turns and become like children, you will never enter the Kingdom of Heaven." Matthew 18:3. Entrance into the kingdom is for the poor in spirit. "I have not come to call the righteous, but sinners to repentance." (Luke 5:32) the point to remember as we go through these comparative terms relating to the two different worlds is that in both cases, the same laws are referred to in each different world of laws, the *Ten Commandments* given to Moses by God. Another point to remember here is that referring to the fall of mankind as in the Garden of Eden, all human beings are guilty of breaking the ten laws God gave Moses. All human beings not aware of the laws of God are doomed to an eternal slavery and death of the one world they inherited from their mother's womb. They are free from death only if they become spiritual, and are given access to that other world of the Spirit, which is of the same substance, presence as God. Hosea 4:6 and John 8:32: "My people are destroyed for lack of knowledge," and Jesus, "Continue in my word, and you shall know the Truth, and the Truth shall make you free."

(3) Judgment: The physical world: In light of the casual interpretations given the other serious and important terms listed here, it is worth asking why is judgment given the same definition in Merriam Webster as it is in the Scriptures and Interpreter Bibles? Judgment: a formal utterance of an authoritative opinion. Judgment: The final judgment of mankind by God. I will try to explain why human beings can easily get an idea of what judgment is without considering its final devastating consequences: Under spiritual conviction versus physical conviction in a court of law, a human being becomes penitent, as in penitentiary. In spiritual penitence, the human being becomes a different person, a complete turn about. With this new spirit-mentality-mind, the person is prepared to accept, in humility, reason (mental powers

needed to form a conclusion) not of their human condition. When this occurs, not only are they prepared to accept their sentence of guilt, which is what the criminal court judge hands down, but if they want to pass on to the spiritual world of eternal life, they must accept the judgment of death on their physical life, the one they have passed from in their acknowledgment of its faults and weakness before the judge, God, becoming penitent (a new person spiritually).

Dr. Elisabeth Kuebler Ross, a medical physician, after studying patients in intensive care and in a hospice (terminally ill housing unit connected with hospitals) discovered and documented five stages of fear in the attitudes of those about to die. (1) the first stage is denial and isolation, (2) The second stage is anger, (3) The third stage is bargaining (with God, which should have come earlier and under much more reasonable circumstances when there was something to bargain with, (4) the fourth stage is depression (Dr. Ross: Never tell a person in this stage that they should not be sad. They know already that they are going to lose everything in this world.), (5) the fifth stage is acceptance, or "The final rest before the long journey" is what one patient had to say. Dr. Ross informs that "This is the time when the family needs more help than the patients."

I hope that those who feel that the statements above about judgment are without substantiation will take time to see the reasoning or the mental powers concerned with forming conclusions are clear here in concluding that faith in God makes a lot of common sense.

For instance: I am going to quote three Scriptures to bring these points from the Word of God, through Jesus Christ and the Holy Spirit:
1) "Verily, verily, I say unto you, he that heareth my word, and believeth on him that sent me, hath everlasting life, and shall not come into condemnation, but is passed from death into life," (John's Gospel 5:24 KJV).
2) "The law and the prophets were until John; since that time the Kingdom of God is preached, and every man presseth into it." (Luke's Gospel 16:16 KJV). The story of Job would be an example. Also Matt 5:1-12, in other words, doing the time you have on earth, rather than letting your time on earth, in human flesh, do you in.

3) "And it is appointed unto man once to die, but after this the judgment," (Hebrews 9:27). You can pay the piper now, or wait until your death. Although it is possible to pay at the last moment, there are two dangers: (a) Your lack of the knowledge of your spiritual condition required before the judge does not change based on time only, but by the condition of your heart. Remember, "You cannot serve two masters." You will always be with the master you love at death; and (b) Beware of sudden death in which case you have no control of time to make your peace with God, the Judge. The Judgment has to do with how you have acknowledged your mistakes in adjustments from your mother's womb, to the immutable perfection of the divine order of His universe. Matthew 5:23-24: "Therefore if thou bring thy gift to the altar, and there rememberest that thy brother hath ought against thee; leave there thy gift before the alter, and go thy way; first be reconciled to thy brother, then come and offer thy gift." This judgment is based on Matthew 25:31-46.

The two world thesis is a no-brainer when it gets to the discussion of intelligent design. It does not take a rocket scientist to figure out how intelligent God's design of Jesus Christ is. Jesus Christ was intelligent enough to find out how to meet all the requirements necessary to be resurrected from the dead after the whole world witnesses him being crucified and put in a tomb perfectly sealed. The reason I give here is the two world phenomena. "Jesus answered and said unto him (Nicodemus), 'Verily, verily I say unto thee, except a man be born again, he cannot see the Kingdom of God,'" (John 3:3 KJV).

"For Christ is the end of the law for righteousness to everyone that believeth," (Romans 10:4 KJV). "Let this mind be in you which was also in Christ Jesus, who being the form of God, thought it not robbery to be equal with God, but made Himself of no reputation, but rather, took upon Himself the form of a servant, and was made in the likeness of man," (Philippians 2:5). Communion with God in flesh and Spirit: Two different worlds made available to human kind: "Take eat, this is my body," (Gospel of Matthew 26:26). This is a perfect example of existentialism or extending one's life beyond the ordinary.

COMMENTS CONTINUED ON JUDGMENT

The life that God has given through His Son, Jesus Christ, can only come after physical death that effects both the mind, spirit, and the body. John's Gospel Chapter 12:23b-25. (23b) The time has come for the Son of Man to enter into his glory. (24) The truth is a kernel of wheat must be planted in the soil. Unless it dies it will be alone—a single seed. But its death will produce many new kernels—a plentiful harvest of new lives. (25) Those who love their life in this world will lose it. Those who despise their life in this world will keep it for eternal life. (26) All those who want to be my disciples must come and follow me, because my servants must be where I am. And if they follow me, the Father will honor them." In other words, life, as it is intended to be understood by Jesus' words to Mary and Martha at the death of their brother, and Jesus' close friend, Lazarus in John 11:21-26, can only come after physical and material death in the worldly sense. "Martha said to Jesus, 'Lord, if you had been here, my brother would not have died.'" (22) But even now I know that God will give you whatever you ask. (23) Jesus told her "Your brother will rise again." (24) "Yes," Martha said, "when everyone else rises, on resurrection day." (25) Jesus told her, "I am the resurrection and the life. Those who believe in me, even though they die like everyone else, will live again." (26) They are given eternal life believing in me and will never perish. Do you believe this Martha?" (Life Application Study Bible).

In other words, life, as it is understood by Jesus Christ, and meant for human beings of the physical world, can only come after death. You must be born again, not of flesh and blood, but on the spirit. Flesh and blood cannot inherit the Kingdom of God. The time that one becomes born again or begins life spiritually is not as important as one's ability to address his condition that is required to come before God, who judges our fitness to coexist in the Kingdom of God with Him, in His presence. The quality of your awareness of your imperfect condition in a perfect universe is more important than the time you chose to change or be changed by the Holy Spirit. Hebrews 9:29 Jesus' statement to Martha at Lazarus's death can be equated with Jesus' statement to the thief on the cross, who was obviously arrested, found guilty, convicted, sentenced, and was in the process of serving out his sentence of death by crucifixion. This is an example of a late case for a plea bargain for Jesus' fellow hangman. Nevertheless, the only thing that mattered in this case, where Jesus is acting on God's behalf as the Judge was the condition of his heart, and as that related to the thief's ability to coexist with God in His perfect universe. This gift has been graciously offered to us while still "existing" in it, this physical world where the Kingdom of Heaven is also available to us. So, Jesus could grant him a pardon that no governor and Supreme Court of the United States could render. This statement covers the thief's exoneration of his crimes on earth. Hebrews 9:27 "And just as it is destined that each person dies only once and after that comes judgment," (*Life Application Bible*). We die to the flesh, eternal death, or to the Spirit of God, eternal life. In either case, a judgment from an all-wise, all-loving and forgiving, and righteous God, has been rendered.

The overriding truth here is life as opposed to death. For death is mental and spiritual, before it is finished physically. When our vital signs, determining that our physical body still exist, or is about to expire, we must understand something else that is going on, or there is nothing else going on, in which case, life is over, expired. Jesus' last words on the cross were not that "It is finished," although he said those words, obviously meaning that He had completed His mission on earth as the Savior. His last words were, "Into Thy hands I commend my Spirit." Unless you or I can say the same thing at the same time in our physical expiration, we will just be headed for yonder's graveyard, or cemetery, unless we purchased a vault at the crematorium. I think the Apostle Paul speaks to this time in the fading life of a human being, who is a believer in Jesus Christ: I Corinthians (53) "For our perishable earthly bodies must be transformed so that we will never die. (54) When this happens—when our perishable earthly bodies have been transformed into heavenly bodies that will never die—then at last the Scriptures will come true. Death is swallowed up in victory. (55) Oh Death, where is your victory? Oh Death, where is your sting? (56) For sin is the sting that results in death, and the law gives sin its power. (57) How we thank God, who gives us victory over sin and death through Jesus Christ our Lord," (I Corinthians 15:54-57, *Life Application Bible*).

THE LAW

As we have mentioned other documents previously written as references tying together the "Law" as it is intended to relate to both the church and the state, theological law references are made here to the following addenda: Death has not been explained sufficiently by theologians and teachers of the Bible and the *Ten Commandments* to make life the center of our being, desire, and lifelong search, so we detest, try to prevent, and shun death. Jesus Christ taught, both by precept and example, Hebrews 4:15, "This High Priest of ours understands our weaknesses, for He faced all the temptations we do, yet He did not sin, or what? Break the laws of God." God, in the first dispensation of His revelation, specified the *Ten Commandments* that were the potential avenue to our death. The second dispensation of His revelation is in Jesus Christ the Savior, who, as I have said, taught by precept and example, and as a result, fulfilled His mission on earth which was to provide us with power to overcome those items listed in God's reminder: *Ten Commandments* of the Law, which if not obeyed, results in death.

God is a Spirit: (John 4:24) We must be spirit if we are to have communion with Him. This has nothing to do, except as a symbol, with the bread and grape juice we serve on the first Sunday of each month, which is of this world, earthly. This is a simple, yet deadly conclusion: If you cannot obey the Law, death is as certain as breathing when you stop. Romans 10:4: "Christ has accomplished the whole purpose of the law. All who believe in him are made right with God," (*Life Application Bible*). The next question might be: How was Jesus able to keep the law? He was sent that we might believe in God. "So, you see, it is impossible to please God without faith. Anyone who wants to come to Him must believe that there is a God and that He rewards those who sincerely seek Him," (Hebrews 11:6, *Life Application Bible*).

Earlier in this chapter, mention is made under "Arrest and Conviction," and the Miranda ruling. No member of the criminal justice system has either the ability or the right to select the legal counsel except to relate the accused to their family or guardian for causes leading to the allegation of guilt. This is the problem we stated at the beginning of this section of Chapter Four. The problem, a gap in the organized process of remedial rehabilitation, and the solution, strengthening the circle that bonds, by bridging the gaps that are created, where the results will be the positive values we seek so that these youth can experience a community shared by all our citizens.

DISCIPLESHIP: ITS RELATIONSHIP TO EACH ONE OF US IS THE SAME AS ITS RELATIONSHIP TO HIS BODY, HIS CHURCH, AND HAS TO BE CARRIED OVER INTO THE COMMUNITY, REPRESENTATIVE OF THE KINGDOM OF GOD

Great crowds were following Jesus. He turned around and said to them, "If you want to be my follower you must love me more than your own father and mother, wife and children, brothers and sisters—yes, more than your own life. Otherwise, you cannot be my disciple.

And you cannot be my disciple if you do not carry your own cross and follow me."

But don't begin until you count the cost. For who would begin construction of a building without getting estimates and checking to see if there is enough money to pay the bills? Otherwise, you might complete only the foundation before running out of funds. And then how everyone would laugh at you! They would say, "There's the person who started that building and ran out of money before it was finished!" Luke 14:25-30 (Life Application Bible).

You must have the example of Jesus Christ in your life; you do not have life if you do not have His Spirit—that is, the Spirit of God, which represents the three dispensations of the eternal presence of God, you or I are outside of the presence of God. Furthermore, if you or I do not have the Spirit, you or I am judged as a violator of the Law, and subsequently the judgment of death is just being deferred by the grace of God. Ephesians 2:8: "By grace we are saved through faith and that not of yourselves, it is the gift of God." I John 5:12: "He that hath the Son hath life, he that hath not the son of God, hath not life." If you or I do not make Jesus Christ the Lord of our life we will certainly, like sheep, stray and eventually wind up far from the shepherd and safety, and security. Whenever this sad situation occurs, eventually we will be arrested by trouble, and convicted by God's perfect judgment of our violations.

God/Christ/Spirit/Christ's Body/The Christian Church, and Discipleship

If these six stages of God's revelation are to be indistinguishable, as we know they are, The Christian Church specifically, and our world generally, are way out of line from where they ought to be. And if what I have said about an individual believer coming to be arrested by trouble and being brought to justice and judgment and convicted, who and which of the two groups mentioned above, the Church of Jesus Christ, or the world, is to be held responsible? Can we blame the government? I Peter 4:17: "For the time has come for judgment, and it must begin first among God's own children, and if even we Christians must be judged, what terrible fate await those who have never believed God's Good News?"

If I did anything serious in this writing, it would be to show, and to as fair a degree as possible, with the hope of proving that there is no difference in the way the laws of the Supreme Court of the United States of America are meant to be understood and interpreted, and the intent of those given to Moses thirty-five hundred years ago by God.

John 3:16: "God so loved the world that He gave His only begotten Son, so that whosoever believeth in Him shall not perish, but shall have everlasting life." God sent Jesus Christ to inaugurate His coming into our lives and times, including eternity, which will extend beyond the understanding of the times we now live in, without this world ending.

Following on from what I hope will be internalized as a life changing reality mentioned just above, there is absolutely no way in this world to be able to keep from violating the laws of God, without the Holy Spirit. If there was some easier way, in His loving kindness and tender mercy, I'm more than sure that our Father, who is also our God, would have made it possible.

Listen to these divine proclamations from Scripture made at Christmas two thousand years ago: Luke 2:14 "Glory to God in the highest, and on earth peace, goodwill toward men." This is God's incarnation—God in flesh appearing. He hath gained strength with his arm. He hath scattered the proud in the imagination of their heart. He hath brought down the mighty from their seats, and exalted them of low degree. The rich he hath sent away empty, the poor he hath filled with great things. Luke 1:54 forward. Luke 2:29-32: "Lord, now lettest thy servant depart in peace, according to thy word: For mine eyes have seen thy salvation, which Thou hath prepared before all people: A light to lighten the Gentiles, and the glory of thy people Israel."

Revelational Reality: I will attempt to do two things: (1) Relate the Trinity, the three dispensations of God's reality, to what He is accomplishing in His world, and (2) Reveal the need for "A" people to "Act" as what we know from reading above, as that church or body of Jesus Christ. The purpose it is to allow us to live in the third dispensation without breaking the laws of God. This means not violating the laws, and being arrested by "trouble," later being brought to justice and being convicted and judged to death, unless we come before God and ask for forgiveness, this by correctly admitting our fault, and guilt of the violation committed. You might notice as you read here, I have not used the word sin. Sin in light of a violation of the law of God is the same. In other words, sin gives everyone in our present day world where the existence of the Kingdom of God is also present, a good excuse for not seeing themselves as violators. I might explain it this way: Sin is a condition of the heart, resulting in a behavior of the body. Psalm 119:11 says, "Thy word have I hid in my heart that I might not sin against Thee." The law is a condition of judgment. A person who sins can be forgiven for that sin, but that person was under the sentence and judgment of death just the same. So, a person is not really off the hook when they are forgiven for their sins. It's the same as having an outstanding warrant in the books at the court house. If you're brought to justice, you will have to answer for that sin, although it was twenty years ago, and you were forgiven during those twenty years.

There is one statement from Scripture that I choose here to show what I have been trying to do in changing our Christian terminology from sin to law, the same law that is used by the government, the state, et al, Romans 10:4: "Jesus Christ is the end of the Law for righteousness to everyone that believeth."

The work and office, administration of the Spirit is the same for the law and sin, and is preeminent in the will of God for establishment of the Kingdom of God. The ten laws—Ten Commandments, are adjudicated by two factors, (1) Repentance, and (2) Obedience to those laws. These characteristics repentance - an attitude of regret for mistakes, and obedience to the laws, in man's heart are to be reinforced through the breaking of bread and prayer, based on John's Gospel 3:3, Jesus answered and said unto him, "Verily, verily, I say unto thee, except a man be born again, he cannot see the Kingdom of God." Jesus' statement is the same whether or not you or I are at the bar of justice before Almighty God, where, hopefully, death of the old self has occurred, or at the court house in Middlesex County, New Brunswick, New Jersey, U.S.A., or Iraq, or Russia, China, etc.

The KINGDOM OF GOD: I could say that the Kingdom of God is Revelational reality. Or that Revelational reality is the Kingdom of God. The Kingdom of God is concrete, Spiritually that is, and Revelational reality is abstract, an explanation in words and thoughts. Nevertheless, they both can be experienced in terms of their meaning, the presence and Spirit of God.

To make this even more confusing, hopefully not, is to say that Jesus Christ formed the Church based on His birth, the incarnation, His life, crucifixion, resurrection, and the giving of the Spirit at Pentecost, and left the church here in the world to act as His body, until He comes again, this time in Judgment. Philippians 1:6: "Being confident of his very thing, that he which hath begun a good work in you will perform it until the day of Jesus Christ."

"It ought not to ever leave the reader's mind here that the story of salvation that Conzelman states very significantly in his book, *The theology of St. Luke*, separates (1) the 'period of Israel,' (2) the ministry of Jesus Christ, and (3) that of the *ecclesia pressa* or church, in time leading toward the *Parousia* or the end time, the consummation of

God's will in time. But in fact all these epochs, if they can be called this, are serving to accomplish the same end and so they represent a different period in time and a different method, rather than a change in direction of purpose," (M.J. Austin; Drew Univ. *To Increase the Congregation's Understanding of Christian Discipleship*; 1976-p. 14).

There are two points that will make this clear, and I will keep them brief:

(1) God called Israel, the twelve tribes, to bring the Kingdom of God into the world, the saving of mankind: The Old Testament, Jesus Christ's coming, the incarnation, God in flesh appearing, was for that same purpose. The proof being that Jesus Himself acknowledged that He had come from God, and His last words from the cross were "Into thy hands I commend my Spirit, from which He had come." God has given Himself by the Spirit, at Pentecost, to His followers, who subsequently became and is the Church we are members of today, of the same substance and Spirit as God, and our Savior Jesus Christ. Before I state number 2 here, there are two points to remember from point number 1, a) Israel in the Old Testament was called to save the world, salvation for mankind; b) It is absolutely conclusive here that God has revealed to us that His Holy Spirit is the only mode of operation to accomplish world salvation, and that through His Christian Church, and in all expectations has resulted in the KINGDOM OF GOD, His original purpose in His universe.

(2) At the time of a person's death, let's say he or she has been a member of the church, the First Baptist Church of Charlotte, North Carolina for the past fifty years. He or she will not likely understand his or her death, as opposed to the opportunity for life in Christ, or anyone else's if he or she did not understand his or her experience as a member, as being a part of Jesus Christ's body, literally in the sense of Jesus' coming into the world physically, as well as Spiritually and making up that world that is here now in degrees. In other words, the small number of true believers now is what Jesus refers to as the Kingdom of God being as leaven in bread that affects the whole loaf, or an acorn growing into a large oak tree. The number of true believers that exist now will become the fullness of the Presence of God and His Kingdom when Christ returns in Judgment. Faith in God

must be seen as surely and as visibly as one's faith in the resurrection of Jesus Christ, and His abiding presence in the world, but also in our hearts and lives. As Apostle Paul would say in Galatians 2:20, "I am crucified with Christ, nevertheless I live; yet not I, but Christ liveth in me, and the life which I now live in the flesh I live by the faith of the Son of God, who loved me, and gave himself for me." The funeral of a believer should be addressed as that person having been Jesus Christ for others by having done all they could to bring the Kingdom of God into its fulfillment as found in St. Matthew 25:31-46.

To reiterate the above two points:
(1) There is no difference between the laws of Moses given by God to His people, and those adjudicated by all judges in this country, including the Supreme Court, and (2) The word "sin" intentionally or unintentionally, has replaced "law" in administering the word of God given to Moses as the answer, should we obey them, to treating our human conditions, and hopefully, saving our soul.

We might be able to assume that many Christians believe that they can sin without breaking God's laws, because they don't go to jail, or are brought before a court of law for sinning. You go to jail only if you break a law that is on the man's books. The problem there is that there are two different sets of books. Not only does God have the true copy, He also audits the other set.

If we use the Bible and Scriptures generally, and the *Ten Commandments* specifically, in the United States of America and our judicial system, to arrest and take into custody a juvenile and charge him or her with a crime, or a violation of the *Ten Commandments*, we are misinterpreting the canons of judicial ethics. If we take the *Ten Commandments* seriously, we must also take Proverbs 22:6 seriously which says, "Train up a child in the way he should go, and when he is old he will not depart from it."

When the president of the United States, at his inauguration, places his hand on the Bible and swears in an oath to uphold the laws of the Constitution so help me God, and he says "I do so help me God!" that is a solemn responsibility when it comes to the *Ten Commandments*, and Proverbs 22:6. When the courts and the judicial system acknowledges that an adolescent is incapable of understanding the full implication and consequences of his choice of behavior as is now the case, it is here that such words as "right to know", "due process", "probable cause", "equal protection of the law", become in question. It seems clear here that when an adolescent is apprehended for violation of the law, and his Miranda rights are read, they should include a clergyman trained in systematic theology, as well as U.S. Constitutional law, and professionally trained in social services otherwise, the question arises as to whether that citizen's rights as an American have been violated.

Should we analyze the New Jersey State Attorney General Peter C. Harvey's 2005 "Station House Adjustment" law for "first offenders," it would be clear that we are not talking separation of church and state, as much as separation of powers." The state gets its power from the *Ten Commandments*, jurisprudence.

As I reiterated in the statement immediately above in reference to the fact that there is no difference to be made between the *Ten Commandments* and the laws on which our United States Constitution are based, those who think they can, as a single taxpayer or citizen, use technicalities recently legislated from the Supreme Court bench, change some basic language on which the freedom of each person was based, are producing one form of hypocrisy after another. Based upon the major premise here, the *Ten Commandments* and the Holy Bible are very clear on individual freedom to be had by individual citizens for which the interpretation God, the Creator of the universe has given to the term "Freedom." The military conflagration going on now in Iraq and the Middle East in general is proof that democracy cannot guarantee freedom to any nation without the justice of the Word of God. Our political heritage confirms the following from The Declaration of Independence, "We hold these truths to be self evident that all men are created equal, and endowed by their Creator with certain inalienable rights, among these are life, liberty, and the pursuit of happiness." As Jesus has said in St. John 8:31-32, "Continue in my words, and you shall know the Truth, and the Truth shall make you free, indeed." We repeat here the Word of God to the Prophet Isaiah, 66:4, "I will choose their delusions, and will bring their fears upon them; because when I called, none did answer; when I spake they did not hear; but they did evil before mine eyes, and chose that in which I delightest not," (KJV).

Let's confirm the paradox of separation of church and state where the laws of God—The *Ten Commandments*—are superseded by the interpretation given to them by the U.S. Supreme Court. The Constitution provides that there will be no test for office, and the First Amendment allows the "free exercise of religion" and prohibits the establishment of an official religion by Congress. Yet there has never been a complete "wall of separation" between the church and state in America. The armed forces have chaplains paid for by Congress; the Supreme Court chambers have a mural of Moses "giving" the *Ten Commandments*; the dollar bill proclaims "In God We Trust." This involvement with religions was extended by President Bush who proposed giving government funds to faith-based groups for their charitable work (*The Basics of American Politics*: GaryWasserman, Person Longman, Pg. 159).

As a former New York governor Mario Cuomo observed, "I protect my right to be a Catholic by preserving your right to be a Jew, or a Protestant, or a non believer, or anything else you choose." That to me, from what I hope to have proven here, is a flat-out cop-out. What this statement says, is that if your religion says America or Israel, or the nation of Palestine is to be destroyed, is that all right, if that's what they choose? Where is the Truth, the *Ten Commandments*? Democracy cannot be defended should we agree to ignore the Truth of the Law of God. Without the Truth, anyone who gets enough people to agree with them gets to interpret what is right.

The Pilgrims broke away from Great Brittan for just the reason we speak of here. They did not want to worship or pay ultimate allegiance to any human agent or government body. Britain was playing willy nilly helter skelter with the laws that governed the people. The king, Edward the Eighth, wanted to get married, and as a Catholic he could not, so he changed the religion to another denomination of religion in order to carry out his own nefarious objectives. This is what happens without the Truth, and this is why the Pilgrims left England for America. THIS IS THE ABSOLUTE TRUTH OF THE FOUNDATION OF OUR GOVERNMENT AND LAWS, AND OUR DEMOCRACY THAT NOW WE ARE READY TO DENY, AND IN FACT LEGISLATE THAT YOU CAN NO LONGER MENTION GOD IF YOU REPRESENT THE GOVERNMENT WHOSE FOUNDATION WAS BASED UPON THE LAWS OF GOD TO SECURE A MORE PERFECT UNION.

I do not believe that Gloria Ward Howe was out of touch with either the goals and objectives of the people of her time, or the government that Abraham Lincoln spoke of in the Gettysburg Address. Ms. Howe wrote:

Mine eyes have seen the Glory of the coming of the Lord,
He is trampling out the vintage where the grapes of wrath are stored,

He has loosed the fateful lightning of His terrible swift sword,
His Truth is marching on.

I have seen Him in the watch fires of a hundred circling camps
They have built Him an altar in the evening dews and damps,
I can read His Righteous sentence by the dim and flaring lamps,
His day is marching on.

He has sounded forth the trumpet that shall never call retreat,
He is sifting out the hearts of men before His judgment seat,
Oh be swift, my soul, to answer Him, be ju-bi-lant, my feet,
Our god is marching on.

In the beauty of the lilies Christ was born across the sea,
With a glory in His bosom that transfigures you and me,
As He died to make men holy, let us die to make men free,
While God is marching on.

Glory! Glory, hal-le-lu-jah, Glory! Glory, hal-le-lu-jah,
Glory! Glory hal-le-lu-jah! His truth is marching on.

We started out sending missionaries around the world with this Good News of the Truth of God. Now we send spies, CIA, and economic advisors as carpetbaggers.

RECESSIONAL - RUDYARD KIPLING - 1897
God of our fathers, known of old,
Lord of our far-flung battle-line,
Beneath whose awful Hand we hold,
Dominion over palm and pine,
Lord God of Hosts, be with us yet,
Lest we forget-lest we forget!

The tumult and the shouting dies,
The captains and the kings depart,
Still stands Thine ancient sacrifice,
An humble and a contrite hart,
Lord God of Hosts, be with us yet,
Lest we forget - lest we forget!

Far-called, our navies melt away,
On dune and headland sinks the fire,

Lo, all our pomp of yesterday
Is one with Nineveh and Tyre,
Judge of the Nations, spare us yet,
Lest we forget - lest we forget!

If drunk with sight of power, we lose,
Wild tongues that have not Thee in awe,
Such boastings as the Gentiles use,
Or lesser breeds without the Law,
Lord God of Hosts, be with us yet,
Lest we forget - lest we forget!

For heathen heart that puts her trust,
In reeking tube and iron shard,
All vigilant dust that builds on dust,
And guarding calls not Thee to guard,
For frantic boast and foolish word,
Thy mercy on Thy people, Lord!

Just as in England, as Kipling so reverently prophesied and as beautiful as the Pilgrims' attempt toward a religious/Christian/spiritual counter culture was, they became disingenuous, being materially swept up in the industrial and economic revolution of the early fifteenth century. Cotton was indeed king. Because of the great demand for products, and the tremendous opportunity for profit, the Negro/Blacks in America became the exploited denominator of the equation in the master/slave politics of the time of the Pilgrims. What had started out as a counter culture with Pilgrims leading the way with religious and spiritual integrity, resulted in the Negro/Black becoming the true counter culture for the Truth as it relates to the communion with God intended by our accepting of Jesus Christ as our Savior. My dissertation required at Drew University for the doctor of ministry degree entitled "To Increase the Congregation's Understanding of Christian Discipleship" would be an excellent instrument to model a good opportunity to look at the sweep of American history up to now, with the serious dichotomy of separation of church and state.

IN CONCLUSION: America will never be able to counteract the judgment of Israel in the Old Testament without being subject to the same judgment as well. No nation will ever remain militarily superior because of the flaws in man's nature without God's saving power. Zechariah 4:6: "Many people believe that to survive in this world a person must be tough, strong, unbending, and harsh. But

God says, "Not by force nor by strength, but by my Spirit." The key words are "by my Spirit." It is only through God's Spirit that anything of lasting value is accomplished. The returned exiles were indeed weak—harassed by their enemies, tired, discouraged, and poor. But actually they had God on their side! As you live for God, determine not to trust in your own strength or abilities, instead depend on God and work in the power of His Spirit," (*Life Application Study Bible*).

UNDERSTANDING THE KINGDOM OF GOD

We will state two essential requirements to exist, or "go in and out and find pasture" in the Kingdom of God, while also existing in flesh and blood as a normal human being. St. John 10:9: "I am the door; by me if any man enter in, he shall be saved, and shall be able to go in and out, and find pasture," (KJV).

UNDERSTANDING THE X FACTOR (1) It appears that the state, or the government in any particular situation involving church and state matters, in the U.S., acts as the Christian Church's proctor, or monitor. We in the Christian Church don't seem aware that we should spend our money, the money we take in on any given Sunday morning to be used for the welfare of human beings. If we applied the very serious judgment Jesus renders in Matthew 25:31, we would be covering both their physical and their spiritual needs, which includes establishing a counter culture as an example of the Kingdom of God. We pay taxes and give our money to the government. In fact, the only way we're going to help our community with their welfare burdens— mind you, we're talking economics here, the things that people depend on for life and survival, is to have the government give a smidgen of our money back to us with the proviso that we not mention God's name as that money—is applied to the problems of the community that we are responsible for. And even if we acknowledge that spirituality is the basic need for true survival, that is not being considered here when it comes to the money we take up in the name of God and on behalf of the body of Christ in the world.

Without teaching our church members their commitment to the Kingdom of God as Jesus Christ died to bring into existence, we are not taking part in Christ's mission, which was to inaugurate the appearing of God, the Creator of this world. We speak here of His direct intervention and personal/spiritual fellowship with mortal human beings of His creation, which He intended would be holy as He is holy. "If any man come to me, and hate not his father, and mother, and wife, and children, and brethren, and sisters, yea, and his own life also, he cannot be my disciple. And whosoever doth not bear his cross, and come after me, cannot be my disciple," (St. Luke 14:26-27 KJV). If it is to be made clear here, we speak of two kinds of needs, one for our physical body, and one for our spiritual body, our soul. It takes as much money to deal with one as it does the other. My question would be: Why have we in the Christian Church chosen not to attend to either one? (Reference: Matthew 25.31 forward).

If we're using the government's money the way they want us to use it, and we agree with them the way they want us to use it, why can't we use our own money? There are two different reasons as to why we need the government to tell us how to use our own money to do what we really in fact want, and even need to do: (1) Motivation; we're not motivated to do it, or we don't see the need, and (2) We don't know how to do what our Savior Jesus Christ has said we should do, "Render unto Caesar the things that are Caesar's, and to God, the things that are God's," (Matthew 22:21 KJV). As a matter of fact, in a very large church, of any denomination, $50,000 could be taken in on a given Sunday. If the fifty thousand is not channeled to the glory of God, rendering to God what is His, it will be rendered to Satan for his destructive purposes. Within a few weeks of that offering of $50,000 being deposited into a bank on Main Street in Any Town U.S.A., it will find its way to Wall Street where bids will be made on it for purposes of raising more interest, which in the times that we face in Iraq and Afghanistan, will wind up in the military industrial complex, specializing in WMD—weapons of mass destruction. The word of God spoken that Sunday and the money that was taken up could very well within a month lead to the death and destruction of an entire village of innocent human beings.

There appears a slightly obscured contradiction here, even a dichotomy. Women are compassionate and in fact positively so. Men tend to ask more questions about the money taken up in church. Maybe it's because men have to go out and bring in the bacon and the flour so to speak. And I think in far too many instances the men see that the minister/pastor seems to be the sole keeper of the funds, of course along with plans on building a bigger sanctuary for more people and of course, more money.

THE BASIC VIOLATION OF THE LAW (NOT "SIN") IS THAT THE MONEY TAKEN UP IN A CHRISTIAN CHURCH GOES TO SOMETHING, ANYTHING, OTHER THAN THE BUILDING UP OF THE KINGDOM OF GOD. I MENTIONED THE X FACTOR AND WILL EXPLAIN IT AS JESUS

INTENDED IT TO BE EXPLAINED IN MATTHEW 25:31 IN CHAPTER ELEVEN

We rob God - Malachi 3:8-9, "Ever since the days of your ancestors, you have scorned my laws and failed to obey them. Now return to me, and I will return to you, says the Lord Almighty. But you ask, How can we return when we have never gone away? Should people cheat God? Yet you have cheated me! But you ask, What do you mean? When did we ever cheat you? You have cheated me of the tithes and offerings due to me. You are under a curse, for your whole nation has been cheating me."

The greatest plague visited upon America will come from our failure to remember the Name of our God to our children (Deuteronomy 6 Chapter), the same God that we know brought us out of England, and against our will out of Africa into the vilest known form of brutal slavery ever practiced by man. Because of false worship of an earthly king, president, or monarch, we now are denied to overtly mention the God of Truth, who has advised us against using His name in vain, we choose not to use it at all.

WHEN WE REJECT THE KINGDOM OF GOD, WE INVITE THE WAGES OF SIN, WHICH IS DEATH. WE HAVE RE-JECTED THE GIFT OF GOD, WHICH IS ETERNAL LIFE, THROUGH HIS SON, JESUS CHRIST. THE SADDEST DAY IN OUR MORAL AND SPIRITUAL LIFE AS A NATION WAS WHEN THE U.S. SUPREME COURT ALLOWED MADELEINE O'HARE TO USE OUR LAWS, FOUNDED ON THE TRUTH OF GOD, TO STOP GOD FROM BEING A PART OF OUR IN-DIVIDUAL AND COLLECTIVE LIVES AS A NATION.

The in-depth thought of the twentieth century mindset has created mental stress from living in our present world with high-tech handheld global positioning systems (GPS) computer software that allows one to use satellite programming linked up with the World Wide Web to literally distance the body from the mind. With this potential for mental and spiritual stress, that's spiritual with a small "s," hallucinations, vicariously experiencing anything that one's demented mind might conjure up. No one should question, at the beginning of the twenty-first century, at the beginning of the new millennium, the contradiction, spiritually and theologically, the old cliché, "Whatever you do, you will not be able to get out of this world alive." This statement is obsolete, and a contradiction to the meaning of Christ's resurrection for our lives, as quiet as it is trying to be kept.

Those of us, who know the Truth, understand the incarnation by God, of Himself, in the Person of Jesus Christ, including His death and resurrection. And that this is not only possible, it is required for any superior understanding of what is, or ought to be expected of life by every human being that lives. The judgment of this reality and truth can be gleaned from a statement made by Dr. Martin Luther King Jr. before his untimely "death," "Unless you find something worth dying for, life is not worth living." So that the judgment of death is understood in the failure of not having found the spiritual relationship made possible by Jesus Christ in this life, in relation to His having met the criteria for His resurrection, and His having made that criteria understandably fool-proof to those who would seek it.

THE KEY HERE IS THAT OUR PHYSICAL LIFE IS INSEPARABLE FROM OUR NEED TO BECOME SPIRITUAL IN ORDER TO EXPERIENCE A MEANINGFUL EXISTENCE DURING OUR THREE SCORE AND TEN YEARS OF EARTH. IF ONE DOES NOT PERCEIVE THE NECESSITY TO SPEND THEIR ENTIRE UNDERSTANDABLE EXISTENCE IN BRINGING THE KINGDOM OF GOD INTO EXISTENCE, AS GOD HAS ORDAINED IT FROM THE FOUNDATIONS OF THE WORLD, THAT PERSON WILL NOT BE ABLE TO ENTER THE KINGDOM OF GOD EITHER. WHAT ONE DOES NOT EXPERIENCE WITH THEIR SPIRITUAL COGNITION AND THE ABILITY TO REASON (MENTAL POWERS CONCERNED WITH FORMING CONCLUSIONS), HERE IN THIS PHYSICAL WORLD ALSO DOES NOT EXIST FOR THAT PERSON IN THE SPIRITUAL WORLD EXISTING IN THE UNINTERRUPTED PRESENCE OF GOD. IN OTHER WORDS, YOU CANNOT ENTER THE KINGDOM OF GOD IF YOU ARE NOT "OF" — IN KIND, THAT IS—WITH THE KINGDOM OF GOD.

And it would seem to me that Dr. Martin Luther King Jr. has made a reasonably logical statement here; "If you have not found something worth dying for, life is not worth living."

If on this Christmas, December 21, 2005, the beginning date of this writing, one cannot get a glimpse of what has been done by God sending His son Jesus Christ into the world, he or she might also draw the conclusion that the generic person we speak of here has also not done any thorough thinking about his life on earth, including the three questions that somehow seem to invade everyone's consciousness somewhere along the way: "Who Am I? Where did I come from? And where am I going?"

(2) An example the counter culture is demonstrated with the X Factor; an intelligent design for the ability to enter, and then become a disciple of Jesus Christ in bringing the Kingdom of God into its final existence, the *eschaton* or the *Parousia*:

There are two premises to be considered here:

(1) Based upon the Law, the *Ten Commandments* were given to the Church, and extrapolated throughout the consequent attempts for good, or perfect government, based on the need to serve those who are governed, rather than those who govern. Documents such as the *Magna Carta*, or our English political heritage, in 1215, made it clear that the power of the king was not absolute. It also concluded that the idea of natural rights, expressed by English philosophers, most notably John Locke, wrote that people were "born free" and formed society to protect their rights.

Central to the position of this first premise, referring to the *Ten Commandments*, in the austere chambers of the U.S. Supreme Court is a replica of Moses handing The *Ten Commandments* to the members of that body. In the light of this continuing heritage of "human rights" over those of the government, we would like to confirm here that a youth, or an adolescent taken into custody means that someone in the chain of responsibility for indoctrinating that child on his or her responsibility to behave as a citizen of the great republic comprising all humanity, has failed. The statutory violations in this lack of due process action are mentioned throughout this book. I add here that the laws on which we arrest or hold these youth in custody are based upon the same laws that should be used to explain to him or her their faults. I will comment later on the possible deficiency of the parental structure in this regard, resulting in the "at risk" status of the child.

As mentioned above, "judgment" is the only term used in the criminal justice system that is understood to be the same as that used in theology, the Bible, and the *Ten Commandments*. We must accept the fact that the political heritage of our system of laws flow from the *Magna Carta*, and it is logical if not imperative that the judgment that we refer to here is to be accepted by both church and state. This judgment has to be legislated for the welfare of human beings, the people, rather than any interpretation or strict construction of the Law. The following statement is made earlier in this chapter that,

"Democracy as an ideal in government cannot be achieved if the ultimate Truth of the laws of God, understood in The *Ten Commandments* are violated." Therefore, no taxpayer, or group thereof, can challenge the laws of our government, applying the separation of church and state statutes to force our government to refrain from mentioning God in order to protect their individual rights. Truth, based upon the above, the judgment of these laws protect that challenger, even if he or she does understand that fact. Unless we apply this truth, considering that both worlds acknowledge the same definition of judgment, there can never be any judgment that would refer to all the people, as their government, all the time.

Conclusion to the second premise: The Church of God has the parameters and the scope to execute the judgments and laws inherent in the *Ten Commandments*. And we add here that the three major faiths involved here, Islam, Judaism, and Christianity, would embrace this determination.

And, if we wait on the state to interpret, and define or legislate the laws and judgments on which our freedom, justice, and peace rests, we will live in disillusionment. Earlier in this chapter mention is made that there has never been a clear wall that separates church and state. I recall from church history, that there were eras in early Christianity, where the pope and the emperor fought each other for the position of final authority on the matters we discuss here. Vatican City in Rome, Italy, is perhaps the clearest example of this dichotomy that still exists today.

Based on the "political heritage" that we speak of above, unless the church accepts full responsibility for the welfare of all of its citizens in any country or nation, there can never be any guaranty of peace, order, justice, and judgment. In other words, forget about due process, equal protection of the laws. The *Bill of Rights* will be a piece of paper unless we can guarantee, or at least admit to trying to guarantee God's intentions for "freedom and justice for all."

In, or around 1964, Madeleine O'Hare was instrumental in having prayer taken out of the public schools. From the results of that event, and what we see in today's news media, any school now could be challenged for allowing prayer in any of its affairs or instructions, or administration, where not led by students, almost exclusively. Furthermore, accepting the logic and truth of the foregoing to start to put both worlds back into "order," the schools of our children would be the place to start, seeing that again, they are the most "at risk" group in our society for violating the very same laws they are denied from learning to obey.

Presently, the New Jersey Division of Youth and Family Services (DYFS) is strapped to the laws that gives them their existence, and which laws they are violating. They need to be strapped to the laws that give human beings their existence. They are trying to stop the water from flowing, instead of going to the handle that turns off the water. There is something wrong with the mentality that does not evaluate a law that says you must take the child out of their home, and that same law says you must put them back, sometimes in a worst home than the one they were taken out of. Until the Church takes over interpreting and making sure that the laws are executed, as they are correctly interpreted, there will always be a blocking of the final outcome or results of the law. THE DEVIL IS IN THE DETAILS. IT IS OBVIOUS, IN THIS CASE, THAT NO ONE OR GROUP, GOVERNMENT OR OTHERWISE, IS IN CONTROL WHO HAS BOTH THE AUTHORITY AND POWER TO SUCCEED, AS IT IS INTENDED BY LAW. THE LAW MUST BE USEDTO MAKE JUDGMENTS AND CONVICTIONS. GOD HAS GIVEN US THE PERFECT LAWS AND WILL EXECUTE THE PERFECT JUDGMENT.

Here we can conclude that there is a double jeopardy, not only for the children taken into custody for breaking the laws of our society, but for society itself, resulting in ruined lives and high taxes for all of us.

THE X FACTOR WE CONCLUDE IS A SINGLE PERFECT SET OF LAWS AND JUDGMENTS THAT ARE NECESSARY IN A COUNTER CULTURE. THE SAME JUDGMENT IS ACCEPTED BY BOTH WORLDS. WE COULD PROCEED TO CONCLUDE THAT BECAUSE THEY ARE FLAWED IN BOTH WORLDS, BASED UPON THIS JUDGMENT, IT'S A NO-BRAINER WHAT THE VERDICT WILL BE WHEN IT COMES IN:

(1) The Secular World: The following statement was made by former New York Governor Mario Cuomo, "How to recognize the sentiments of the people, yet ensure that government does not infringe on religious freedom or favor one group over another, is a delicate matter. 'I protect my right to be Catholic by preserving your right to be a Jew, or a Protestant, or a non believer, or anything else you chose,'" (Gary Wasserman *The Basics of American Politics* - Page 161; *See page 19 bottom of page*)

(2) The Ecumenical Church Movement: The Spiritual World: "The radical source of the denominational system does not lie in our theological differences, but in the presumptuous assertion of the right to erect and maintain separate churches on the basis of variant interpretations of certain aspects of the Christian faith. It is the assertion of such a right that has broken the body of Christ into sectarian fragments. This is the sin of Protestantism. The churchism of the denomination is utterly and absolutely inassimilable in the true Church of Christ." and "The ecumenical movement is the resurgence in Protestantism of the spirit and rationale of the Reformation of the sixteenth century. The radical and inspiring intention of the great Reformers was to release the hidden and submerged Church of Christ's people from apostasy into which it had been led captive by a sacerdotal hierarchy which had usurped the functions of the true Church. Despite the heroic efforts of the Reformers to complete their work, they were compelled to leave to us an unfinished Reformation. The denominational system is the Protestant counterpart to the Roman hierarchy. The ecumenical movement in our time is engaged in releasing the same Church of Christ's people from Protestant apostasy into which it has been lead by the evil spirit of sectarianism."

I would emphatically disagree with former Governor Mario Cuomo who says that to have his freedom of choice in religions, he must also allow others theirs. There is no freedom of choice when it comes to the Truth in religion, either a man or woman is free or they are not, otherwise we have several judgments. We have agreed that there is only one judgment. Morrison goes on, "Also in passing, we ought to note that a united church would restore to the Holy Spirit the field and condition necessary for its complete and most fruitful manifestation. Our sectarian fragmentation of the Christian fellowship denies to the Spirit the essential condition upon which its exercise chiefly depends. The Holy Spirit is the spirit of the whole body of Christ; it is the spirit of the whole and not of a part. Its manifestation is necessarily partial and curbed by our denominational separatism. WHAT THE SPIRIT OF GOD COULD DO WITH A UNITED CHURCH IS BEYOND OUR POWER TO IMAGINE: *The Unfinished Reformation* - Charles Clayton Morrison - Harper & Brothers Publishers, New York - 1953 - Pages 220-221, and Page 76.

With this kind of accepting of correct and responsible justice and judgment, the church and the state owes all those young people taken into custody and held, based on flawed due process and equal protection under the law statues, some form of pardon or reparations. If we get money from the government, we can't mention the real problem, which is to omit the real answer in applying the law. So we must conclude that the government is the problem.

WHAT SHOULD BE TAUGHT TO OUR CHILDREN IN PUBLIC SCHOOLS?

Recently in the State of Delaware, a Federal Judge ruled against intelligent design, or the obvious conclusion that there has to have been a higher power involved in our creation. Those who disagree with intelligent design believe in the hypothesis put forth by Charles Darwin. The judge's ruling, approved by a portion of the country, says that only science, that which can be proven, should be considered a science, and should be allowed for the teaching of science in public schools.

Science is a systematic study of available information in order to arrive at a conclusion of the answer to a problem. My question would be to those who believe that the conclusions of Darwin are correct, "Where did Darwin get his information from? How did he arrive at his conclusions? Who created the knowledge he used, or did he create it? Does his knowledge begin and end with the physical world, and since he used all knowledge available to him, is there knowledge available that he did not use?" There is with us presently the questioning of psychiatry as a science by the Church of Scientology, as with Mr. Tom Cruise, the famous actor.

I mentioned earlier the convincing proof that the Twelve Steps of Alcohol Anonymous and Narcotics Anonymous are scientific as it relates to meeting all the requirements God has set for a person to have power over the desires of his flesh. This power is also necessary to enter the Kingdom of God. And now, compare the first three steps of AA and NA, or the Twelve Steps: (1) We admitted we were powerless over alcohol, drugs, that our lives have become unmanageable, (2) Came to believe that a power greater than ourselves could restore us to sanity, (3) Made a decision to turn our will and our lives over to the care of God as we understood Him. The other nine steps are just that, tasks to remind us of the steps necessary to remain sober. If these steps and tasks are considered closely, they will lead us to prayer, and what it does to keep us sober, or obedient and penitent. This is an intelligent design.

CONCLUSION

In the Old Testament, God gave Moses *Ten Commandments*. During the time of Micah, the prophet, these ten had mushroomed to 360 commandments. Micah, realizing how hard and confusing it would be to obey all these, reduced them to three, 6:8. "What doth the Lord require of thee but to love mercy, do justly, and walk humbly with Thy God." The last and most perfect comprehensive understanding of the *Ten Commandments* given to Moses, and forms the basis of our judicial system today comes from Mark 12:29-31, "And Jesus answered him, 'The first of all commandments is, Hear, Oh Israel; The Lord our God is one Lord; And thou shalt love the Lord thy God will all thy heart, and with all thy soul, and with all thy mind, and with all thy strength;' this is the first commandment." And the second is like, namely this, "Thou shalt love thy neighbor as thyself." There is none other commandment greater than these.

If, as Jesus Christ explained, these two commandments were obeyed, intelligent design would also be explained (1) there would not have been two world wars or the one we are involved in now in Iraq and Afghanistan; (2) there would be no hunger in the world, or malnutrition; (3) there would be no homelessness in the world; (4) there would be no crime or corruption, greed; (5) the Tsunami in Indian Islands that killed 165,000 people could have been prevented. They needed an early warning system that exists at the cost of three million dollars; (6) Hurricane Katrina would not have devastated the gulf coast, the money for an efficient dam was not provided. And there probably would not be the concern for global warming, which our country does not care to discuss in International summits on the matter.

INTELLIGENT DESIGN, EXPLAINED BY GOD, CALLS INTO QUESTION MAN'S USE OF THE CONCLUSION, "AN ACT OF GOD"

CONCLUSION: It is logical to see how this "great controversy" will lead to a period in time of great conflict and tribulation.

Chapter Five
EVERY LIFE EXPERIENCES
A TURNING POINT

Hopefully after that turning point, the person will accept the truth that the final analysis of their eventual physical death can never be left out of any serious decision made, regardless of the degree of temptation. Every decision mankind makes must be based on the gravity of his "conviction war" conclusion, or else he, or she, is subject to the sure death ignored at that moment, but recurring as the physical body loses its vitality, absolutely. The term referred to here is existentialism, or the ability of one to extend the understanding of his existence beyond his present understanding, or mode of existence. Hebrews 9:27: It is appointed unto man once to die, but after that the judgment.

THE PROBLEM: Because of the lack of spiritual enabling, the three citadels of authority in the world, the church, the state, and the citizens of the community have all failed. Their failed responsibility results from the disingenuous obfuscation apparent in hiding behind the excuse for the separation of church and state.

Seeing that man by nature is not righteous in the Spirit that God is, the power that man aspires to is corrupt, and in his absolute achievements, man is corrupt absolutely.

THIS IS THE FOCAL POINT OF CONTACT EFFORT FOR MINISTRY ON BEHALF OF THE CHURCH OF JESUS CHRIST.

We begin by observing the station in life where being unable to see the perfectly ordered universe as friendly. Or, we might observe the immoral actions of another and reject the opportunity for a broken spirit, a humble and contrite heart before God, which is our only gift to be brought to Him, acknowledging the perfection that we confirm here. The acknowledgement of God's perfect universe is attainable under any set of circumstances, even death, if we bring to Him these gifts mentioned above. In so doing, we inherit love, joy, peace, as we enter the Kingdom of God. Those who reject this opportunity experiences fear, depression, anxiety, and death is the final judgment. The Sermon on the Mount; Matthew 5:1-12 is the condition of a broken spirit, a humble and contrite heart.

Matthew 25:31-46 represent the judgment of Jesus Christ as He returns in final judgment. In this Scripture mentioned here we see those who are in a sense infirm and are also without wisdom. The strong shall bear the infirmities of the weak - Romans 15:1. Even though the infirm, mentioned in these verses, might be breaking the law of love in experiencing the perfect world/universe as a hostile place, we, the children of God, the body of Christ in the world, a counter culture to the dominant unbelieving culture, will be judged as having failed to represent Jesus Christ Himself to them, in these situations mentioned. By our faith in Him, as He has charged us to act on His behalf, we then accept His solemn charge of becoming a counter culture rejecting the dominant culture, 1 Peter 4:17.

JESUS CHRIST IS GOD'S INTELLIGENT DESIGN FOR ACCOMPLISHING THE ABOVE, HIS KINGDOM ON EARTH

The following statement is made to clarify this position in my mind. That is, the connection, and the relationship between the church and the state: A key fact and truth is that when the Supreme Court of the United States of America adopts the *Ten Commandments* as its guide to upholding the laws given to Moses by God, it also committed itself to making sure that in doing so, acknowledges that any offensive behavior by one person toward another would violate those same laws. I take that position to mean that, as we know, God's laws, in the *Ten Commandments* were given to make us free (John 8:31-32). It would be clear and unequivocal that to deny any American that God given right is a violation of the laws of God. For emphasis here, I reiterate a statement from Chapter Four where I say,

Mario Cuomo's statement is contradictory to this. He says democracy means to protect a Jew's right to be a Jew, as I protect my right to be a Catholic. Then we say the Supreme Court must be taken out of the picture in a democracy, and any group that gets the most power determines what a democracy is. The present debacle on January 1, 2006 involving the election between Hamas, and the regular part in that Palestinian area proved my point here when Hamas won. Americans and our national elected leaders did not think this would happen because of the simple fact that this is not supposed to happen in a democracy where a free and open election is held. That is not what is said and understood in the *Ten Commandments*. This is the exact juncture where intelligent design becomes the fulcrum for the Ten commandments, which is the lever to deliver stability and Justice and Peace to all mankind, finalized in the three dispensations of (1) God's revelation in the Old Testament, (2) Jesus Christ and His body in the world today, and (3) the Holy Spirit that constitutes the Christian Church as stated just above.

THE FLASH POINT FOR OUR WORK IS AS FOLLOWS:

We refer to this stage in the work of the foundation as the flash point because there has to be a clear point of emphasis for the crystallization of our efforts to occur in the mind of the casual observer. To do this we state a question and three accompanying statements leading up to or are necessary for casual the observer to get the point, the flash point."

(1) Why are both the church and the state responsible for the executing the judgments based on the laws God has given to mankind for justice, peace, and order, in the *Ten Commandments*?

(2) Accepting that fact that same casual observer must be convinced of the moral imperative for both to obey God's laws of repentance and obedience, but also accepting the fact that the Church is held to a higher standard of applying the *Ten Commandments*, leaving the judge in administering justice to only have to appreciate remorse in his judgment, with a small "j." The key here is that the state is also held to some high standards of morality based on the *Bill of Rights*. Such words as "probable cause", and "equal protection of the law", hold them to at least be sure that they deny no American citizen, regardless of age, color, religion, or previous conditions of servitude, those same rights that are intended by God in the *Ten Commandments*. "We hold these

truths to be self evident that all men are created equal, and that they are endowed by their Creator with certain inalienable rights, that among these are life, liberty, and the pursuit of happiness."

(3) Proverbs 22:6: "Train up a child in the way he should go and when he is old he will not depart from it." We could exempt the parents from this responsibility if there is lack of education, finance, or privilege necessary to accomplish same. The key here is that the two citadels of authority and power in the community, the church and the state, have failed to administer justice fairly or equitably.

When we look at the Law, the *Ten Commandments* that guide the world that is America, and when we take a nine to seventeen-year-old child or adolescent who has no knowledge of improper behavior, because he or she has never been taught, this is the flash point because it is also a violation of equal protection of the law, and violation of due process. Based upon the law entitled "Impairing the Morals of a Minor" or "Child Abuse," the church and the state are guilty of these violations if the person punished is unable to understand their guilt and therefore what they are being punished for. The same statute that prevents a child or an adolescent from being tried as an adult should prevent them from being tried at all. The exception would be under the conditions of their lack of the necessary cognitive ability to understand the law they have violated, and knowledge of their not having been instructed properly on the significance and usefulness obeying the *Ten Commandments*. The human understanding of these concerns that we advocate for children is now in force for persons committing crimes who are not psychologically competent to be tried in a court of law. Rather, they are referred for psychiatric treatment. THE COUNTRY IS IN VIOLATION OF THE RIGHTS OF CHILDREN AND ADOLESCENTS WHEN WE INCARCERATE THEM UNJUSTLY, AND IN DISPROPORTIONATE NUMBERS BASED ON THEIR LACK OF HAVING BEEN GIVEN THE OPPORTUNITY FOR THOSE RIGHTS GUARANTEED TO THEM IN THE CONSTITUTION OF THE UNITED STATES OF AMERICA. THE PROGRAM OF THE LIFE FOR CHRIST FOUNDATION, INC. AND ITS ATTEMPT TO INVOLVE THE CHURCHES OF THE COMMUNITY IS THE ONLY WAY TO INVOLVE THE CHURCH WITH THE STATE, INSTEAD OF "SEPARATION OF CHURCH AND STATE."

In *Parting the Waters* by Taylor Branch, "America in the King Years," page 85, Rhienhold Niebuhr helped Dr. King to separate the rather fundamental biblical truth of Count Leo Tolstoy whose eyes had locked on three familiar words from the Sermon on the Mount: "Resist not evil." "Resist not evil" means never resist, never oppose violence; or, in other words, never do anything contrary to the law of love. And, of course, we know that Tolstoy went on to become the father of the modern pacifism. His book, *The Kingdom of God is within You* had a profound influence on young Mohandas Gandhi when he was a student in England.

In his book, Niebuhr attacked pacifists and idealists for the assumption that Gandhi had invented an approach that allowed religious people to be politically effective while avoiding the corruption of the world. For Niebuhr, Gandhi had abandoned Tolstoy the moment he began to resist the color laws in South Africa. Gandhi's strikes, marches, boycotts, and demonstrations were all forms of coercion, which, though nonviolent, were contrary to the explicit meaning of "Resist not evil." The Final Judgment of God by Jesus Christ in establishing His kingdom on earth, mentioned in Matthew 25: beginning at verse 31, diametrically refutes the "Resist no evil." In all too many of the conditions Jesus cites here are caused deliberately by evil actions of the "haves" against those who "have not." Matthew 10:34: "Think not I am come to send peace on earth: I came not to send peace, but a sword."

Like Niebuhr, King allowed his religious and political thoughts to run along the same moral edge. Questions about the existence and nature of God seemed to merge with a simpler, more existential question: Is the universe friendly? (See the first line of this chapter.) Although Niebuhr distinguished sharply between the realms of love, perfection, and God on the one hand and justice, reality, and man on the other, he tried with his moral man and immoral society to place them along a single continuum. As King would paraphrase him in a student paper, "Justice is never discontinuously related to love. Justice is a negative application of Love.... Justice is a check (by force if necessary) upon ambitions of individuals seeking to overcome their own insecurity at the expense of others. Justice is love's message for the collective mind."

In Chapter Four, I mention the Pilgrims coming to this land because they refused to serve in a democracy where the king represented the final authority. They left England because the Church of England was just that, a church of the nation, not a Church of God. Mention is made of Julia Ward Howe's "Battle Hymn of the

Republic," which, by the laws on which our nation is founded, should be the national anthem. Also mentioned there is Rudyard Kipling's *The Processional*. The *Magna Carta*, framed in 1215, declared that the power of the king was not absolute. The English philosopher, John Locke, wrote that people were "born free." The U.S. *Bill of Rights* is perhaps civilization's greatest example of a nation where the *Ten Commandments* (Where the same as in the Judgment of Jesus Christ in Matthew 25:31-46) could actually be realized. That is freedom, that is the Law, and that is love, that is peace, as understood in Jesus' indictment against those would be his disciples as he states in Matthew 25:31 forward, and this makes the possibility of the Kingdom of God a reality. And this precludes the separation of church and state. This was Dr. King's dream. He referred to himself as a drum major for justice, and quoting from the "Battle Hymn of the Republic," "Mine eyes have seen the glory of the coming of the Lord. The promised land - I might not get there with you, but as a people, we'll get to the promised land, I've been to the mountain top, looked over, and I've seen the promised land."

Following from the previous statement, there is a definite theological margin of error ceding to the chronological error understood in the erroneous application of strict construction applied to the Supreme Court of the United States of America.

The Canons of Judicial Ethics (Deuteronomy 1:16-18) are the foundation on which jurisprudence rests, as they are derived from the *Ten Commandments*. When the laws of the Supreme Court are adjudicated based on a time in our ancestry as a nation, we must moreover conclude that this ancestry consisted of involuntary slavery of African Americans. The dichotomy here is to apply strict construction to a chronological era:

(1) Legislation from that history has been acknowledged to be in error, such as not considering slaves as fully human beings, and

(2) Theologically, an attempt is made here in this writing, to become absolute, applying the *Ten Commandments* that God handed down to Moses as the only strict construction.

When national politics elect conservative judiciary, we as a nation, must qualify a correct application of the correct laws in order to ensure divine justice, or we have no justice at all. The danger here is that a chronological, as opposed to a theological application of legislation, intentionally or unintentionally, are steps to return the republic to the times when this unjust legislation prevailed.

I would like to refer here to my dissertation for the doctoral degree from Drew University, the title being "To Increase the Congregation's Understanding of Christian Discipleship." The following quote is inserted to prove decisively that the laws that govern the universe, the *Ten Commandments*, cannot be applied separately, between the church and the state. There is only one set of laws, on understanding of peace, salvation, and justice.

"The danger of the Reformation lies in the fact that it devotes its whole attention to the mandate of the proclamation of the word and, consequently, almost entirely neglects the proper domain and function of the church as an end in itself, and this consists precisely in her existence for the sake of the world (Godsey, John D. *The Theology of Dietrich Bonhoeffer*, Westminster Press, Philadelphia, 1960, pages 264-265).

God called Israel, the twelve tribes, allowed them to wander in a wilderness and be set upon by world governments. His classic battle on their behalf was Midian, Egypt, where He broke the yoke of their heavy burden once and for all times. This was really God's first congregation, a counter culture, a remnant.

SUMMARY OF THE CHRISTIAN LIFESTYLES: THIS IS THE CONTACT POINT OF THE EFFORTS FOR MINISTRY IN JESUS' NAME:

JUSTICE: The maintenance of administration of what is just. The impartial decision where conflicting claims are presented.

Justice understood, perceived, discerned, is to accept God's creation, universe, both physical and spiritual, as being friendly. It might appear not so when in Matthew 5:1, where it begins by saying, "Blessed are the poor in spirit, for theirs is the Kingdom of Heaven," "Blessed are they that mourn, for they shall be comforted." Jesus Christ taught this by both precept and example. If we chose to be existential here we would explain the resurrection of Jesus Christ that He spoke of in John 11:26. "I am the resurrection and the life, he that believeth in me though he were dead, yet shall he live, and he that liveth and believeth in me shall never die." Let's admit that existentialism is a twentieth-century philosophy having to do with the total ethical responsibility for life at any moment in time, and under any set of circumstances. In other words without this meaning to life, one has not lived at all. Jesus Christ went beyond life as we know it, but as we should know it. This is how in Ephesians 4:8, it is said that Jesus Christ led captivity captive and gave us the same gift. And in

Luke 11:20, Jesus remarks, "But if I with the finger of God cast out devils, no doubt the Kingdom of God is come among you."

Under this topic, Contact Point of Ministry, we call your attention to the quote by Godsey on Bonhoeffer—page 57 of my dissertation. This is about the church of Jesus Christ, His body in the world. What Niebuhr, Gandhi, and Dr. King are saying, Niebuhr's contentions in his book, *Moral Man and Immoral Society* are applicable here. This is of course challenging Count Tolstoy's contention that Jesus' statement, "Resist not evil" meant exactly that. This Scripture was meant or referred to one person's individual behavior against a disciple of Christ. We make no judgment against another person. God has said, vengeance is mine, I will repay (Romans 12:19). The reference Niebuhr, Gandhi, and Dr. King refer to here has to do with the meaning of the church, the body of Jesus Christ in the world as God called Israel to be. This is not about moral man, but rather, about immoral society. This is where in acting on the faith required to bring the Kingdom of God into reality, we overthrow Satan or Beelzebub with our power given by God: Ephesians 4:8, and John 11:26 above.

What will inexorably bring, in time, the tribulation of Christians suffering along with immoral society, is the conclusion that they, the dominant society or culture is in opposition to the counter culture of Jesus' body, His church. And this makes clear God's intelligent design in creating a perfect whole, His Kingdom. Leaven in the bread of Luke 13:20-21, and again He said, "Whereunto shall I like the Kingdom of God? It is like leaven, which a woman took and hid in three measures of meal, till the whole was leavened."

God has ordained that we act on behalf of His church that now is the body of His Christ and our Savior. This should be the center of the controversy, but we are not to appear helpless. Each one of us in that counter culture should be able to tell the same story of Jesus and God's love. "By this they will know that you are my disciple."

"Teach us, good Lord, to serve thee as thou deserves, to give and not to count the cost; to fight and not to heed the wounds, to toil and not to seek for rest; to labor and not to ask for any reward, save that of knowing that we do thy will; through Jesus Christ our Lord" (M.J. Austin, *Theology of Ministry* paper: Drew University. See for credit to the author - unknown)

"RIGHTEOUSNESS EXALTS A NATION, SIN IS A REPROACH TO ANY PEOPLE."

THE REJECTION OF GOD'S COMMANDMENTS HAS LED TO THE JUDGMENT SEEN IN THE NEGATIVE IMPACT OF THE FAILED RESPONSIBILITY OF THE THREE CITADELS

OF AUTHORITY—THE CHURCH, THE STATE, AND THE CITIZENS OF OUR SOCIETY.
RELIGION AND LAW
FLASH POINT

Jesus Christ is a unifying force in the universe (Colossians 1:14-22).

The religion that does not recognize, in its service of worship, the critical demand by God to obey his laws, the *Ten Commandments*, is doing its members a disservice leading to their spiritual death.

This statement is to act as a spiritually cognizant monitor as to whether or not, when we as human beings hear the word of God spoken, or come into its presence, exhibits a broken spirit, an humble or a contrite heart. This condition, upon hearing or acknowledging the presence of the Word of God, the *Ten Commandments*, will either lead to fear, instability, and death, or to affirmation, and witness to the presence of God in our lives under any set of threatening situations and circumstances, even death. We either see the situation as it is, with God's power over it, through us, or our faith is without meaning, support, and understanding of salvation through belief in Jesus Christ. For God hath not given us the spirit fear; but of power, and of love, and of a sound mind (II Timothy 1:7).

SEARCH YOUR HEART, FOR OUT OF IT ARE THE ISSUES OF LIFE. KEEP THY HEART WITH ALL DILIGENCE (Proverbs 4:23) MY PEOPLE ARE DESTROYED FOR LACK OF KNOWLEDGE (Hosea 4:6).

Let's compare a minister, rabbi, imam, to a policeman. All three are to assist us in obeying God's laws, or we could be arrested if we violate, or disobey the Law, the *Ten Commandments* ("By grace we are saved through faith, and this not of ourselves, it is the gift of God," (Ephesians 2:8).

Let's imagine you ran a red light by mistake, and a policeman, lights flashing, siren blaring, runs up beside you and asks you to pull over. What does your heart say? By flipping the situation, if you were in danger of being robbed on a deserted street late at night, and just as the would-be-robber approaches you, a police car rolled up next to you, in an unmarked squad car, and says to you "Are you okay? Would you like a lift home?"

The minister reads from the Word of God as you are sitting in the pews, you've joined a church for the first time. You've confessed to the congregation that you have been out in the world doing some crazy things, and want to get your life together. You've gone through baptism, and attend church regularly. Now, let's say that you, or I, for that matter, knowingly commit a sin, which is a violation of the Law, or disobedience to God's Word. If you are serious about getting your life together, what does your heart say when the minister, rabbi, or imam, in his sermon for the day, reminds the congregation, without calling your name, that if any of you are guilty of one of these sins, or violations of the law, you must come before God, just as you did before the police officer that could have thrown you in jail for running the red light, you having a driving license that has expired? If there is a difference, you or I are in danger of getting a death sentence when we come before the bar of justice before an all-wise, all-loving Creator who is concerned about our soul salvation, and our ability to live and commune, and exist with Him in His Kingdom. God has already begun His Earthly Kingdom as we are taught through His Son Jesus Christ, Muhammad, Moses, and several other religious leaders of other world religions.

The other side of this scenario is this: what you should feel towards your minister, rabbi, imam, is the same as what you felt when the policeman rolled up on you just as you were about to be robbed, and possibly killed. They both were trying to save your physical life in one scenario, and your soul in the spiritual sense. Both violations are derived from the *Ten Commandments* and involve a possible offense against another human being.

THE IMPACT OF THESE LAWS, AS STATED ABOVE, AS ADJUDICATED OR TAUGHT, BY BOTH CHURCH AND STATE

There is no difference in the way the laws of the Supreme Court of the United States of America are meant to be understood, interpreted, and obeyed, and the intent of those given to Moses thirty-five hundred years ago by God.

CONCLUSIONS:

The Church of The Living God has the parameters and the scope, and power to execute the judgments and laws inherent in the *Ten Commandments*. And we add here that the three major faiths—Islam, Judaism, and Christianity, would embrace this determination. The fact exists that we in these three faiths are not to judge, but to warn that there is a judgment outstanding.

Furthermore, accepting the logic and truth of the foregoing to start to put both worlds back into "order," the spiritual, and the non-believing, the schools of our children would be the place to start, seeing that again, they are the most "at risk" group in our society to commit violations. They are without the correct training that would empower them to obey, and not violate the laws that are essential for their peace of mind, body, and the salvation of their soul. The church and the state could be found negligent by profiling or violating the morals of a minor. Laws such as violation of due process and equal protection of the law are being violated.

This is the dilemma we now face in America after the 1964 Civil Rights Act. Minority Concerns, profiling by the New Jersey State Troopers, DYFS threatening to be taken over by the National Children's Rights Group, the administrative offices of the courts have acknowledged unfairness in the handling of minorities by judges disproportionate to demographic formulas. Several departments of the state are presently under consent decrees for these types of acknowledged violations.

Until the Church, Muslim, Christian, Judaism, or other religion take over to make sure that the laws are executed as they should be correctly interpreted, there will always be systemic intentional or unintentional blocking of the final outcome of results of the Law. The Devil is in the details. It is obvious in this case that no one, government or otherwise, who has both the authority and power to succeed, as intended and interpreted by Law, is in control. The law must be used to make judgments, convictions, and sentences. God has given us the perfect Law, and He will, if we obey Him, execute the perfect judgment. Our failure does not annul the law, rather a death sentence is made against civilization as a whole. The X Factor, which we conclude, is a single perfect set of laws and judgments that are necessary in the forming of a counter culture began with the Hebrew, or Jewish people brought out of bondage in Egypt from under an evil Pharaoh 3,500 years ago, and is witnessed in our time by four hundred years of slavery of black people in early American History.

The counter culture, which understands its obligations to God's Law given to Moses, and sets the judgment for the dominant culture to observe, will be persecuted for acting as their—the dominant culture's—judge. We proceed to conclude that these standards of acknowledging and interpreting the absolute revelation of the reality of the laws are flawed in both cultures, that is, church and state. There is no secret as to why confusion and disaster that followed Hurricane Katrina will always pop up in one form or another. The fact is, because of this inherent systemic flaw in man's nature without God, it has been acknowledged that only three million dollars could have developed a first warning system that would have prevented the devastating effects of the tsunami that killed over one hundred and fifty thousand people. The result was bad planning or warped minds and spirits, or both? In fact, how can the two be separated?

Hurricane Katrina was not an act of God as some have declared. It was an act of man violating the Acts of God given to Moses, and supposedly adjudicated by man in the Supreme Court of the greatest nation in God's universe.

"The Christian ideal has not been tried and found wanting. It has been found difficult, and left untried," G.K. Chesterton, *What's Wrong with the World*.

"What the Spirit of God could do with a United Church is beyond our power to imagine," Charles Clayton Morrison, *The Unfinished Reformation*.

LET MY PEOPLE GO • ON THIS ROCK I BUILD I BUILD MY CHURCH • VOX POPULI • A MAN FOR ALL SEASONS • MAN WAS BORN TO BE FREE • I WILL NOT RECANT, HERE I STAND GOD HAVE MERCY ON MY SOUL • THE COST OF DISCIPLESHIP • HE NOW BELONGS TO THE AGES • FREE AT LAST, FREE AT LAST, THANK GOD ALMIGHTY, FREE AT LAST • THE PRICE OF PEACE IS ETERNAL VIGILANCE

The true Reformers all stood in the martyrdom's path facing off against injustice, greed, and mediocrity. Power corrupts, and absolute power corrupts absolutely.

God, the Creator of the universe was the very first Reformer. Hearing the cry of the Children of Israel, He set out to free them from bondage out of Egypt. "Go down, Moses, into Egypt, and tell Pharaoh, 'Let my people go.'"

THE CONSTITUTION OFTHE UNITED STATES OF AMERICA

On July 4, 1776, the Declaration of Independence proclaimed the American colonies "Free and Independent States." This symbolized the beginning not only of a bitter fight for independence from Great Britain, but also of a struggle to unify the separate and often conflicting interests, regions, and states of America.

The politicians who gathered in Philadelphia in May 1787 to write the Constitution were not starting from scratch. They were able to draw on (1) an English legal heritage, (2) American models of colonial and state governments, and (3) their experience with the Articles of Confederation.

THE CIVIL WAR

When we become involved with "MINORITY CONCERNS" from Washington D.C. to the smallest most obscure precinct of government, there are two major defining epochs that precipitated the 1964 Civil Rights Act, they are:

(1) The Constitution of the United States of America - The Declaration of Independence; "And for the support of this Declaration, with a firm reliance on the Protection of Divine Providence, we mutually pledge to each other our lives, our fortunes, and our Sacred Honor."

(2) The infamous institution of slavery, The Civil War.

The latter caused Abraham Lincoln, a great president, his life. He saved the Union, the republic. He salvaged everything America was supposed to have fought and died for in the Revolutionary War.

We can also say that another great reformer, Dr. Martin Luther King, Jr., salvaged everything America still needs to stand for. The world now can watch as we demonstrate before all men why Gloria Ward Howe chose the words she did in the "Battle Hymn of the Republic." There is no question why Dr. King referred to these words in most of his celebrated oratory.

We can say, without fear of equivocation that Dr. King went to John F. Kennedy with the very same message Fredrick Douglas went to Lincoln with. Ironically, Kennedy was assassinated in the same politically complex climate in which Lincoln was assassinated.

In the flotsam and jetsam of history after the Middle Ages, this is where we'd reintroduce Rudyard Kipling's "Processional." We are at the point in history where it might appear, or does appear that we have tried to make God a liar by twisting the truth of His ten laws that were given to Moses.

I don't see how we, mortals, could miss the fact that God created a perfect world/universe by intelligent design, and we have methodically dismantled it, and would lie by saying that it just came into being by itself. Luke 20:10, "Jesus Tells the Parable of the Evil Farmers: now Jesus turned to the people again and told them this story 'A man planted a vineyard, leased it out to tenant farmers, and moved to another country to live for several years. At grape picking time, he sent one of his servants to collect his share of the crop. But the farmers attacked the servant, beat him up, and sent him back empty-handed." To shorten the story, this happened three other times "What shall I do? The owner asked himself. 'I know! I'll send my cherished son. Surely they will respect him.' But when the farmers saw his son, they said to each other, 'Here comes the heir to this estate. Let's kill him and get the estate for ourselves!' So they dragged him out of the vineyard and murdered him." "What do you suppose the owner of the vineyard will do to those farmers?" Jesus asked. "I'll tell you, he will come and kill them all and lease the vineyard to others." "But God forbid that such a thing should happen," his listeners protested. Jesus looked at them and said, "Then what do the Scriptures mean? 'The stone rejected by the builders has now become the cornerstone.' All who stumble over that stone will be broken to pieces, and it will crush anyone on whom it falls."

Isaiah 28:15: "Because ye have said, we have made a covenant with death, and with hell are we at agreement; when the overflowing scourge shall pass through, it shall not come unto us; for we have made lies our refuge, and under falsehood have we hid ourselves."

Isaiah 28:16: "Therefore thus saith the Lord God, Behold I lay in Zion for a foundation a stone, a tried 'stone,' a precious corner 'stone,' a sure foundation; he that believeth shall not make haste."

Isaiah 28:17: "Judgment also will I lay to the line, and righteousness to the plummet; and the hail shall sweep away the refuge of lies, and the waters shall overflow the hiding place."

Jesus Christ has this to say about our rejection of God's intelligent design in John 8:44: "Ye are of 'your' father the devil, and the lust of your father ye will do. He was a murderer from the beginning, and abode not in the truth, because there is no truth in him. When he speaketh a lie, he speaketh of his own; for he is a liar, and the father of it."

John 1:10: "If we say we have not sinned, we make Him a liar, and His Truth is not in us."

Chapter Six

Jesus Christ, God's Gift for the Execution of His Will in Bringing into Existence His Perfect Universe

It took me sixty years to get my life together.

I was licensed to preach the gospel of Jesus Christ in 1960. I knew, during the golden years of the black revolution, that God had a precise locust of power for the freedom for all human beings regardless of their color, income, geography, sex, religious denomination, or even whether they were married, and of the same sex. I feared God's judgment if I put words in his mouth. From 1992 through 2007, I spent fifteen years searching, while focusing on Jesus Christ who is the light of the world. He led me to the truth of God.

THE PROBLEM: Because of the lack of spiritual enabling, mankind is without the truth about who we are as a civilization. As a result, collectively, we are without the enabling energy to function in everyday life situations without outside stimulants too numerous to mention, understood as psychoactive, mind altering chemicals supposedly to relieve stress, pressure in order to cope. The overarching question, "Does Jesus care?" corroborates a resounding yes to the question on which the book's title is based. "I have come that they might have life, and that they might have it more abundantly," (John 10:10).

I was always convinced that God's love, and His justice for humanity can never be separated without the omen of divine judgment. II Timothy 2:15: "Work hard so God can approve you.

Be a good worker, one who does not need to be ashamed and who correctly explains the word of truth," (*Life Application Study Bible*).

THEOLOGICAL DISCUSSIONS LEADING TO THE DESCRIPTION OF THE ROLE OF THE CHRISTIAN CHURCH IN THE WORLD

In the beginning of this book, I mentioned that God is unalterably opposed to oppression of humanity by the natural, or material world in the form of our temptation to worship the creation rather than the Creator. Mankind failed to keep God's commandments, and the epoch of this failure is explained as the *fall*, Genesis 3. This condition considered the *fall* can be deducted from what God is enumerating in the *Ten Commandments* as our weaknesses or inclinations for *falling* instead of keeping His Commandments, or otherwise being in the acceptable nature of Spirit to coexist with Him in His perfect presence and universe/world.

These violations in our human nature after the *fall* can be surmised from the first five laws of the *Ten Commandments* which are as follows, verses of Exodus 20: (1) And God spoke all these words, saying, (2) I am the Lord thy God, which have brought thee out of the land of Egypt, out of the house of bondage, (3) Thou shalt have no other gods before me, (4) Thou shalt not make unto thee any graven image, or any likeness of anything that is in heaven above, or that is in the earth beneath, or that is in the water under the earth, (5) Thou shalt not bow down thyself to them, nor serve them, for I the Lord thy God am a jealous God, visiting the iniquity of the fathers unto the children unto the third and fourth generation of them that hate me.

The theme for this part of the book implies that Jesus Christ is God's gift to the world for implementing this perfection that has been inaugurated by God, and as II Corinthians 5:19 states, "God was in Christ reconciling the world to Himself." This has to do with His way of life that we should, and must observe, obey, and live in order to avoid an eternal death. Jesus Christ makes this statement in Luke 14:25-27 (25) "And there went a great multitudes with him, and he turned and said unto them"(26) "If you want to be my follower you must love me more than your own father or mother, wife and children, brothers and sisters - yes, more than your own life. Otherwise, you cannot be my disciple" (27) "And you cannot be my disciple if you do not carry your own cross and follow me."

I mention these two statements, the first and second persons of God's revelation of Himself, and His purpose, control, and judgment of our world to show that Jesus Christ is God's revealed "precept" for our obedience to the ten laws given to Moses in Exodus 20, leading to our ability to live with Him in His perfect universe, or we face the judgment of eternal death. The following explains the third dispensation for our survival and opportunity extended by God for Christian discipleship. Acts 1:6-8: "When they therefore were come together, they asked of him, saying, Lord, will thou at this time restore the kingdom of Israel? And he said unto them, it is not for you to know the times or the seasons, which the Father has put in his own power. But you shall receive power when the Holy Spirit is come upon you, and you shall tell people about me everywhere, Jerusalem, throughout Judea, in Samaria, and to the ends of the earth." The event of Pentecost, or the third Person of the Trinity, God's presence in the world, His Holy Spirit, is recognized throughout Christianity.

The oppression of the Hebrew people in Egypt, and the political matrix with one of Jacob's sons, Joseph, being sold by his jealous brothers into Egypt, and he later becoming second only to pharaoh in power, and authority, was the backdrop of God's deliverance as stated in Exodus 20, leading to giving Moses the *Ten Commandments*.

The judgmental significance to Christian discipleship is that God is unalterably opposed to (1) oppression brought on by any human being putting his interest for himself ahead of the interest that God has in his soul's salvation as Jesus Christ states above. Luke 14:25-27: This possibility of our soul's salvation rests on Jesus' demand that we "follow Him" in renouncing self service and eventual destruction. Because we already know what God does when society creates structures of oppression, as He brought the Hebrew people out of Egypt, it is only as we, followers of Christ, resists both personal physical, and material self aggrandizement, can we be with Christ as He has left His body, the Christian Church to act as His proxy in the deliverance of mankind. Isaiah 54:17: "No weapon that is formed against thee shall prosper, and every tongue that shall rise against thee in judgment thou shall condemn. This is the heritage of the servants of the Lord, and their righteousness is of me, saith the Lord."

This explanation of the precept for deliverance of the oppressed in society by those who say they are followers of Christ is stated emphatically by a Jesus in Matthew 25:31-46.

A key opportunity essential to the book's objective in answering the question "How Was I Supposed to Know that God has Created a Perfect World/Universe?" is supplied in Chapter Six, "Theological Discussions Leading to the Description of the Role of the Church in the World."

The original revelation by God of His *Ten Commandments* is to have mankind that had fallen in disgrace by violating His commandment in the Garden of Eden, to be returned to that same paradise that was lost, as Milton's great novel states. If I made an over arching judgment of God for this to happen it would come from God, and His son Jesus Christ. (1) God, by His son Jesus Christ, Matthew 5:17-18: "Think not that I am come to destroy the law, or the prophets, I am come not to destroy, but to fulfill. For verily I say unto you, till heaven and earth pass, one jot or one tittle shall in no wise pass from the law, till all be fulfilled." (2) Jesus' Words about himself, Matthew 16:13-18: "When Jesus came into the coasts of Caesarea Philippi, he asked his disciples, saying, Whom do men say that I the Son of man am? And they said, Some say that thou art John the Baptist, some, Elias, and other, Jeremiah, or one of the prophets. He said unto them, But who say ye that I am? And Simon Peter answered and said, Thou art the Christ, the Son of the Living God. And Jesus answered and said unto him, Blessed art thou, Simon Bar Jona, for flesh and blood hath not revealed it unto thee, but my Father which is in heaven. And I say unto thee, That thou are Peter, and upon this rock I build my church, and the gates of hell shall not prevail against it."

STATED HERE IS THE SIGNIFICANCE OF JESUS CHRIST'S REVELATION OF THE PRESENCE OF THE KINGDOM OF GOD, HEAVEN. THE TABERNACLE OF GOD IS WITH MEN (Revelations 21:3)

Matthew 12:28:30: "But if I cast out devils by the Spirit of God, then the Kingdom of God is come unto you. Or else how can one enter into a strong man's house, and spoil his goods, except he first bind the strong man? And then he will spoil his house. And he that is not with me is against me; and he that gathereth not with me scattereth abroad."

I WOULD LIKE TO SPEAK TO THREE NOTIONS THAT ARE ACCEPTED IN CHRISTIAN CHURCHES THAT DO NOT STAND UNDER THE TRUTHS STATED ABOVE:

(1) That to become involved in the political arena in America is the best way to improve the morals and integrity in government and society. The children of Israel were called by God to be guided specifically involving the smallest detail required in the *Decalogue*, the *Ten Commandments*. What is needed is a counter culture to the dominant culture, obedient

to these laws, and bringing to truth, and justice the failure of the dominant culture with the Judgment of God as being imminent. Proverbs 14:34: "Righteousness exalteth a nation, sin is a reproach to any people." Isaiah 28:17: "Judgment will I lay to the line, and righteousness to the plummet, and hale shall sweep away the refuge of lies, and water shall overflow the hiding place."

(2) That somehow, predicting the end of time, or when Christ will return will bring judgment to the sin in the world. We, the body of Christ in the world will cause God to bring down His judgment on the church's failure as stated immediately above in #1. First Peter 4:17, "For the time is come that judgment must begin at the house of God; and if it first begin at us, what shall be the end of them that obey not the gospel of God?" The Kingdom of God here as stated above, Ephesians 3:20, "Now unto him that is able to do exceeding abundantly above all that we ask or think, according to the power that worketh in us. Unto him be glory in the church by Christ Jesus throughout all ages, world without end."

(3) The sorrow, and grief entered into, and experienced by those gathered to express their condolences at a funeral of a Christian defies Jesus Christ's resurrection. Unless a Christian has grown in the grace, and knowledge of Christ Jesus it is unlikely that he or she will have "put on Christ" as Paul speaks of. Jesus' reminder to Mary and Martha at Lazarus's death shows Jesus' warning to those who do not "put Him on." I am the resurrection and the life. He that believeth in me, though he were dead, yet shall he live. And he that liveth and believeth in me shall never die. Broad is the way that leadeth to destruction, and many go that way. "Straight is the gate, and narrow is the way that leadeth into life, and few there be that find it," (Matthew 7:13).

What is needed to offset the judgment of death is a paradigm of life that has been developed and grounded in the existential cognition of one's daily and continual engagement in the divine eternal presence of almighty God, recognizing the actuality of this in Christian discipleship. Hebrews 9:27: "As it is appointed unto men once to die, but after this, the judgment."

The following Scriptures should inform the reader of a bridge rather than a breach between the saved and unsaved:

(1) Philippians 1:6: "He that hath begun a good work in you will perform it until the day of Jesus Christ."

(2) Philippians 2:12: "Work out your soul salvation in fear and trembling."

(3) Luke 16:16: "The law and the prophets were until John, since then the Kingdom of God is preached, and men press into it."

(4) I Corinthians 1:18: "The preaching of the Gospel is to them that perish foolishness, but to us who are saved, it is the power of God."

(5) Romans 1:16: "For I am not ashamed of the Gospel of Christ, for it is the power of God unto salvation."

(6) II Corinthians 10:6: "For the weapons of our warfare are not carnal, but mighty through God to the pulling down of strongholds."

(7) Ephesians 2:8: "For by grace we are saved through faith, and that not of ourselves it is the gift of God."

(8) Philippians 2:5: "Let this mind be in you which was also in Christ Jesus, who being in the form of God, thought it not robbery to equal with God, made himself of no reputation and took upon himself the form of a servant, and was made in the fashion of a man. And being found in the fashion of a man, he humbled himself and became obedient unto death, even the death of a cross. From which God has highly exalted Him, and given Him a name above all others, for at the name of Jesus every knee must bow, and every tongue confess, that Jesus Christ is Lord, to the glory of God the Father."

(9) Philippians 3:10: "That I might know Him, and the power of His resurrection, and the fellowship of His suffering, being made conformable unto His death, that I might be raised with Him. Not as though I might attain or be perfect, but that I press on towards the mark for the prize of the high calling in Christ Jesus."

Elizabeth Kublar Ross, a medical physician, after studying those in intensive care, and in a hospice, a terminally ill area of many hospitals, discovered and documented five stages of fear in the attitudes of those about to die. The first stage is denial and isolation. The second stage is anger. The third stage is bargaining (with God, which should have been done earlier, or even in these circumstances by coming with a broken spirit, a humble and contrite heart, which in fact is the law that is required by God under any set of circumstances). The fourth stage is depression. Dr. Ross never tells a dying person that he or she should not be sad. He or she has come to the conclusion that nothing in this world matters anymore. The fifth stage is acceptance, "The final rest before the long journey" is what one patient had to say. Dr. Ross came to the conclusion that at this time, the family needs more help than the patient.

FIVE BRIEF SERMON PROFILES AND FOUR ACTUAL SERMONS PREACHED, LEADING TO THE DESCRIPTION OF THE ROLE OF THE CHURCH IN THE WORLD
A SERMON PROFILE - I
DOES JESUS CARE?

The answer to this question is a resounding YES! I'm sure all of you agree with me on my answer. However, if each person had to explain, his or her answer would be different.

Ninety percent of Americans say they believe in God. But they must be able to understand that God is the Father of Jesus Christ. And He, God, must become our Father if we are to live with Him in Spirit throughout eternity. And if God sent Jesus Christ to save us and the world, we cannot believe in God without also believing in Jesus Christ. John 11:25-31: "I am the resurrection and the life...."

We must discern, interpret mentally, reason (mental powers necessary to form a conclusion) that God is a spirit, and that he intended through this three way Trinitarian hook-up, that we, those 90 percent of Americans who believe in Him, would also become spiritual human beings.

Let's agree that Jesus cares about our soul's salvation—in other words, our becoming spiritual. If you see a contradiction here by human beings becoming spiritual, born from a woman's body, I do, too. But look at the statement above. God sent Jesus Christ to show us the "way" to accomplish this miracle, being human, at the same time being spiritual.

We can't do what Jesus did, but He walked us through all the steps, including death, in order to come into the presence of God, or to become both human and spiritual at the same time, on earth, prefiguring and preparing for God's reign in His Kingdom on earth, Heaven.

If the 90 percent of Americans that say they believe in God, believe also in Jesus Christ, they, those 90 percent of Americans, would be carrying out God's will for the world as Jesus was when He was crucified in the process of carrying out that *will* and *mission*.

Webster says to believe in something or somebody, you must have confidence in the truth, existence, or reliability, or value of that something, or somebody.

In other words, I, you, or the 90 percent of Americans who say they believe in God, can be truthful only if they understand Jesus Christ, and in His Holy Spirit, and are living the "way" He intended for them to live, as they work towards the establishment of the Kingdom of God, and His heaven on earth, here and now.

Right here I am going to exempt the 90 percent of Americans who say they believe in God from the guilt because they are not here to defend themselves. I'm just concerned with those who can hear me and say for themselves that they are or are not living the "way" Jesus did. And, we could say if you or I are not in His, God's, and Jesus' Spirit here today.

Turn in your Bibles to Matthew 25:31-46. I have a Rainbow bible that uses colors to interpret the theological meaning of the passage. Verses 31-34 (Salvation) is a serious judgment by Jesus Christ for what I have said He means for "the way" those 90 percent of Americans who believe in God and the Christians sitting here today, "believe" in what God has inaugurated for His Kingdom. They must see the Heaven He expects those of us who "believe" in him to experience as we live in the physical world of death and dying.

This judgment Jesus explains by using words that are imaginary, sheep and goats. It is based on those of us who "say" we believe in God, our relationship to one another when we are in trouble. God's paradigm is Hebrews out of bondage in Egypt, and Black people from slavery in America. Jesus Christ was sent to save all who are oppressed trying to make sense in his perfectly designed universe.

From my Rainbow Bible, this passage means God's LOVE: Matthew 22:35-40, "Then one of them, which was lawyer, asked him a question, tempting him, and saying, Master, which is the great commandment in the Law? Jesus said unto him, THOU SHALT LOVE THE LORD THY GOD WITH ALL THY HEART, AND WITH ALL THY SOUL, AND WITH ALL THY MIND. THIS IS THE FIRST AND GREAT COMMANDMENT. AND THE SECOND IS LIKE UNTO IT, THOU SHALT LOVE THY NEIGHBOR ASTHYSELF. ON THESE TWO COMMANDMENTS HANG ALL THE LAW AND THE PROPHETS.

Verses 41-46A is about sin. To verse 46A the 90 percent who say they believe in God, but did not respond to the needs mentioned here, were the goats turned away in God's judgment. From verse 46B, those who responded to the oppression of God's people were the righteous: "But the righteous into life eternal."

THIS IS A SERIOUS INDICTMENT ON THOSE OF US WHO CALL OURSELVES CHRISTIAN. IT MIGHT BE BETTER IF WE CALLED OURSELVES A PERSON OF THE "WAY," BASED ON THE LIFE OF JESUS CHRIST.

God in Jesus Christ has become one of us. "Take, eat, this is my body," (Matthew 26:26). Paul, I Corinthians 11:29-30: "Color here is sin, or breaking the law of God." "For he that eateth and drinketh unworthily, eateth and drinketh damnation to himself, not discerning the Lord's body. For this cause many are weak and sickly among you, and many sleep." UNLESS WE ARE SPIRITUALLY IN JESUS CHRIST'S BODY, AS HE IS STILL IN THE WORLD THROUGH GOD'S SPIRIT, WE ARE SLEEP IN CONFUSION, FRACTURED MENTALLY WITH PSYCHIC STRESS, PRES-SURE AND ANXIETY. THIS LEADS TO DEATH AS EX-PLAINED IN HEBREWS 9:27, IT IS APPOINTED UNTO MAN ONCE TO DIE, AND THEN THE JUDGMENT.

Paul above talks about people who cannot discern the Lord's body in the communion of the bread and the wine become weak and sickly. If those of us who are Christian are not busy doing the works of the Kingdom of God and Heaven spoken of by Jesus in Matthew 25:35-40, we are involved in hypocrisy, idolatry, apostasy. We have become backsliders. Look at the great commandment above. Because our very lives are ties to the Kingdom of God for salvation, we cannot separate the two. The Spirit of God is in all of us, from the foundation of the world. That same Spirit has also been slain from the foundation of the world. God has sent Jesus Christ to reinstate it, without sin. Jesus was slain from the foundation of the world, but in the New Testament He is given victory over His tormentors, death. Revelations 13:7-8 (7) "And it was given unto Him to make war with the saints, and to overcome them, and power was given Him over all kindreds, and tongues, and nations" (8) "And all that dwell upon the earth shall worship Him, whose names are written in the book of life of the lamb slain from the foundation of the world."

Because of the *fall*, Paul had to write in I Corinthians 15:22, "As in Adam all die, in Christ, all are made alive."

Can we agree that Jesus Christ was sent by God, after seeing us "fall" in the Garden of Eden, to pick us up again? The following is the mission statement in Matthew 28:18-20, referred to as the Great Commission; Jesus says, "All power is given unto me in heaven and earth. Go ye therefore, and teach all nations, baptizing them in the name of the Father, and of the Son, and of the Holy Ghost; teaching them to observe all things whatsoever I have commanded you, and lo, I am with you always, even to the end of the world."

King Constantine joined the Christian Church in its early centuries. He left the impression that had to be corrected by Jesus to the rich young ruler. To follow Jesus Christ and be "saved," one had to go sell what they possessed, give it to the poor, and then come follow Him. After the celebratory acceptance of the King into Christendom, the faith became form and fashion to this evil generation rather than suffering like the Master did to bring the Kingdom of God into reality as stated in Matthew 25:35-40.

I mentioned the Scripture immediately above, Matthew 25:35-40, as representing Love based on my Rainbow Bible for study. God is Love. And the establishing of the Kingdom of God is based upon Love. Interpersonal relationships are God's intentions for us in this establishment. Jesus explained "Who is my neighbor" in Luke 10:29 of a Jewish man traveling the Jericho road. Now that road would be in the heart of an inner city at two in the morning. We all know the story. If you are close enough to see need of the things mentioned in Matthew 25:35-40, that person is your neighbor.

DOES JESUS CARE? OH, YES, HE CARES, HIS HEART IS TOUCHED WITH OUR GRIEF. IF THAT PERSON IS GRIEVING, IT DOES NOT MATTER IF HE, OR SHE IS A MUSLIM, A CHRISTIAN, A JEW, OR A NOBODY. Jesus knows if you cared about them. And will say later when you seek to enter as He has explained in Matthew 25:31, "You did not see me, and I did not see you. Depart from me ye workers of iniquity."
HOW WAS I SUPPOSED TO KNOW CHRISTOLOGY
A SERMON PROFILE - II
THE LAW OF CHRIST: SEEK FIRST THE KINGDOM OF GOD!
A NEW DECALOGUE; LAW: TESTAMENT.
THE KEY TO THIS CONNECTION TO THE PREVIOUS SERMON PROFILE IS SEEING JESUS' (1) PASSION UNTO DEATH, (2) The impact of (a) the Passion, (b) a beatitude, (c) the death of man born of a woman, (d) Hebrews 9:27, the appointment of death in the life of man born of woman, (e) the structures of oppression resulting in man's establishment of an "immoral society" applying the figment of his imagination, prompting God, after hearing their prayers, to deliver the Hebrews out of slavery as a paradigm/fore-shadowing: the two examples here are the nation of Israel, and slavery of black people in America.

There are three dispensations of God's Revelation. The Christian Ethics applicable in the birth, life, suffering-passion, death, resurrection, and Holy Spirit, is meant to be adhered to by each Born Again Christian. They are to repent and become obedient to God's will, resulting in communion with God, which is His will for his Sovereign love and power to govern His Kingdom, the Kingdom of Heaven. (3) JUDGMENT: MATTHEW 25:31-46 MAKES DISCIPLESHIP A PREREQUISITE FOR SALVATION, RATHER THAN AN OPTION. THESE SCRIPTURES HAVE BEEN LEFT OUT OF SERMON APPLICATIONS BY PASTORS AND MINISTERS OF THE GOSPEL, THE GOOD NEWS.

We say destruction from disasters, including death from disasters is an act of God. This is true only when we explain that it was His judgment resulting from our failure to obey.

The following statements, mentioned above, make the Gospel the Good News of God's magnificent obsession, a magnificent processional. As Isaiah in 35:8 states "And an highway shall be there, and a way, and it shall be called the way of holiness; the unclean shall not pass over it; but it shall be for those, the wayfaring men, through fools, shall not err therein."

The following excerpt is taken from the dissertation of Dr. Miles J. Austin, "To Increase the Congregation's Understanding of Christian Discipleship," Drew University, Madison, New Jersey October 8, 1976.

The call was to Abraham, he responded and became the father of the faith, the beginning of a people of a covenant that carried with it a premise that would, in spite of their efforts or the lack of same, reveal ultimately, the promise to Abraham in the covenant. Conzelman states it this way:

"The extent of this revelation is determined not by speculation but by soteriology. Plan and promise correspond. Acts 3:18: "For the latter is made possible only by the former. This means that fulfillment is certain."

In this chapter, the doctrine of the Church as a prerequisite to discipleship, I have mentioned faith which is the umbrella covering all component aspects of the requirement for discipleship. But more specifically, I have mentioned repentance and obedience.

In the Old Testament, the misunderstanding of the prerequisite for discipleship which is total commitment to the plan and will of God for salvation of the world, led to Israel's apostasy. Faith is important, but as the Epistles of James point out, faith without works is dead. The works of faith can only come from a "heart" converted to the will and plan of God for salvation of the world. The basis of the preparation for this work of faith is repentance and obedience. In fact, at this point, one has then responded to the call of God for his purpose in the world.

The misunderstanding of the mission of church by the Children of Israel in the Old Testament carries right over into the New Testament and is the major basis of the need to write the Gospels and the introduction to the Gospel of St. Luke points out. "Forasmuch as many have taken in hand to set forth in order a declaration of those things which are most surely believed among us, it seemed good to me also, having had perfect understanding of all things from the very first, to write unto thee in order, most excellent Theophilus, that thou mightiest know the certainty of those things, wherein thou hast been instructed," (Luke 1:1-3 and 4, KJV).

CONNECTING OBSERVATIONS OF THIS CHRISTOLOGY

"Take, eat: this is my body," (Matthew 26:26). "Behold, I stand at the door, and knock; if any man hear my voice, and open the door, I will come in to him, and will sup with him, and he with me," (Revelations 3:20).

In the first paragraph above, I say Jesus' Passion and death actualized the same conditions of the people in the suffering conditions mentioned in Matthew 25:35-40. The difference only, is His mission in the world to save us from our sins, which are violations of the Law, which would be to act contrary to Him, Jesus Christ, in the very same, or similar, situation of stress, suffering, and death. This being true, we must acknowledge that the violations of the Law that Jesus obeyed, is also the requirements for discipleship. And if His way, Jesus' way required in discipleship is not followed, enduring His suffering and Passion, we are not only in opposition to the conditions, the apparent way, we are workers of iniquity. The pain of our suffering being the very same as Jesus' and for the same reason, a judgment has to be rendered resulting from our violations of the laws of God in The New Testament, "Actualized" failing as Jesus' Body, the Christian Church.

This is why Jesus in this Scripture can say, "If you did this for the least of these my brethren, you did it to me, and if you did not, you did not do it for me." The Christology of the Kingdom of God has to be actualized in the organized Christian Church, as it is explained in the soteriology of the way God is executing in the world today. The Christian Church has to embody the will of God in the world today, or it is not the body of Jesus Christ. I Peter 4:17 says, "For the time is come that Judgment must begin at the house of God; and if it begin first at us, what shall the end be of them that obey not the Gospel of God?"

THE CONTACT POINT OF EFFORT FOR THE CHRISTIAN CHURCH IS ACTUALIZED BY RELIEVING STRUCTURES OF MAN MADE OPPRESSION WHICH DIAMETRICALLY OPPOSES THE SPIRITUAL LAWS ON WHICH THE KINGDOM OF GOD HAS BEEN ESTABLISHED. THERE IS A DEADLY JUDGMENT FOR THESE VIOLATIONS AND JESUS READS THE RIGHTEOUS SENTENCE IN MATTHEW 25:31-46.

Beatification is considered the condition of glorifying God, the creator of a perfect universe while experiencing the oppression created by the sins of human beings in violations of those perfect laws that establishes His Kingdom. Jesus' Passion unto physical death demands through discipleship, that we experience, and overcome those same passions as He did. The beatitudes of Matthew 5:1 forward is Jesus' sermon on Matthew 25:31-46, but with the demand in our discipleship. By existentially experiencing the Kingdom of God while in flesh and blood, we show faith by our works as in Matthew 25:31-40. "This is my body," the Church. The following is in fact and truth, the baptism Jesus meant when he left for us a symbol of His death and resurrection. Jesus says in I Corinthians 11:25, "This cup is the New Testament in my blood; this do ye, as oft as ye drink it, in remembrance of me." Paul, of necessity, explains for the believer and disciple, what Jesus means for the individual, and the Church, His body in the world. "For as often as ye eat this bread, and drink this cup, ye do show the Lord's death until He comes. IF WE FAIL AS "WOULD BE DISCIPLES" of Jesus Christ, along with the organized Christian Church, we will be judged by Jesus in the following Scripture as being workers of iniquity, "I never knew you," (Matthew 7:20-24). "Wherefore by their fruits you shall know them. Not everyone that saith unto me, Lord. Lord, shall enter into the Kingdom of Heaven; but he that doeth the will of my Father which is in heaven." Many will say to me in that day, Matthew 25:31-46, "Lord, Lord, have we not prophesied in thy name? And in thy name have we cast out devils? And in thy name done many wonderful works? And then will I profess unto them, I never knew you; depart from me, ye that work iniquity. Therefore whosoever that heareth these sayings of mine, and doeth them, I will liken him to a wise man, which built his house upon a rock."

The thread of the Trinity is the Holy Spirit. Judging the authenticity of discipleship is a by-product. The call of two great nations in history, Israel, and Black People in America identifies with the Passion and suffering of Jesus Christ. It is unmistakably clear whose side God is on in the suffering from oppression as seen in these two great peoples in human history, and we can thereby justifiably compare them with the suffering in Matthew 25:31-46.

On the cross, during his crucifixion, Jesus accepted the malefactor's identification with him. There are two points that I will mention here: (1) As I mention i n my dissertation beginning with Abraham, repentance and obedience are keys to following Jesus Christ, and (2) We must be born again to identify with Jesus Christ in his suffering continuously in saving humanity, the world. Most Christian's conversion experience begins with a conviction war experience coming from some form of crisis or suffering. However, when they fail in a beatitude, as in Matthew 5:1 forward, they fall back into a sense of spiritual weakness, wherein by the Satanic deception and temptation from their experience of feeling stress and pressure dictates the need to practice the beatitudes. The downside is that they become victims of the temptation of impending suffering in the death of the flesh at some time in the future, a false paradigm of reality. Jesus' resurrection was the true paradigm of reality. The only true security comes from the possibility of Christian Discipleship, the Life in Christ Jesus. Paul puts it this way, "I live, but not I, but Christ who lives in me." Galatians 2:20. The eventual death results from the failure of the flesh and blood on which they had depended for "life."

Christians who admit their sins before God, and are changed by repentance and obedience, as well as overcoming oppression of some sort in conviction war, and later fall away after the crisis and suffering is overcome, or appears to have gone away, is called a backslider. Jesus has this to say about such people, Matthew 12:43-45 "When the unclean spirit is gone out of a man, he (that unclean spirit) walketh through dry places, seeking rest, and findeth none. Then he saith, I will return into my house from whence I came out, and when he is come, he findeth it empty, swept, and garnished. Then goeth he, and taketh with himself seven other spirits more wicked than himself, and they enter in and dwell there. And the last state of that man is worse than the first."

Footnote: We could compare the above tragedy of backsliding with that of America, becoming free from evil and sin coming here from England to seek freedom of Religion, but later, amid The Industrial progress of the early twentieth century, forgetting how the process of spiritual integrity was achieved, and this forgetfulness resulting in a judgment of backsliding and death. Righteousness exalts a nation, sin is a reproach to any people. The evil spirit we gave up will return, and the latter "state" will be worse than the former. (Rudyard Kipling, "The Processional.") (Julia Ward Howe's "The Battle Hymn of the Republic.")

A SERMON PROFILE - III
BRIDGING AND CONNECTING THE GAP BETWEEN THE BOY IN FLORIDA AND THE WILL OF GOD IN THREE DISPENSATIONS OF HIS PERSON, THE TRINITY.
SUBJECT: THE X FACTOR IS GOD'S LOVE FOR HIS PEOPLE IN HIS WORLD.
THE WAY HE ACCOMPLISHES THIS IS THROUGH JESUS CHRIST AND HIS BODY AND BLOOD, THE CHRISTIAN CHURCH (ISLAM, JUDAISM, ET AL)

The X factor in civilization, "the salt of the earth," as understood in Christianity, is Jesus' body, that is, spiritually. He is still in the world. This body of Christ is a body of organized believers in Him, only if there are two or three gathered together and agree in His Name (Key insight? The Spirit of God is everywhere at the same time.)

In order for what God has willed to come to pass or be accomplished, the following must take place: A group of disciples of Jesus Christ must be committed to intentionally organizing to be present where there are human beings struggling to take care of themselves, in prison, sick, hungry, or naked, or homeless. The idea is to help those in these situations adjust to God's perfect universe, resulting in resurrection from the "dead," salvation from the wrath of Judgment to come for those who cannot make this adjustment.

Propitiation, expiation, atonement, is in fact the exemptions from the violations of the Law by man born of a woman as in exoneration from the judgment of death. This death is from the fall in the Garden of Eden from that first disobedience to the laws of God by Adam and Eve.

The following Scriptures explain how Jesus Christ stands between us and God, the Father, to make us acceptable in God's perfect universe, free from the death of the soul and spirit:

- When we consider the *Decalogue* or the *Ten Commandments* of God's immutable laws governing His universe, we recite Luke 16:16 "The Law and the prophets were until John; since that time the Kingdom of God is preached, and every man presseth into it."

- The understanding of these terms results from man's attempt to understand God's expression of His Love, and His three dispensations to bring us into His presence, and Kingdom for an eternity. We search for His omnipotence, omniscience, and omnipresence in propitiation, expiation, atonement, as well as exoneration of these immutable laws of an all wise, all loving God. We can begin to see the Truth in Ephesians 2:8, "For by grace we are saved through faith, and that not of ourselves, it is the gift of God."

- The above Scriptures should lead us to understand why (1)The Sermon on the Mount by Jesus sounds so challenging, even to a born again believer, Matthew 5:1, "Blessed are they that 'mourn,' for they shall be comforted." We see in Philippians 2:12b "Work out your soul salvation with fear and trembling." and (2) in the three dispensations, and Persons of God, the Father, the Son, and the Holy Spirit, in Matthew 25:31-46, we can understand why Jesus Christ connects God's Judgment to the unequivocal commandment to assist others in trying to keep these commands in spite of their struggles, vicissitudes, tribulations and temptations. The Judgment consists in two ways, (1) Oppression from slavery of human beings is contrived against the principles of the Kingdom of God in these three dispensations, and (2) In order for us not to be one of those Jesus Christ was referring to in this statement," Depart from me ye that work iniquity I never knew you." He, Jesus, identifies so closely with the sick, those in prison, the hungry, the naked, that we cannot separate Him from them. "I never knew you," "When did we see you?" "As often as you did not do this for the 'least' of these my brethren, you did not do it to me"

- The ways man has tried to explain the great transaction in redeeming us through Jesus' broken body, and spilled blood, propitiation, expiation, atonement, and exoneration from death continues to be seen unmistakably clear in Philippians 1:6: "Being confident of this very thing, that He that hath begun a good work in you will perform it until the day of Jesus Christ." That work is explained as our personal piety in Matthew 5 and 6, and collectively as a group of baptized believers in Matthew 25:31-46.

- This Scripture is my evidence that discipleship of Jesus Christ is mandatory for our salvation, not an option seen in being "born again." I Corinthians 1:18, "For the preaching of the cross is to them that perish foolishness, but unto us which are saved, it is the power of God."

- If a born again Christian wants to evaluate the assurance of his salvation from the natural birth given by a woman, this Scripture touches on the possibility of doubt. II Corinthians 10:3-4, "For though we walk in the flesh, we do not war after the flesh, for the weapons of our warfare are not carnal, but mighty through God for the pulling down of strongholds; casting down imaginations, and every high thing that exhalteth itself against the knowledge of God, and bringing into captivity every thought to the obedience to Christ."

- How broad is this judgment expressed in Matthew 5:1-12 and 25:31-46, and how clear is our individual and collective responsibility to become disciples of Jesus Christ? I Peter 4:17 "For the time is come that that judgment must begin at the house of God, and it first begin at us, what shall the end be of them that obey not the Gospel of God?"

On October 24, 1994, 1095 Park Drive, Hammonton, New Jersey, I committed my energies and focus to bringing into existence the Life For Christ Foundation, Inc. I mentioned the three citadels of authority including the juxtaposition between church and state rather than a cohesive relationship leading towards their mutually acknowledged goals and objectives based on both their acknowledgments that these goals and objectives concern the welfare of the community, and are derived from the *Ten Commandments* given to Moses by God.

Having been taken before a civil magistrate while preaching the Gospel of Jesus Christ by several deacons of the Bethel Baptist in 1977, puts the commitment mentioned immediately above in 1994 in an emotional as well as a factual perspective.
HISTORICAL PERSPECTIVE: I KNEW WHERE GOD WAS AT WORK IN THE WORLD, I NEEDED INSIGHTS INTO CONNECTING THE DOTS LEADING TO THE HOUSE OF GOD; I PETER 4:17, JUDGMENT BEGINS THERE.

A SERMON PROFILE - IV
STATED HERE IS AN UNDERSTANDING OF DISCIPLESHIP THROUGH JESUS CHRIST IN THE WORLD WITH THE TRINITARIAN INAUGURATION OF THE KINGDOM OF GOD ON EARTH.

THEME FOR THIS FOURTH SERMON PROFILE: "LET MY PEOPLE GO" OUT OF BONDAGE: HEBREWS OUT OF EGYPT AND BLACK PEOPLE OUT OF SLAVERY IN AMERICA WITH THE EMPOWERMENT AGAINST OPPRESSION, WHICH DIAMETRICALLY OPPOSES THE SPIRIT OF THE KINGDOM OF GOD. THE EMPOWERMENT, SPIRITUALLY, OF THOSE WHO FOLLOW JESUS CHRIST BECOME THE FIRST FRUITS OF ETERNITY. THE PREFIGURING OF THOSE THAT ARE TO BE RESURRECTED IS ALSO THE TRINITY, GOD IN THREE PERSONS, UNDERTAKING GOD'S ESTABLISHMENT OF THE KINGDOM OF GOD, HEAVEN ON EARTH.

EXODUS 2:23: "And it came about in the course of those many days that the king of Egypt died. And the sons of Israel sighed because of the bondage, and they cried out; and their cry for help because of their bondage rose up to God. So God heard their groaning; and God remembered His covenant with Abraham, Isaac, and Jacob."

EXODUS 3:7: "And the Lord said, 'I have certainly seen the affliction of my People who are in Egypt, and have given heed to their cry because of their taskmasters, for I am aware of their sufferings. So I have come down to deliver them from the power of the Egyptians, and to bring them up from that land' unto a land that flows with milk and honey."

EXODUS 3:9: "And now behold, the cry of the sons of Israel has come to Me, furthermore, I have seen the oppression with which the Egyptians are oppressing them."

JESUS WAS SENT BY God to deliver mankind from (1) The oppression of God's people by the figment of man's imagination in his structuring a society that violates the first and second Commandments of God's laws specifically. That is "to have no other gods before Me," second, Thou shalt not create any graven images or any likeness of anything that is in the heaven above, or that is in the earth beneath, or that is in the water under the earth. Thou shalt not bow down to them or serve them. For I the Lord thy God am a jealous God, visiting the iniquity of the fathers unto the children to the third and fourth generation of them that hate me; and (2) for the spiritual empowerment of God's people, those who are oppressed. Beginning with the people of Israel, and of Africans coming to this country in slavery, and more commonly expressed in the judgment of Jesus Christ against the Christian Church in Matthew 25:31-46, develops a paradigm for God's promise to Abraham, Isaac, and Jacob.

THE KEY TO THIS SERMON PROFILE IV IS AS FOLLOWS:

I believe that in comparison between Dietrich Bonhoeffer's story and mine, he understood the need for a Black theology. I believe he understood the reality of suffering and oppression being appropriated in his well documented steps to costly grace. In *The Cost of Discipleship*, where Bonhoeffer's visit to this country took him to the South in the early part of the twentieth century when the evil vestiges of slavery were visible not only in the minds of black oppressed people but structures - segregation and discrimination permeated black and white society. It was during this visit that Bonhoeffer heard Negro spirituals and observed in them something that obviously he related to his own people (I refer here to Germany during the "Rise of the Third Reich" of Adolf Hitler, and his oppression of Christianity and the Holocaust, or the destruction of the Jews.) I believe he recorded these and later used them in his underground seminary in Germany."

John A. T. Robinson, bishop of Woolwich, leaned to Bonhoeffer in his writings, one of which was *Honest to God*. The observation is made in this context that Robinson buttressed his interpretation of Bonhoeffer with the theology of Paul Tillich, and later, Bultmann. This being the case, and as Bonhoeffer himself states in so many words, Tillich did not understand the world. I would say that Bonhoeffer moves towards a philosophical interpretation of God's action in the world that I have interpreted here as a "Black theology." Then in light of John A. T. Robinson, it might be correct to say that Bonhoeffer understood what they were saying and why, but this was not so vice versa.

Godsey, who has interpreted Bonhoeffer's theology in a book by that same title, will be mentioned later. In the context with J. A. T. Robinson, Bultmann and Tillich, all of whom are neo-orthodox theologians strictly of the "Western tradition," and for the purpose of my disagreeing with Robinson who interpreted Bonheoffer in this light, I quote Godsey here: "The danger of the Reformation…lies in the fact that it devotes its whole attention to the mandate of the proclamation of the word and, consequently, almost entirely neglects the proper domain and function of the church as an end in itself, and this consists precisely in her existence for the sake of the world," (E 267) Thirty-two doctoral dissertation of Miles J. Austin, entitled "To Increase the Congregation's Understanding of Christian Discipleship," Drew University, October 8, 1976.

KEY INSIGHT FOR THE LITERAL DEFENSE OF MATTHEW 25:31-46 AND THE JUDGMENT THAT JESUS CHRIST STATES:

Based upon the tempo, direction, and interpretation of the human beings mentioned in the Scriptures directly above, they need no credentials to be eligible for Salvation brought about by Christian disciples of Jesus Christ mentioned in these Scriptures (See Sermon Profile II and III for detail insights into identifying the person of Jesus Christ inextricably as God would have it, to the conditions mentioned in Matthew 25:31-46.)

THE ACKNOWLEDGED UNDERSTANDING OF "THOSE WHO CALL UPON THE NAME OF THE LORD SHALL BE SAVED" IN THE NEWTESTAMENT, HAS TO BE ACKNOWL-EDGED IN THE CONTEXT OF GOD'S LISTENING TO MAN'S FEELINGS OF BEING OPPRESSED BY OTHER HUMAN BE-INGS AS IN EXODUS 2:24, IN THE OLD TESTAMENT, "SO GOD HEARD THEIR GROANING; AND GOD REMEMBERED HIS COVENANTWITH ABRAHAM, ISAAC, AND JACOB."

SERMON PROFILE - V
THE MIRACLE OF OUR SALVATION EXPLAINED AS A METAMORPHOSIS:

After dark one evening, a Jewish religious leader named Nicodemus, a Pharisee, came to speak with Jesus. "Teacher," he said, "we all know that God has sent you to teach us. Your miraculous signs are proof that God is with you." Jesus replied, "I assure you, unless you are born again, you can never see the Kingdom of God."

"What do you mean?" exclaimed Nicodemus. "How can an old man go back into his mother's womb and be born again?" Jesus replied, "The truth is, no one can enter the Kingdom of God without being born of water and the Spirit. Humans can reproduce only human life, but the Holy Spirit gives new life from heaven. So don't be surprised at my statement that you must be born again," (John 3:1-7, *Life Application Study Bible*).

Although we do not have to experience physical death to inherit eternal life as Jesus Christ did as he exemplified on the cross, our prior life before our spiritual resurrection was death in a real sense. And our eternal life after our spiritually resurrected life is real in every sense of the word.

The things that we treasured as supposedly being essential to life, could, and will in fact lead to our death. Hebrews 9:27: "It is appointed unto man once to die, and then the Judgment" What this

Scripture is saying that regardless to how long you live, or whether you die during this day, a judgment must be rendered based on whether you have been born again, of the water, and Spirit Jesus mentions. Not born again? Death today, or death later. In other words, since Jesus actually did not have to die for his own salvation in order to have eternal life and be free from sin, physical temptations, he died for us. His death for himself was not death. The following words of Jesus Christ were not only for his disciples, but for those who would be a disciple of his, John 16:33, "Be of good cheer, I have overcome the world." "It was a real physical death for us to vicariously experience. And in so doing, we can in reality, experience His life" "I have come that you may have life, and that more abundantly."

DISCERNMENT: "But let a man examine himself, and let him eat of that bread, and drink of that cup. For he that eateth and drinketh unworthily, eateth and drinketh damnation to himself, no discerning the Lord's body. For this cause many are weak and sickly among you, and many sleep," (I Corinthians 11:28-30 KJV)

So if anyone eats this bread or drinks this cup of the Lord unworthily, that person is guilty of sinning against the body and the blood of the Lord. That is why you should examine yourself before eating the bread and drinking from the cup. For if you eat the bread and drink the cup unworthily, not honoring the body of Christ, you are eating and drinking God's judgment upon yourself. That is why many of you are weak and sick and some have even died," (I Corinthians 11:27-30, *Life Application Bible*).

The key to metamorphosis must be seen both in our individual and personal salvation. Then we must be about saving society and the world as God called Israel first, and has sent Jesus Christ as the second person or dispensation of the Trinity to accomplish individual, and world salvation. Only as a disciple of Jesus Christ can we be saved from the Judgment and the wrath to come.

SPRINGS OF LIVING WATER CHURCH
440 CHURCH LANE
NORTH BRUNSWICK, NEW JERSEY
Reverend Dr. Young Kim, Sr. Pastor
Sunday July 3, 2005 - 1:00 P.M.
Dr. Miles J. Austin, Preaching

Subject: My feet would have slipped, had it not been for God's intelligent design.

OT Scripture: Psalms 73:1-5, "Truly God is good to Israel, even to such as are of a clean heart. (2) But as for me, my feet were almost gone; my steps had well nigh slipped. (3) For I was envious of the foolish, when I saw the prosperity of the wicked. (4) For there are no bands in their death; but their strength is firm. (5) They are not in trouble as other men; neither are they plagued like other men. (17) Until I went into the sanctuary of God; then understood I their end. (18) Surely thou did set them in slippery places; thou castedst them down into destruction. (19) How they are brought into desolation, as in a moment! They are utterly consumed with terrors."

"My feet would have slipped." I'm comparing myself here with King David, if it were not for God's intelligent design, in Jesus Christ, His only begotten Son.

The discussion of intelligent design is being discussed in religious and political circles. David did not get his understanding of his problem with the world from just going to church/sanctuary, He went to the sanctuary of God. Can we agree here that David must not have been going to the sanctuary before this problem? Or if He were, there was a different reason for Him to go at this time.

In other words, unless we come to God with a question about life and death, we tend to come with a question that has nothing to do with life and death. This is the question I hear David asking God. How can I be right and be wrong, and they be wrong and be right?

You see, David was thinking and reasoning with his rational mind. He used the mind and reason we develop as natural human beings born of a woman, using five senses to draw conclusions, hear, taste, feel, smell, and see. These five senses will never allow us, by themselves, to enter the presence of God. David himself admits in Psalm 51:16-17, "For Thou desireth not sacrifice; else would I give it; thou delightest not in burnt offering." (17) "The sacrifices of God are a broken spirit; a broken and contrite heart, Oh God, thou wilt not despise." There is no way to come into a broken spirit and a contrite heart from reasoning the way the world is with what we know from our five senses, from our natural growing up in a crazy mixed up world. We must come into the knowledge of how we look to God, who made us and the crazy mixed up world that we made crazy and mixed up.

John 4:24 "God is a spirit; and they that worship Him must worship Him in Spirit and Truth." Let us listen to verse 22: "So foolish was I, and ignorant; I was as a beast before thee." This is the danger of going back to being rational, after a "born again believer" has overcome in "conviction war." If we have been born again, we must have come into the knowledge of God, with the right sacrifice, a broken spirit, and a contrite heart. Without the constant awareness of this need to overcome our weak convictions from a rational mind, we backslide, or turn back.

I'd like to mention something here about convictions. We all know what a convict is. A convict is a person who has been found guilty of breaking a law. Based upon how our convictions must be constantly regenerated with the Spirit of God, we are all lawbreakers; it's just that we have not been brought to trial, and I don't mean before the Middlesex County judge. Based upon what we have concluded here with David, God is the only Judge we should be really concerned about, and if we pass that bar, we never have to worry about the one in New Brunswick, New Jersey.

We need different convictions to stay out of trouble like David was in. It's one thing to need to be able to make a living. To get an education, learn a skill and become marketable for earning a living. When we see prosperity, people appearing to have nothing to worry about in life, unless our convictions, our sworn knowledge can attest to the fact that they are workers of iniquity, we are bound to envy them, and wonder why our nights are long and our days are dreary. The reason why we know they are working iniquity, David speaks of in verse 18-19, "Surely thou didst set them in slippery places; Thou castedst them down into destruction, (19) How they are brought into desolation, as in a moment! They are utterly consumed with terrors." We know, the sentence before the bar of God's judgment is a death without meaning, eternal damnation.

As Apostle Paul would say, I would not have you frightened by my explanation of God's judgment. The Word from the same God says, "Seek first the Kingdom of God and its righteousness, and all these other things that seem to bring joy and happiness, will be added unto you." In other words, if you have accepted the judgment and conviction that guides your choices of behavior, you and I are aware that to save our soul far exceeds the joy and happiness for a season, and sometimes for a fleeting moment.

Unbelievers, spiritually unconvinced persons who wantonly enjoy themselves and seek happiness, thrill seekers, break the spiritual laws of God's creation, and can lead to having their physical freedom taken away. And in these situations, going to court, corporate executives who made millions in an honest job, blame some situation as a turning point in their loss of self control. They are made to be penitent, being sent to the penitentiary. To be righteous before God means that you or I must be convicted that the moral integrity and ethics that we apply in our daily lives and in business is the only way to live. We know the spiritual tragedy of breaking those laws that God gave Moses, the *Ten Commandments*. Being good requires the sacrifice resulting from a "broken spirit, and humble and a contrite heart" seek first the Kingdom of God," and we are made whole in mind, body, and spirit. This is the Law God gave to Moses, and was made intelligent and understandable in the birth, life, death, resurrection, and the giving of the Holy Spirit. This is in the ministry and teachings of Jesus Christ in the New Testament, with the teachings of Apostle Paul.

We see David here at first being confused by people who broke God's Law and just enjoyed life while he, keeping God's Law always seemed to be in trouble. That's a problem right here today, now. There are people on the golf course, at the casino, flying in and out of faraway places with not a care in the world, while we sit here on a beautiful day, concerned about what is right. We are trying to save our souls. I'd rather have Jesus than houses and land, I'd rather be held by his nail scarred hands, than to be the king of a vast domain, and dwell in sin's dread sway. I'd rather have Jesus than anything this world affords today (These verses are from one of my favorite hymns.).

In the *Newark Star Ledger*, Thursday, June 23, 2005, page 13, a national survey revealed that 90 percent of Americans believe in God. But do they know the difference between believing in God, and being able to be found acceptable, in a spiritual sense, before God? In other words, if they died, would their spirits find rest with God? In other words, do they have a conviction that the laws of God that they may be breaking does not allow them to separate from this world as it is which leads to death? And do they understand that as they lived physically, they should have been "working out their soul salvation in fear and trembling" preparing for its coexistence with the Creator, God, Spiritually, in another medium, or mode of life?

I don't think so. As a matter of truth, I know so. And my conviction is based on the condition of America. And I will not blame anyone, or mention any specific condition or situation. I think you will either agree with me or not that this country would be exalted to God's glory if 90 percent of its citizens practiced being spiritual in their relationship with God. "Righteousness exalts a nation, sin is a reproach to any people," (Proverbs 14:34). In the New Testament, we find Jesus saying, "You cannot serve two masters. Either you will love one and hate the other or vice versa."

The people who came up with finding "intelligent design" in our world, from whence did they get their intelligence? Did they create it, or did the Creator create it. Does their intelligence start and end with the physical world, or have they concluded that based on the Truth of God's creation, there are two worlds, separate and distinct, and never the twain shall meet. You or I will not be able to leave one and go to the other just because we want to, or feel we should be able to. I cannot tell if the universe is intelligent, unless I understand its intelligence, and if I did not make, or create it, how do I know what is intelligent about it?

David almost slipped because of his misunderstanding of the intelligence of God's creation and its intelligent design. His convictions were faulty, and they almost caused him to slip and fall, in a spiritual sense. This would have lead to his, David's cognitive awareness of himself being fragmented disconnected from reality, the opposite of the way Jesus Christ perceived of himself as mentioned in Philippians 2:5, "Let this mind be in you, which was also in Christ Jesus…"

If there's anyone here struggling with intelligent design or, if you are dissatisfied with how you feel during the day or many days in your life, listen to this: When it comes to the way we are made when we are born, God did not make a mistake. God does not make mistakes, and He does not make junk to be recalled during the life of the product as having been manufactured defectively. God expects that our parents or guardians, or church school teachers, pastor, at nine, ten, or twelve years of age will "Train us up in the way that we should go, so that when we are old, we will not depart from it." As Colin Powell has so boldly put it, "you break it, and you own it." We see a human being fail in life as he or she comes down to his or her last days. With death being imminent, the Judgment is also imminent that he or she has failed to come into the knowledge of an all wise, all-powerful, all loving Creator. We can conclude here with the experience of David that he or she has failed, and not their Creator, and their God. If you don't want your children's feet to slip, read and adhere to Proverbs 22:6, which we quoted from just above.

I hope I've made a case for the fact that there is nothing wrong with your body if you don't like the life you experience as it relates to eternal life, it's your mind that is confused, and it could cause you to let your feet slip. Without a sound mind, you cannot be held responsible for your decisions and your choices of behavior. Proof: Before eighteen years of age, a violator of the laws of the State of New Jersey cannot be held responsible for an incorrect choice that led to his violation. This decision by the courts is corroborated by the Word of God as I read from Proverbs 22:6.

II Timothy 1:7: "For God hath not given us the spirit of fear; but of power, and of love, and of a sound mind." If we conclude, as we must, that the body without a sound mind is subject to errors, we must also conclude why Apostle Paul attribute all true knowledge to Jesus Christ when it comes to having a sound mind. (1) Philippians 2:5: "Let this mind be in you which was also in Christ Jesus; (6) who being in the form of God, thought it not robbery to be equal with God; (7) but made himself of no reputation and took upon himself the form of a servant, and was made in the likeness of men; (8) And being found in the fashion as a man, he humbled himself, and became obedient unto death, even the death of the cross; (9) Wherefore God hath highly exalted him, and given him a name which is above every name; (10) That at the name of Jesus every knee should bow, of things in heaven, of things in earth, and things under the earth; (11) And that every tongue should confess that Jesus Christ is Lord, to the Glory of God the Father."

Philippians 3:10: "That I may know Him, and the power of His resurrection, and the fellowship of His sufferings, being made conformable unto His death, (11) If by any means I might attain unto the resurrection of the dead."

Would you listen to this statement and tell me if this is not a true statement of intelligent design? In Jesus Christ, God came out of a woman, and walked us through the steps necessary for life here and salvation after death, and then returned to His original self, and is set down at the right hand of God, His Father. By doing so in love, power, justice, and salvation, He has convinced us that the laws of the *Ten Commandments* that He gave us to survive even the final judgment of eternal death, He himself also had to obey.

And consider this: There is one exception, and this is proof of the preceding statement, Jesus the Christ did not have to change based on His lack of spiritual awareness. He came to save us from the death that God warned Adam and Eve of in the Garden, resulting from the fall. We use words like propitiation for our sins, and atonement in order for our soul to be saved. All these high sounding words come to the Truth that we must change and become like His glorious body in resurrection the righteousness of His resurrection, "Take eat, this is my body, as we agree on the first Sunday of every month to commemorate our confession of being in constant, daily communion with Him.

IS THIS MAN JESUS CHRIST WORTHY OF THE EXAMPLE OF AN INTELLIGENT DESIGN? THERE IS IN OUR AN-SWER, OUR OWN CONVICTION, EITHER AS OUR SEN-TENCE OF LIFE EVERLASTING, OR OF AN ETERNAL DAMNATION, AND ETERNAL DEATH.

Some might say, well, that sounds good, but how can that simple principle change the world? The story is told of an executive who took his son to work lacking a "child care" attendant. While executing company business involving an important client, his son kept asking questions about things in the office that caught his attention. After several interruptions from his son, he gave him a puzzle that appeared in each day's newspaper. This particular day the puzzle was a picture of the world. His son took the puzzle and came back in fifteen minutes all finished. His father and the client looked at each other in amazement. How did you do that so fast his father asked. It was nothing. I turned the paper over and on the other side there was a large picture of a man. I put the man together, and the world also came together.

I Kings 18:21 "And Elijah came unto all the people, and said, how long halt ye between two opinions? If the Lord be God, follow him; but if Ba'al, then follow him. And the people answered him not a word." I can't speak for anyone here, but My hope is built on nothing less, than Jesus' blood and righteousness, on Christ the solid rock I stand, all other ground is sinking sand.

FAITH HOPE BAPTIST CHURCH
40 GEORGES ROAD
NEW BRUNSWICK, NEW JERSEY
REV. WILLIAM CURTIS RIDDICK, PASTOR
SUNDAY JUNE 24, 2007 - 11:00 A.M. SERVICE
REV. DR. MILES J. AUSTIN, PREACHING

SUBJECT: A long day's journey into light "All the way, my Savior leads me…," "With a love that will not let me go!" Isaiah 9 and John 3:16-21.

There are three parts: (I) Follow me, (II) I Am the Way, and (III) I never knew you. That I might know Him…!

I - JESUS: FOLLOW ME!

I am a sinner. I once was lost, but now I'm found, was blind, but now I see. But first I want to tell you about my sickness. You see, sin, which is separation from the Spirit of God, is a sickness. Matthew 9:12-13: "When Jesus heard that, he said to them, 'Those that are well have no need of a physician, but those who are sick. (13) But go and learn what this means; I desire mercy and not sacrifice: For I am not come to call the righteous, but sinners to repentance."

I was born in Sanford, Florida, many years ago. My father was a primitive Baptist minister. They washed feet like Jesus did with his disciples, every first Sunday. I was told to get up on Sunday early and get ready for church, and I did. But, I was a sinner still.

I was baptized at nine years of age, grew up fighting with my sisters and brothers like all young people. Graduated from high school, had a lot of fun with the young girls like any young boy does, you see, I was a sinner, even after my baptism, in and out of the army with the wilding out that soldiers do, you see, I was a sinner.

Right here today, this morning, I'm a sinner, but I'm saved by *grace*, and this is not of myself, it is the gift of an almighty God. As the little girl in high school said, "Our God is an Awesome God!"

I got married, tried with all my strength to make a living and raise my children, and take care of my wife, went to the universities of the world, earning top credentials studying about Jesus Christ, but I was still a sinner. I was not saved by grace, because I did not call upon Jesus with all my heart, and with all my soul, and with all my mind and strength.

I was a pastor in two different Baptist Churches for all of twenty years, successfully. I was given honor and respect, and material wealth. And although the last church I pastured gave me a wholesale headache, they never broke my spirit.

Be careful what you ask for when you decide to be saved by God, and become a disciple of Jesus Christ. After I came to a cross-road in my life, filled with frustration, and possible failure to be what I knew Jesus expected from me, becoming trashed because of the success standards of the world that I had adopted from growing up in America, I could imagine right now, seeing Jesus with Peter after they had gone fishing, back to their daily way of living, Jesus saying, "Loveth thou me more than these? I will make you fishers of men, feed "My sheep."

I'm convinced after trying to save others for sixty years of my life, I came face to face with Him. Lovest thou me more than these? Right then I had to make a choice. I was a dead man if I had not chosen

Jesus Christ right then and there! This was in 1991, but I had been taken down by a very high fever, a viral infection in Divinity School at Washington D.C. in 1964, helpless, and yet not knowing which way to turn. I thought then, that civil rights was a good enough gift in following Jesus Christ, and I was wrong.

II - I A.M. THE WAY, TRUTH

Make sure your sins find you out. David was a mighty warrior, later in life said after watching the sinful prosper, and enjoy life while committing evil against the weak, "my feet had almost slipped, until I went into the Sanctuary alone. Everybody had gone. He that dwellest in the secret place of the most high shall abide under the shadow of the Almighty. The Lord is my Light."

My life, you can call it "Midlife Crisis" or not, at sixty, life will become strangely dim. It will move year by year towards total darkness, job, fame, fortune, even family goes away. I'm here as a witness that like Isaiah, I saw that there were people who had walked in the darkness, but had seen a great light, a light to lighten the Gentiles, and a glory unto the people of Israel.

I used to wonder why God did not make us perfect from the Creation so we could commune with Him in His Spirit. He did. The fall, involving Adam and Eve in the Garden in Genesis 3, is a discussion for theologians. I tell my grandson and granddaughters that man or woman born of a woman is fashioned from flesh and blood. Water cannot rise higher than its source. As the conversation between Jesus and Nicodemus goes, Jesus reminds us here, that which is born of the flesh is flesh, that which is born of the Spirit is Spirit. Unless you are born of the water and the Spirit, you cannot enter the Kingdom of Heaven.

I Corinthians 15:22, "As in Adam, all died, in Christ, all are made alive. God so loved the world...," verse 19, "This is the condemnation, that Light has come into the world, but men love darkness rather than light, because their deeds are evil."

I've said enough about me as a sinner, saved by grace. The challenge is to you today, if you have not already accepted it. When the young Jewish girl, Mary, heard Angel Gabriel assign her the honor of becoming the mother of the Savior of the world, this is her response, referred to by great thinkers, as the Magnificent. Luke 1:52-53, "He has put down the mighty from their thrones, and exalted the lowly. He has filled the hungry with good things, and the rich he has sent away empty."

If I challenged each of us here with the dilemma of choosing life for Christ, you will be either one of these two people: (1) a rich young ruler in Matthew 19:17, Good Master, what must I do to be saved? Why call me good? There's only One Good. You know the Law. He had kept the Law as well as he could understand. Jesus' challenge to each one of us today, "Go sell what you have, give it to the poor, and come and follow Me." He went way in "sorrow," for he had much wealth.

Mark 12:41-44: "This is the poor widow." Verse 44: "For they all put in out of their abundance, but she out of her poverty put in all that she had, her whole livelihood." Was she crazy, or was the rich young ruler crazy?

This is where my life took a turn for my salvation. You cannot serve two masters. And I am not necessarily talking about money, but rather, time, the time of the day, week, month, years. It's just simple enough for me to admit, as I said I was a sinner, not even saved by grace for sixty years, even after being saved by grace, I must spend time in the presence of God, or I am serving another master. Wherever my thoughts and my time are, there, they are my master.

III - I NEVER KNEW YOU!

And when Jesus comes back as stated in Matthew 25:31-46, I want to connect what Jesus would be doing if He were here now, and what He left the Church to do, and what each of us should be doing with our time during the week. If we do not meet Jesus somewhere out there in one of those places he mentions, the sick, in jail, hungry, naked, he has already said what He will say to us in the Judgment, depart from me ye that work iniquity, I never knew you.

Can we all agree here today that Jesus is more concerned about New Brunswick right now, the people who fit the description in Matthew 25:31-46, than He is with what is happening here, including the words that I speak? Can anything "good" come out of New Brunswick? I say, yes, because they thought nothing good could come out of Nazareth: "Take, eat, this is my body, given for you."

Can anything good come out of Edison? It might. If someone here says you know, I didn't know Reverend Austin was such a bad kid when he was little, and even up to sixty years of age. God saved him, maybe there's hope for me, too. And he preached to people for twenty years, talking about God but he was not in the Light of Jesus' cross on Calvary. Maybe since I have not totally committed myself to God, through Jesus Christ, His blood and broken body, and spilled blood given for me, maybe it's not too late for me either.

I won't ask what auxiliary you are a member of at Faith Hope. But ask yourself the life or death question today, can any good come out of my auxiliary it is possible that I might keep someone from falling down in their walk in life, by telling them how I fell, and God through Jesus Christ picked me up, dusted me off, gave me walking and talking, put a song in my mouth, a prayer of thanksgiving in my heart and on my lips.

Can any good come out of me going to work tomorrow morning? Could it be that I am just tired of getting up and going to work for thirty years? Or could it be that if I helped a young boy or girl to stick it out, in spite of all the temptations young people have today, drugs, sex, unemployment, racism, youth gangs, sin everywhere, there but for the *grace* of God would be me? By God's Awesome *grace*, I have been saved by faith in His great salvation toward all men.

This is my final testimony today. I see myself in all those people who are suffering from hunger from unemployment, sick from malnutrition and poor living habits, naked from either not having clothes, or not being motivated to wash them, or nowhere to wash them. I was sick, I have been homeless, even if for a short season, I was in prison identifying with those who were in prison for Justice's sake. I have been without the clothes I wanted to wear, without money to live in ease. It was grace, amazing grace that saved a wretch like me.

It was love that would not let me go! I rest my weary soul in thee, I give thee back the life I owe.

This was the life of Christ of the cross, and it must be your life and mine. I know why George Fredrick Handel could write the entire score of the spiritual musical entitled "The Messiah" in twenty-nine days. He no doubt wanted to prove to God that something good could come out of Nazareth.

I don't know about you today, but I'm glad I don't have to go back to 79 Keystone Court the same way I came. I come to the garden alone…I heard of a city called heaven, I'm trying to make it in, they tell me of a home where no storm clouds rise, an unclouded day.

Beams of heaven as I go, guide my feet in peaceful ways, turn my midnights into day, I do not know how long it will be, not what the future holds for me, but this I know, that if Jesus goes with me I shall get home someday.

Stony the road we trod, bitter the chastening rod, felt in the days when hope unborn had died, yet with a steady beat, have not our weary feet, come to place for which our fathers sighed. Sing a song, full of the hope that the dark past has taught us, sing a song full of the hope that the present has brought us, facing the rising sun, of our new day begun, let us march on till victory is won.

Mine eyes have seen the glory of the coming of the Lord. It's good to be able to say with our brother, Martin, God has allowed me to go up to the mountaintop. Look over and see the Promised Land. We might not all get there together.

But, when we all get together, what day of rejoicing, when we all see Jesus, we'll sing and shout the victory.

FIRST BAPTIST CHURCH
SOUTH BOUND BROOK, NEW JERSEY
Reverend I. Earle Bright, Pastor
GOOD FRIDAY SERVICE
Friday, March 21, 2008 - 12:00 noon
THE SEVEN LASTWORDS FROM THE CROSS OF JESUS CHRIST
SUBJECT: TALKING THE TALK AND WALKING THE WALK

Luke 23:34: "Then said Jesus, 'Father, forgive them; for they know not what they do.' And they parted his raiment, and cast lots."

When it comes to forgiveness, not only must we talk the talk, we have to be able to walk the walk. Perhaps the most powerful question put to Jesus Christ was "Master, teach us how to pray: And Our Savior responded, "Our Farther, Who art in Heaven, Hallowed be thy name, Thy Kingdom come, thy will be done on earth as it is in Heaven, give us this day our daily bread, and forgive us our trespasses, as we forgive those who trespass against us, lead us not into temptation, and deliver us from evil, for thine is the Kingdom, the power, and the glory, Amen.

Now, you ask any English professor if that's not putting a lot of stuff into a few words. As a lesson, let's take Job. The people of his time knew he could talk the talk, because God had been good to him and his family.

But listen to this. Job could not forgive his miserable comforters, because he had not been forgiven his sins, before Almighty God.

Because of his faith in the God he trusted, he was cut off from his generation. Do you know what it means to be cut off from your family when they tempt you to sin, by not cursing them out when they get on your nerves, day in, and day out.

It's easy under those conditions to talk the talk.

Jesus was out there by himself—hanging between heaven and earth. Father, forgive them, they have not yet learned to "hang in there" while Satan tries to get them to turn loose. "Let go," without letting God come with their rescue.

The only true peace of mind and spirit can be experienced in this world, which is now, and without end, is done within the presence of the Holy Spirit of the True and Living God. When Jesus Christ opened the seven seals of Revelation 5, not only was life assured, but death to those outside of the Arch of the Covenant as well.

In John 10:9, Jesus says, "I am the door; by me if any man enter in, he shall be saved, and shall go in and out and find pasture, or peace." It would be almost impossible for a follower of Jesus Christ to go in and out, from time to time of the mind, body, and Spirit of Jesus Christ, and not understand what is taking place. In other words, to be forgiven of my sins, knowing how and why, makes me ever careful, and mindful of Jesus' prayer for us, "Forgive us our trespasses, as we forgive those who trespass against us.

This is the essence, substance, and the Truth of the Kingdom of GOD.

THIS MIGHT SOUND CRAZY, OR FUNNY, BUT IF I LOST MY MIND, I'D WANT, THROUGH THERAPY TO REMEMBER ONE WORD, FORGIVEN. IN ANY CRISIS, TROUBLE, ARGUMENT, LOSS, FACING THE CRUELEST AND THE EXCRUCIATING PAIN OF DEATH, I WOULD PRAY TO GOD TO NEVER LET ME FORGET THAT I WAS FORGIVEN.

Matthew 6:33: "Seek first the Kingdom of God and its righteousness, and all the other things in life will be added unto you." Matthew 22:36: "Master, which is the great commandment in the law? Jesus said unto him…"

It is impossible to love God unless our sins are forgiven. Sin is separation between us and God. I Timothy 2:5: "For there is one God, and one mediator between God and men, the man Christ Jesus."

If I were lost today, or if I had lost all my money, my health, and the last friend on earth, the one hope left would be for me to sit down, think about who, and what God is for me just then, I'm forgiven. WHEN PEACE LIKE A RIVER, ATTENDETH MY WAY, WHEN SORROWS LIKE SEA BILLOWS ROLL, WHATEVER MY LOT, THOU HATH TAUGHT ME TO SAY…

CAN YOU IMAGINE A SLAVE SAYING IN THE FACE OF THE WORLD'S CRUELEST SLAVERY, JUST GIVE ME JESUS, THAT'S ENOUGH. I'VE GOT SHOES, YOU GOT SHOES, ALL OF GOD'S CHILDREN GOT SHOES.

I BELIEVE FROM THE DEPTH OF MY HEART HERE TODAY WHY JESUS SAID "FATHER, FORGIVE THEM, FOR THEY KNOW NOT WHAT THE DO."

Father, maybe, just maybe, under the most dire circumstances, they will see me, as you had me show them not only my love, but your love.

There was a lady, they tell me she had an issue with her blood, and had spent all her money on a cure that had failed her. She could have been paralyzed with hatred against her physician, and those who looked the other way when they saw her, but she heard that Jesus was coming her way. Physically crippled, and emotionally de-energized, she maneuvered her way until she could just see the hem of his garment. SHE WAS THROUGH WITH ALL THAT OTHER STUFF THAT CAUSES PEOPLE TO LOSE THEIR SOULS FROM HATRED AND CONFUSION.

Beams of heaven as I go, through this wilderness below, guide my feet in peaceful ways, turn my midnights into day, I do not know how long it will be, nor what the future holds for me, but this I know, that if Jesus goes with me, I shall get home some day.

STELTON BAPTIST CHURCH
334 Plainfield Avenue, Edison, New Jersey 08817
Sunday, July 20, 2008 - 10:00 A.M. Worship Service
Reverend Kathleen Tice, St., Pastor
Reverend Dr. Miles J. Austin, Preaching
SUBJECT: Relying on the God of all Comfort
SCRIPTURE: Psalm 23 and II Corinthians 1:1-6

This letter is from Paul, appointed by God to be an apostle of Jesus Christ, and from our dear brother, Timothy. We are writing to God's church in Corinth and to all the churches throughout Greece. May the God and Father of our Lord Jesus Christ give you his grace and peace.

All praises to the God and Father of our Lord and Savior Jesus Christ. He is the source of every mercy and the God who comforts us. He comforts us in all troubles so that we can comfort others. When others are troubled, we will be able to give them the same comfort God has given us. You can be sure that the more we suffer for Christ, the more God will shower us with his comfort through Christ. So when we are weighted down with troubles, it is for your benefit and salvation! For when God comforts us, it is so that we, in turn, can be an encouragement to you. Then you can patiently endure the same things we suffer. We are confident that as you share in suffering, you will also share in God's comfort.

Good morning, Stelton. Please pray, as I have always done, for Pastor Tice, David, and her daughter in the hospital in Virginia. I understand Laverne is speaking on this Sunday at another church.

I have been writing a book on behalf of the Life For Christ Foundation, and will not take up your time here to outline the thrust and theological meaning for our time. However, you can rely on the fact that the meaning of this subject that I have chosen is the bedrock of the book's contribution to society. I want to thank Charles for inspiring me on in this very significant effort.

Since 9/11, there has been an uneasy anxiety, or worry on my mind about the loss of the security America had been used to for over four hundred years. Then there was the looming threat of global warming forecasts that appears to be affecting our climate changes dramatically, especially in the mid-west. There are floods in the flatlands and mud-slides, and forest fires in California.

But what I want to highlight in my sermon today is a problem that affects every one of us sitting within the sound of my voice, and that is the housing mortgage melt-down. There are a lot of people in America today who need to know God for themselves. One of them, the late Luther Van Dross, the famous singer, had a songs that says a chair is just a chair unless there's someone sitting there, a house is not a home unless there's someone waiting there.

The Children of Israel, God's people, he delivered from evil oppression of pharaoh out of Egypt in the Old Testament, were never to have a home as we know one today. Pilgrims were their way of life, they were to move through the earth towards the Promised Land.

Hebrews 11:10 says, "It was by faith Abraham obeyed when God called him to leave home and go to another land that God would give him as an inheritance." He went without knowing where he was going. And even when he reached the land God promised him, he lived there by faith - for he was like a foreigner, living in a tent. Abraham did this because he was confidently looking for a city with eternal foundations, a city designed and built by God.

One of the great hymns of our faith depicts what it means to be on our way as a pilgrim to the Kingdom of Heaven, "Guide me, Oh, thou great Jehovah, Pilgrims through this barren land, I am weak but thou art mighty, Hold me with Thy powerful hand."

Some of the greatest blessings have come to me when I thought things were most miserable, and I thought one or two things were the problem: (1) either God had left, or (2) I had never known Him well enough to know that He was right there, I just did not acknowledge Him. David; Acknowledge Him in all thy Ways and He will direct thy path. I found amid the chaos of the jangling discords of my unprofitable life that "The Lord is my shepherd I shall not want..."

Can you imagine, I think it's really impossible to feel what a man feels standing in front of the home he and his wife has worked for all their life that now has been foreclosed on. A home is the focal point of one's existence, unless that family is grounded in another existence. You lose your house, where will you put your belongings, what happens to your children, your job that you have to report to in eight hours.

ABRAHAM IS CALLED THE FATHER OF THE FAITHFUL, NOT BY SLIGHT OR FAVORITISM BY GOD, HE ACTUALLY LOOKED FOR A CITY THAT HAD A FOUNDATION. THERE CAN BE NO FORECLOSURE IN THE KINGDOM OF GOD. JESUS SAID IN JOHN 14, "LET NOT YOUR HEART BE TROUBLED, IN MY FATHER'S HOUSE THERE ARE MANY MANSIONS, IF IT WERE NOT SO I WOULD HAVE TOLD YOU." "I HEARD OF A CITY CALLED HEAVEN, AND I'M TRYING TO MAKE IT MY HOME." "WHATEVER MY LOT, THOU HAST TAUGHT ME TO SAY, IT IS WELL, IT IS WELL, WITH MY SOUL"

Black people in America, living like the Children of Israel living in tents, I guess they lived in huts, or shacks, children taken way to be sold as chattel only for earthly riches. They sang, "Soon I will be done with the troubles of the world, going home to live with God."

Like the Hebrew people coming out of Egypt into the stress and pressure of the desert, wanted to return to the flesh pots of Egypt, the slaves sang, "Deep river, my home is over Jordan. Go down, Moses, way down into Egypt's land, tell Oh, Pharaoh, let my people go!"

At my age I understand what it means to a family to have a beautiful home to live in, but when your health begins to fail, you don't need a home, you need another body. And that's where God comes in by sending us another body, through forty-two generations.

My hope is built on nothing less than Jesus' blood and righteousness, on Christ the solid rock I stand, all other ground is sinking sand.

I don't know about your faith, and beliefs, but on the first Sunday of the month during Holy Communion, I take Jesus' offer of God's communion with me, through His broken body and spilled blood very seriously. TAKE, EAT, THIS IS MY BODY. ALL I CAN SAY RIGHT HERE, AND RIGHT NOW IS THANK YOU, JESUS.

I was at my wife's family reunion a couple years ago, and an older person of the family came over and grabbed me with both arms as I began to lead them in a closing prayer. He whispered in my ear that he was sick, and that I should include him in that prayer. For some reason later, as I have kept him in my prayers, I believe he was a Christian but perhaps not as serious about his faith as he should have been.

My continuing prayer for him, I have not heard from him since, is that his body was just doing its job. Warning him that it could only go with him so far, from dust thou art, and from dust thou shall return. We brought nothing into this world, and we shall not take anything out. God gave, and although God taketh away, Paul puts it this way.

Romans 7:24-25: "Who shall deliver us from this body of death, thanks be to God, who giveth us the victory through our lord Jesus Christ.

Don't get me wrong, when it comes to foreclosure, it is trouble, and it is not easy. There's a cliché I'd like to use here that has the truth I want to give you. "The family that prays together, stays together." The member of the family that is not grounded in their faith in God, through Jesus Christ can break under the strain, right before your eyes. They can run away, take anti-depressants, drugs, cocaine, heroin, or at worse commit suicide, take their own life.

This is exactly what job's wife wanted him to do. Curse God and die, Job 2:9.

Will the loss of a house, or a job, or your health cause you to leave God, and Jesus Christ he has sent to save you?

Romans 8:35-39: "Can anything separate us from Christ's love? Does it mean that he no longer loves us if we have trouble or calamity, or are persecuted, or are hungry or cold, or in danger or are threatened with death? And I am convinced that nothing can separate us from his love. Death can't, and life can't. The angels can't, and the demons can't. Our fears for today, and our worries about tomorrow, and even the powers of hell can't keep God's love away.

Whether we are high or in deepest ocean, nothing in all creation will ever be able to separate us from the love of God that is revealed in Christ Jesus our lord."

I hope that I have convicted you in hearing the gospel to believe in God's love through his son, and our savior Jesus Christ. And since all faith is personal, so I cannot talk, or sing about yours, as I have acted more or less as a demonstrator, or a witness, professed to the truth of these words, I sing about my faith, and hope that yours is similar to mine. Oh, love that will not let me go! I rest my weary soul in thee…. I give back the love I owe…that in thine ocean depths, its flow may richer, fuller be.

Chapter Seven

Jesus Christ Is the Manifestation of God's Intentions for a Perfect World/Universe, or Our Judgment and Destruction

Being born in America in 1933, and raised in the southern state of Florida, I experienced physically, mentally, and morally, what justice and freedom would mean for my life. The cross-the-culture notion of God being just and all powerful left me with the in-depth desire to search for this truth. I remember vaguely my mother working for a white family by the name of Anderson in Sanford, Florida while I was four or five years old. My father worked both at a lumberyard as a brick maker. He also was called to serve as a Primitive Baptist minister, and pastor at the same time in the Mount Dora, and Ormand Beach, Florida areas. This chapter spells out the passionate struggles of my life to reach the Absolute Truth of God's Divine and Righteous Truth with freedom and Justice for all mankind. Because of the need to find the justice, and judgment of the failed relationships between human beings, in this book, I asked the question, and hopefully give satisfying answers for all of us: How Was I Supposed to Know that God Has Created a Perfect World/Universe?

THE PROBLEM: Because of the lack of spiritual enabling, we humans accept a simple answer to life. We can be players in a game, *Games People Play* by Eric Berne, or as in Pirandello's play, *The Rules of the Game, from the Book, The Myth of Mental Illness*, by Thomas S. Szasz.

This scenario, among other benchmarks of southern segregation led me to accept a scholarship to study religion at the Divinity School of Howard University in the nation's capital, Washington, D.C. in September 1960. It should be made clear here that I accepted this event as the God of Abraham, Isaac, and Jacob delivering me and my family from the oppression elaborated on at the same time in Alabama, Mississippi, and Georgia.

When I arrived in Washington, D.C. for the fall semester at Howard University, I felt that Almighty God had set me up to experience, and become a part of what is now understood as "The Sixties." I refer to them as the golden years of the Black revolution in America. As these years have been succeeded by a half century, they are fast becoming acknowledged as the defining years succeeding the American Revolution itself.

It was in Washington, DC, Howard University, the capstone of Black education, I diligently searched through the copious volumes at Founders Library to find an answer to the blatant absence of either the government of man or divine justice, to reach out to the young black boy in Florida. But then the ominous conclusion was that the young black boy in Florida was just a sign of the millions and millions of young black boys in the ghettoes of metropolitan complexes across our nation.

Founders Library at Howard University was not the only place I searched for answers. As the assistant pastor of the Greater First Baptist Church of Mount Pleasant Plains, just off the campus of Howard University, I was asked to preach the Word of God at least once a month. Regardless to the successful presentation of my sermons and their delivery, I desperately needed an answer, in the Word of God, for the fact that the power to save, that was so beautifully expressed in that Sunday morning service, had no effect outside of the Church, in the dungeons where young boys, who had never had a chance to make anything out of their lives, were beaten down by an uncaring world.

I did not stop there. I wrote about the problem. I chose a topic in a course, "Race Relations," at the Divinity School at Howard. The subject of my paper was entitled "Some Insights into the Phenomenon of Juvenile Delinquency." I do not need to tell you what the outcome of my findings were, we all know that as the Bible states in Proverbs 22:6: "Train up a child in the way he should go, and when he is old he will not depart from it." Interestingly enough, for a couple of years I took a job as a youth counselor with the Department of Corrections in Washington, D.C., at the Cedar Knolls Children's

Center in Laurel, Maryland. This counseling job involved being a part of a system to change the value judgment of these youths. An article appeared in the *Washington Post*, the leading newspaper in Washington, DC, where a young boy had been killed due to negligence at Cedar Knolls, and that there was doubt that elaborate therapy would help in alleviating juvenile delinquency. I immediately shot off a letter to the editor because I had left Cedar Knolls for the very reasons that led to that young boy's death. There was no program existing there to alter negative behavior patterns.

My struggles at Howard University during the early sixties were very troubling. In the thick of the sit-ins and the freedom rides to the deep southern part of the nation, Birmingham, Alabama; bloodshed and the total rejection of basic principles of justice by southern whites, God had given me the privilege of being in the crucible of cataclysmic change facing the greatest nation in the world.

The church of Jesus Christ became the increasing center of my focus for the power and the authority to effect the change that was needed to free that young boy in Florida and millions of others like him across our nation. My research project required to graduate with the masters of divinity degree was entitled, "The Implications of Black Nationalism for the Negro Church." The conclusion of that research was that unless the Christian church came into its own based on the Power of God vested in it to save to the uttermost, that young black boy in Florida had every right to become a "Black Muslim" and get any help he could from them.

During my last semester at Howard University's Divinity School, I became very ill with a fever of 105°. I had hallucinations, and was packed in ice for days to bring down the temperature. I lost my memory for a short period of time. I was very ill. My sister came from Virginia, Bch, VA., and all my family and friends were anxiously awaiting the outcome of my condition.

Around Easter Sunday in 1964, the fever broke. I never will forget the gift of a big, beautiful Easter lily sent by one or more of the students from Howard's Divinity School. The doctors had no explanation except to say that I had a virus and that my system was not capable of throwing off the attack. Before that fever threw me down I was on a mission. I was doing too much and my body said you go ahead, I am stopping right here, right now, and it did. As God would have it, this experience opened my eyes to the Will of God forever. I will mention this illumination of the Holy Spirit later, as I later sought further wisdom from God while studying for the doctor of ministry degree at Drew University in Madison, New Jersey.

KEY: I had thought that the Christian Church, as an institution, had some power, perhaps in its denominational or ecclesiastical orders, to bring about justice, as in the power to get relief for the young black boy in Florida. As God allowed me to proceed to another level of his wisdom, while searching at Drew University, it became clear, as I will elaborate further later on, that the only way I, or anyone else for that matter, can help our young black son in Florida and the millions of other across the nation, is to teach them that they must learn to pray and call upon God, to save their soul. That part of them that God breathed life into at birth, and which will stand the loss of everything about them until God asks for that breath back that was loaned to them for a season. We can and it is our responsibility and our obligation to help them to become "somebody" with the "gifts" that God has given them. He should become a successful professional in life in the best sense of the word. But as Jesus cautions us in Mark 8:36, "What doth it profit a man to gain the whole world and lose his own soul?"

In December 1970, I was called to the Calvary Baptist in Vaux Hall, New Jersey. Between 1964, when I graduated from the Divinity School in Washington, DC, and then I held very responsible executive positions with the Young Mens and Womens Christian Association of Newark, New Jersey and vicinity, and the American National Red Cross of Essex County.

HOWARD UNIVERSITY DIRECTED RESEARCH
PROJECT TITLE: THE IMPLICATION OF BLACK NATIONALISM FOR THE NEGRO CHURCH, May 7, 1964
Instructor: Mr. Gene Rice
Student: Miles J. Austin
Advisor: Dr. Benjamin Payton
Introduction

The purpose of this paper is to show the relationship between our present social revolution and the historical patterns set by the early white church in America, and the standards set by the Negro church in response. I am attempting to assemble several strains of material to accomplish my objective. For instance, I think Professor Kyle Haselden has done much to show how the White church in the South and the North have mothered the racial patterns of our country in his revealing research in the racial problem in Christian Prospective. B.E. Mays and J.W. Nicholson in *The Negro Church* is used to show how the Negro, after slavery, demanded much in terms of freedom but to no avail. The church became his only fortress, and we show

how and why there were certain obstacles arising out of the Negro's church that prevented his quest for freedom. The otherworldly or eschatological nature of the Negro church offset the "genius" that was referred to by the authors.

Black Bourgeoisie by E.F. Frazier is a controversial study of the Negro of the last two decades (circa 1944-1964). The study is penetrating, unveiling, and does much to convert the lethargy of the growing potential of the Negro leadership. I am using this book to bridge a gap between the old and the New Negro. It was obvious in the middle fifties, after the foreign scholar, Gunnar Myrdal, finished a critical study of the racial problem in America that a dilemma was being faced. This book substantiates the fact that there has never been a serious attempt in America to solve a problem that was earlier mentioned to have originated in the church of God. I am striving in this paper to prove that the social revolution is evidence that, as Victor Hugo has said, and as Louis Lomax uses in his *The Negro Revolt*, that there is an "idea whose time has arrived."

The 1954 Supreme Court's decision declaring segregation in public schools to be illegal was to be the one of a long list of answers sought in the growing discontent of the Negroes for the same answers that had been sought in their spirituals and prayers of four hundred years of suffering. The Montgomery, Alabama 1955 bus boycott led by Martin L. King, Jr. was but the beginning of what was to come in the struggle for freedom. The sit-ins sparked by students at A&T College in Greensborough, North Carolina, further voiced the sentiment of the restlessness of the so-called New Negro. Greensborough, N.C. 1960. Just recently, the threatened stall-ins of the militant CORE group to confuse the opening of the World's Fair in New York City in 1964 is a commentary to the growing extremism of the quest for freedom by the Negroes of this country.

My purpose for taking these incidents to relate to others is as follows. If Dr. Martin Luther King Jr. or some other minister had not entered the scene at the explosive state of this rise of discontent, where would the non-violent principle and the country be today? Fortunately, Professor C. Eric Lincoln, and Essien-Udom have published studies of the Black Muslims and their influence on the uneducated masses. Recently, Malcolm X and some of his followers have advocated violence in their defense of civil rights in Negro demonstrations. It is worth mentioning that there has always been a desire on the part of the nationalist movement to have all the civil rights movements, including Negro movements to coalesce.

My continuing thesis in this paper is that without religious dedicated leadership in the civil rights movement, which will continue indefinitely, what will become of the non-violent, rational element that is necessary for survival? This, then, is the role of the church in the moral crisis.

(1) - The Background of the Church in America on the Racial Issue
The Church as we know it had a very constructive as well as a traumatic experience on the lives and culture of the early Americans in this country. How was this "Church," that we remember as being the sole force in founding and establishing this great country, to treat the problem of slavery? How was it to regard the religion and its worship by those who were slave masters and later these slaves after they had become freedmen?

Gathering from the fact that there was integration in the church from the beginning of slavery until a year following the Civil War, my implication here is that as long as the master-slave relationship existed, security was rendered safe by the status-quo. This is not unlike the antagonism the Negro aroused with Northern whites and Southerners after the Supreme Court's Decision and the successful launching on the part of the Negro, a drive for equal rights as guaranteed by the Constitution. What is more interesting to us is not the fact that there was a kind of integration in the antebellum church but the fact that segregation of the races had its beginning in the church quite as early as its emergence in secular society," (K. Haselden).

(2) - The Negro denied integrated worship services (after slavery)
Providence or prudential, the Negro church had its beginning in 1779 when George Liele formed the first Negro Baptist Church in Georgia. Great restrictions were put on the Negro worshippers in the South by white members of mixed churches. This led to the Negro's split, and left with less in economic value and continued oppression, he developed an inferiority complex, but nothing like those Negroes who stayed in the mixed situation. Peculiarly, but naturally, in the North, in colonial days, Negro freedmen were separated in worship services, wherein in the days before the emancipation of the Negro, there was integrated services. Haselden states in reference to the North: "Where a master-slave relationship did not exist to maintain status between Negroes and whites within the same church, artificial distinctions arose; and they arose first, not between masters and slaves, but between whites and freedmen."

(3) - How basic patterns were set by whites to prevent worshipping together

Kyle Haselden continues: "To be sure, under the circumstances nothing could have been more fortunate for the Negro than the establishing of the Negro church. The separated church became the center around which the Negro found his solidarity; it became the school in which Negro leadership was trained and developed; it became his refuge and shelter from the otherwise constant hammering of an indifferent and hostile white society; it became the source of power, inspiring him toward full expression of his humanity and under-girding his claims for complete integration into American life with an inflexible conviction of divine approval; it became his first and fundamental institution, antedating as Dubois said, "by many decades the monogamic Negro home." The Negro church stands as the power of the Gospel and to the faith of the Negro. West Turner, an ex-slave, said to an interviewer, "Dey law us out of church, but dey couldn't law way Christ." Signs marked "White only" and "Colored" were used in the church long before they were seen in public places.

Perhaps there are some, and I include myself, who feel that the Negro church, as it is today, is not only not upholding the faith of the tradition it represents, but that it offers nothing promising for the twenty million Negroes in America. Some examples of the relevance here are referred to in Benjamin E. Mays and Joseph William Nicholson's book, *The Negro's Church*. (1) The Negro's church is in part the result of the failure of American Christianity in the realm of race-relations; (2) the church's program, except in rare instances, is static, non progressive, and fails to challenge the loyalty of many of the most critically minded Negroes; (3) the vast majority of its pastors are poorly trained theologically; (4) more than half of the sermons analyzed are abstract, other-worldly, and imbued with magical conceptions of religion; (5) that in the church school less than one-tenth of the teachers are college graduates; (6) that there are too many Negro churches; (7) that the percentage of Negro churches in debt are high; (8) that for the most part the Negro church is little concerned with juvenile delinquency and other social problems in its environment; (9) that only half of the reported membership can be relied upon to finance the church regularly; (10) and that the rural church suffers most because of the instability and poverty of the rural Negro." Yet there is hope and soul in the Negro church that give it life and vitality that makes it stand out significantly above its creeds, buildings, rituals, and doctrines, something that makes it a unique institution.

There is also, perhaps, a sneer of chagrin or shame on the face and heart of the average leader and those responsible members of the average Negro church. I say this for their betrayal of the heritage and trust portent in the sufferings and prayers during those days of oppression, by former slaves and so called freedmen. During this present social revolution, and if any analogy can be drawn between the period immediately after the Emancipation Proclamation, in proportion as the success of the Negro can be measured, will restrictions and hostility of whites be seen to increase.

(4) - The Negro Church finds its solidarity in suffering

The men mentioned previously in relation to establishing Negro churches were the real trail-blazers of the New Quest for freedom. Benjamin Mays in his book "Negroes Church" concludes that the freedom in church activities that were won immediately before emancipation has persisted through the years. "And the proscriptions hampering him in respect to his social, economic, and civic life, due to slavery, were not removed when Lincoln signed the Emancipation Proclamation in 1863." It was in reaction to these crippling restrictions that the freedom in the church assumed larger proportions and accounted in good part for the continuous development of the Negro church.

(5) - The Eschatological, (other worldly) nature of Negro religion

Nevertheless, the church remains the one institution in which man is obligated to cherish and find salvation. Then what is meant by salvation? It doesn't mean eschatological, or the end of time. "And I tell you, you are Peter, and on this rock I will build my church, and the powers of death shall not prevail against it." One can never put too much emphasis on the second commandment without having fulfilled the first. The church has as its primary responsibility, the worship of God through Jesus Christ, and then the second is like unto it, to love thy neighbor as thyself. Having said that, it would appear that the Negro worshipper is in search of some method of escape from this world if mention is made of some Negro Spirituals; "Soon I will be done with the troubles of the world," "Swing low sweet chariot, coming for to carry me home," "Oh Lord, I want two wings to veil my face, two wings to fly away," "Steal away, steal away, steal away to Jesus," "Go down, Moses, way down in Egypt land, tell old Pharaoh, let my people go." Reflection should be made on the great contributions and emotional insights of Langston Hughes on life in Harlem after dark, and on week-ends after hard living among cold and hostile white people, who were almost without exception, our bosses.

(6) - Can the genius of the Negro Church free him from the bonds of oppression?

The tendency is, and may continue to be, for the intellectual Negroes to break away from many of our churches because they are not attracted to services that differ so widely from those on the campus of the college or university. On the other hand many of these people stay in the Negro church, see great possibility in them and work in them weekly. Many college students work in churches that are not what they think they should be, but they survive to improve them and thereby develop the overall situation. It is a fact that Dr. Martin Luther King Jr. left Ebenezer Baptist Church in Atlanta, Georgia on Sunday as a young man where his father was preaching, to attend the neighboring church pastured by the renowned William Holmes Borders. Borders preached on the issues of the day and times in which we live and were dissatisfied with injustice.

(7) - The Negro Church as regards Negro myths of prosperity

E. Franklin Frazier, the author of very controversial commentary on the impact of slavery and its aftershocks on the Negro, *Black Bourgeoisie*, states that it is impossible for the Negro to escape from the religious tradition of the Negro masses. The reason was that too many of those who achieved middle-class status had come from the masses. They are often haunted by the fears and beliefs that were instilled in them during their childhood. However, they are glad to escape from the prohibitions which the Baptists and Methodists placed upon dancing, card playing, and gambling. The real questions concerning religion are left to a few queer Negroes who should spend their time more profitably in money-making. "When the middle-class Negro abandons the traditional religion of his ancestors, he seldom adopts a new philosophical orientation in regards to existence and the world about him."

(8) - An American Dilemma, a Supreme Court Decision, and the Negro Revolt.

In the early fifties, the Negro found himself to be the infant in a fast-moving and fully developed society. The "mask" has been removed and the Negro, who just recently was living a make-believe life, was on his way to "becoming of age." Nevertheless, there are many obstacles to be faced in a world of space-age technology and automation. The renowned Swedish scholar, Gunnar Myrdal, in his classical study, *The American Dilemma*, has this to say concerning the Negro in this crucial period in American history. "It is true for instance, that the decreasing demand for unskilled work, compared with skilled and semi-skilled, and the change of much dirty and heavy labor to labor that is clean and easy have dangerous implications for the Negroes employment opportunities.

(9) - As of May 17, 1954, "separate but equal" was the law of the land; however, "separate but unequal" was, and still is, the practice and reality.

The American Negro of the fifties lived in a state of constant humiliation. His dignity as an individual was not admitted, in the North or the South, and his worth was so demeaned that even other nonwhite peoples of the world had little respect for him. School segregation, disenfranchisement, segregation of public facilities, and overt police brutality aside, the condition of the Negro is best reflected by his relative position as a wage earner and professional man in American society.

(10) - An Idea Whose Time Has Arrived

"Lord, child," the author professes to have overheard, "we colored people ain't nothing but a bundle of resentment going somewhere to explode." The explosion came on December 1, 1955, the day Mrs. Rosa Parks boarded the Cleveland Avenue Bus in Montgomery, Alabama. And the Negro Revolt is properly dated from the moment Mrs. Parks said "No" to the bus driver's demand that she get up and let a white man have her seat. Montgomery was the launching pad for Martin Luther King, Jr.; he soared into orbit before he himself realized what had happened. He gained international fame, the applause of the world was ringing in his ears, eighteen million Negroes were calling him "savior" and world ethicists were comparing him to Gandhi and Thoreau. The rest is American history.

(11) - The Rise of Black Nationalism in the United States.

I can say that it was providential that Martin Luther King, Jr. came along when he did. I also suspect that Elijah Muhammad would be much better off if he hadn't. If such men as King in Alabama, Kelly Miller Smith in Nashville, Reverend E. Franklin Jackson in Washington, DC, had not come along, I'd suspect that every prediction that the radicals made would have come true. I think the challenge to the Negro church is to keep abreast of the civil rights front, and if necessary, produce the leadership in this moral crisis. This is the seriousness of what faces the Christian Church in preventing distortion of moral facts and Truths and the sin of omission. The only way this can be prevented is for the Christian Church to take the lead in giving moral and spiritual influence to the movement on all levels of society. Essien-Udom has done scholarly research on the search for identity of thousands of Negros in America who call themselves Black Muslims. The focus of his study is the Nation of Islam, a movement led by Georgia born Elijah Muhammad, who is known by his followers as the Messenger of Allah and whom they believe to be divinely chosen and divinely inspired to lead American Negroes under the Crescent of Islam.

CONCLUSION: Unless the Christian Church answers the call to the millions of needy Negroes in the ghettos of the North, they will surely seek the hand that is extended. The role of the Church is being continually defined and redefined. The question of our hearts as to whether we have answered the call in our particular situation and time will be important in the final analysis.

Excerpted June 30, 2006 ** Dr. Miles J. Austin

CONCLUSION: If what I have said above holds true in the wisdom of God, then, the slavery of black people in America, and their response to it, by calling upon God, demonstrates the only "Contact point of effort to be used in ministry in the name of Jesus Christ, to the Glory of God."

CONCLUSION: If we put the "contact point of efforts in Jesus'" words, we would find them in Matthew 25:31 and forward: "When the Son of Man shall come in his glory, and all the holy angels with him, then shall he sit upon the throne of his glory; and before Him shall be gathered all nations; and He shall separate them one from another, as a shepherd divideth his sheep from the goats; and He shall set the sheep on the right hand, but the goats on the left, then shall the king say to them on his right hand, come, ye blessed of my father, inherit the kingdom prepared for you from the foundation of the world; for I was hungered and ye gave me meat; I was thirsty, and ye gave me drink; I was a stranger, and ye took me in; naked, and ye clothed me; I was sick and ye visited me; I was in prison, and ye came unto me.

"Then shall the righteous answer him, saying, Lord, when saw we thee an hungred, and fed thee? Or thirsty, and gave thee drink? When saw we thee a stranger, and took thee in? Or naked, and clothed thee? And the king shall answer and say unto them, verily I say unto you, inasmuch as ye have done it unto one of the least of these my brethren, ye have done it unto me.

"Then shall he say unto them on the left hand, depart from me, ye cursed, into everlasting fire, prepared for the devil and his angels: for I was an hungred, and ye gave me no meat; I was thirsty, and ye gave me no drink; I was a stranger, and ye took me not in; naked, and ye clothed me not; sick, and in prison, and ye visited me not. Then shall they answer him, saying, Lord, when saw we thee an hungred, or athirst, or a stranger, or naked, or sick, or in prison, and did not minister unto thee? Then shall he answer them, saying, verily I say unto you, inasmuch as ye did it not to one of the last of these ye did it not to me. And these shall go away into everlasting punishment; but the righteous into life eternal," (Matthew 25:31-46 KJV).

The Doctor of Ministry Continuing Education Program at Drew University specifically, and across the country generally, was designed not only to raise the level of action for ministry in the church, as it should have, but also to elevate the status and reputation for those attaining the degree to that level of any doctoral degree in any profession.

After my first pastorate of three years at the Calvary Baptist Church of Vaux Hall, New Jersey, I accepted a call to the Bethel Baptist Church of Westfield, New Jersey, in April 1974.

The challenge awaiting me in Westfield could not have been either anticipated, or prepared for.

Of all the extraordinary challenges afforded me by God to minister, this experience at the Bethel Baptist Church of Westfield, New Jersey was exceptional.

There were intense emotional behavior demonstrated by the church members, but for my rescue there was the Divine Intervention by Almighty God, appropriately mentioned in some detail in this very significant chapter.

A fitting preview of these observations could be prefaced with the words of author G. K. Chesterton: "The Christian ideal has not been tried and found wanting. It has been found difficult, and left untried." WHAT'S WRONG WITH THE WORLD.

Spiritual encouragement from God at this time came through the many letters, biblical tracts, and Holy Scriptures. The most lasting and time-honored gift came from the State of California. A Christian gentleman sent for my reliance at this time *The Great Controversy* by Ellen G. White. Although first published in 1884, today, December 29, 2008, I was able to call Barnes & Noble Book Sellers and order a copy.

If it seems that there are several starting points to my story of the young boy in Florida, that is definitely the case. I hope that the foregoing in this statement makes that clear. In my resume, everything about me centers on the Life For Christ Foundation and its goals and objectives. And I refer to my dissertation done at Drew University entitled, "To Increase the Congregation's Understanding of Christian Discipleship," to make the ministry to the young black boy in Florida as relevant as having worship service to Almighty God on Sunday morning and having Communion on the first Sunday of every month.

In my life's story, the following statement is an integral part of my experiences and preparation for ministry:

"As several serious efforts were put forth by Dr. Austin, as outlined above, continued to unfold with opportunities to be involved in several non-traditional types of Christian ministries, in the struggles of 1977 and early 1978, The Life For Christ Foundation came into existence, incorporated April 4, 1978 in Union County."

I have explained my fault-perception involving the wisdom God has chosen to save the world. I have also corrected and narrowed that perception to the "contact point of efforts" or a counter-culture where men and women are met at the critical juncture in their lives when they must, I repeat, they must choose between doing something to save themselves using their own efforts and wisdom while either rejecting or being ignorant of the wisdom of God made real and available in the life of Jesus Christ on Calvary.

I could say that it was a coincidence that when my church took me to civil court before a federal magistrate in January 1978, resulting from several deacons in my church being dissatisfied with the Word of God that I presented as their pastor leading up to Advent 1977, I say that it was God's providence that Elliott Moorman, a young black boy in Newark at the YM-YWCA that I had counseled ten years earlier, who had gone to Princeton University and graduated from Columbia Law School wrote an encouraging letter, and was instrumental with legal expertise in incorporating the Life For Christ Foundation.

Life for Christ Foundation
To Increase the Congregation's Understanding of Christian Discipleship
Bethel Baptist Church, 539 Trinity Place, Westfield, New Jersey
Sunday January 8, 1978 - 11:00 A.M. Worship Service
Sermon: A New Path
Scripture

OT - Joshua 3:1-4: "And Joshua rose up early in the morning; and they removed from shittim, and came to Jordan, he and all the children of Israel, and lodged there before they passed over. And it came to pass after three days, that the officers went through the host; and they commanded the people, saying, When you see the Ark of the Covenant of the Lord your God, and the priests and the Levites bearing it, then you shall remove from your place, and go after it. Yet there shall be a space between you and it, about two thousand cubits by measure: come not near unto it, that you might know the way by which we must go: for we have not passed this way before."

NT - Romans 11:25-33: "For I would not, brethren, that you should be ignorant of this mystery, lest ye should be wise in your own conceits; that blindness in part has happened to Israel, until the fullness of the Gentiles be come in. And so all Israel shall be saved: There shall come out of Zion the Deliverer, and shall turn away ungodliness from Jacob: For this is my covenant unto them, when I shall take away their sins. As concerning the Gospel, they are enemies for your sakes: but touching the election, they are beloved for the fathers' sake. For the gifts and calling of God are without repentance. For as ye in times past have not believed God, yet have obtained mercy through their unbelief: Even so have these also now not believed, that through your mercy they also may obtain mercy. For God hath concluded them all in unbelief, that he may have mercy upon all. Oh the depth of the riches both of the wisdom and knowledge of God! How unsearchable are his judgments, and his ways are past finding out."

PART 1 - A NEW PATH

It is good for me to be back in the pulpit. I would like for you to know that I never felt as though I had left. The reason I say that is because the work we shared together here in ministry which preaching is but a part, continued while I sat out there with you for three Sundays.

God does not start a job with a preacher or leader and let someone or anyone stop the job just because the leader is removed temporarily. What we began with you back at the beginning of 1977 was a great task in God's eyes. We started out together with a "Guide to the Scriptures." We used a little green book in search of God—the God of Abraham, the God of Isaac, and the God of Jacob. Each member was given a copy, and we read together, and studied together, and we worshipped together in God's presence here each Sunday. But we did something else. We waited for the wonder of God's Word to become full among us.

We waited on the fullness of God, in the fullness of man, in the fullness of time. We did not know that God would come this year. Perhaps He would not come in our lifetime to the Bethel Baptist Church, in His fullness!

I was just a leader, an instrument—I did not bring about the excitement you see here today. There were newspaper reporters, and photographers. I have never seen news travel so fast. The news of whatever was happening here at Bethel was causing a conflict in the spirit of the congregation so intense that some of the members could not listen to the Truth of God's near approach.

I am the target of this controversy, but I am not the cause. The word of God as summed up in Jesus Christ that we are going to talk about today will either convict, change a stubborn conceited heart to penitence and humility, or it will lead to anger that consumes in our flesh to all manner of evil.

As we proceed to our lesson or sermon for the day, I would like to remind the listener that the umbrella under which I will unfold the sermon today will be "God's will in our world." Under that umbrella, I will mention an Old Testament example. In this example, Joshua 3:1-8, "And they commanded the people, saying, when you see the ark of covenant of the Lord your God, and the priests and the Levites bringing it, then you shall remove from your place, and go after it. Yet, there shall be a space between you and it, about two thousand cubits by measure, that you may know the way by which we must go; for ye have not passed this way heretofore."

This subject, "A New Path" is a good one for today's sermon. With God as our umbrella of faith, and a new path as our concern, we start a new year.

This is the second Sunday in 1978. We have closed the books on 1977. We are all continually entering new paths, which, afterwards, turn out to have some reminders of the old paths.

Religious experiences move by crisis. Israel had not many years before gone across this same desert and then been abruptly turned back to Sinai, because of the rebelliousness of their will.

Now they were to go to Canaan, but by another route altogether. We are always beginning new experiences. The point of emphasis in Verse 3 and 4, of Joshua three, is not Israel's failure, but a new path, "for you have not passed this way before."

Watch for the details of the journey, not the outer scenery and trappings that catch our eyes at a glance. One of the great insights of this story of Israel's crossing over into Canaan is that Moses, the great lawgiver, was not with them.

Moses is remembered in history for molding a nation out of a motley group of rebellious people. Joshua is hardly mentioned in the same light. But, as our lesson today says, Joshua carried out the great hope of his people. But as we look closer Joshua followed closely God's Word. We are not saying that Moses could not have done the same, but there comes a time for God to bring to pass His will.

The "New Path" was not so much the way they went, for it says in the interpretation, they had been this very same route before. However, this time the difference is "how" they went, not the way, or the route they went.

The word of God is terribly powerful and it must be brought to pass. I'm sure that the rebelliousness of some of the people were ever greater during this second attempt to cross over into the land of promise. Forty years of mumbling and grumbling had grieved the heart of Moses and God, but it also served to chasten the stubborn will of the people of Israel.

God had not only prepared the Way, He had prepared their wills. I have yet to find a place in Scripture where God sets a leader before His people for them to follow His will, and then undermine the leader by giving authority to a lesser person or group. Joshua number 3 and 4, says, "But let the leader go before you. Give them the Ark, let the people stay 2,000 cubits behind.

This distancing of leader from people was to keep down confusion. The obstacles that were put in their path was no sign that God had not put them there. A leader who like Solomon, wished from God an understanding heart, can go on beyond obstacles and misunderstandings, but when he has to struggle with those he leads who do not have the vision to stop, pause, or go forward, this becomes the confusion.

Because of this lack of spiritual leadership in the Christian Church in 1964, the Supreme Court of America rendered a decision taking prayer out of the public schools. There was no challenge to this colossal mistake then by the leadership of the Christian Church. The state kept its authority and the church relented in defeat, and as a result our nation has suffered exponentially from that day until now. The further result is that we, as a world, have taken our eyes off the "Ark of the Covenant."

PART 2 - A NEW PATH - NEW TESTAMENT SCRIPTURE:
Romans 11:26

"And so all Israel will be saved; as it is written, 'The deliverer will come from Zion, he will banish ungodliness from Jacob,' and this will be my covenant with them when I take away their sins.

God gave Jesus Christ to the world to get at the depth of our sin. He came to our hearts. Perhaps Christmas is best seen as the doorway into this experience. JESUS CHRIST IS THE DESIRE OF ALL AGES. All souls that have not yielded to the mighty power of God to save from death. A God, through Jesus Christ and His Spirit, can be with us at any time, and in any trial or conflict, and above all, prepare us to stand before Him blameless unto eternal life.

Before I generalize about what is happening in our church and the world, let me tell you the story of a man who was a Jew. He studied at the feet of the best scholars in Rabbinical Judaism, a strict follower of the Law of Moses. This man followed that Law to the letter. He felt that he knew what the life of Jesus Christ meant after his death on Calvary. The Law was in his bones, his heart, he lived, walked, talked it.

As small group of Christians, followers of the Spirit of Jesus Christ were worshipping and drawing converts to God through His Spirit left after the death of His Son Jesus Christ. This strict follower of Judaism set out with orders from the governor of his province to go to Damascus and bind and secure those who appeared to violate the laws of Moses, for prosecution by the local magistrate.

But, on his way there with his contingent of men, a blinding light fell from Heaven, and a voice said, Saul, why persecutest thou are? Why kick against the pricks? At the twinkling of an eye as the light fell—on this man who had become strict in his worship of the Law of Moses, for the very first time, felt the Spirit of the Law.

All the Rabbinical exactness of his past, the interpretation of the Levitical priesthood, went out the door. All of his degrees of learning and studies diminished in the "Light" of that moment. A New World dawned right before his very eyes. This same man, Apostle Paul, was heard years later to profess, "Oh the depth of the riches both of the wisdom and knowledge of God! How unsearchable are His Judgments, and His ways are past finding out."

That Ark of the Covenant that the Israelites and Hebrews, and Jewish people of old were told to follow and not let out of their sight, has now become a Man whose Spirit abides with us. Born of a virgin, crucified by the government of His time, raised from the dead by God, His Father, lives today in the three persons of our own lives.

That "Ark of the Covenant" has now become our Savior, our only salvation. "He who would come after me, let him deny himself and take up his cross and follow me." "I am the way, the Truth, and the Life, no man comes to the Father but by me."

That same man, Apostle Paul, who set out to persecute the Truth can now say, "I count not myself to have apprehended but there is one thing I do, forgetting the things behind, I press toward the mark for the prize of the high calling in Jesus Christ."

And when this man who set out to persecute those who followed Christ, was himself persecuted by those he had been loyal to in following the Law of Moses; when he had been beaten, shipwrecked, run out of several towns for preaching Christ and Him crucified, his testimony in Romans 8:36 is a source of strength for many of us who share with him, even now, "Who shall separate us from the love of Christ. Shall tribulation or distress, or nakedness or peril or sword - Nay! For in all these things we are more than conquerors through Him who loved us. For I am persuaded, that neither death, nor life, nor angels, nor principalities, nor powers, nor things present, nor things to come, nor height, nor depth, nor any other creature, shall be able to separate us from the love of God, which is in Christ Jesus our Lord."

The Judge might stop me from preaching, but that "Ark of the Covenant" carried out of the desert in Egypt, towards the Promised Land, will go forward. As Kipling has reminded us, "God of our far flung 'battle line,' dominion over palm and pine - Lord God of Host, be with us yet, lest we forget!"

Judges can stop preachers, but not Jesus Christ. He has gone on before us. "Lo I am with you always! Even to the end of the world."

Quote: *New York Time* reporter at the service: The time is coming when Judge Ackerman will not be able to tell Reverend Austin to stop, not to preach anymore!

A crucial point to make here is that only God could have allowed me the exposure that followed on from my situation in Florida with the young black boy trying to make something out of his life. In my earlier writings I have stated that I have never been far away from the controversy between church and state. The tie-in is with the criminal justice system or the Departments of Correction in three different states if the District of Columbia can be included.

To continue with this crucial point of God's guidance into positions of influence in the most prestigious organizations in America, the Young Men and Women Christian Association and the American

National Red Cross, the results of this exposure leading to expertise in the areas of professionalism and recognition are inestimable.

And then to have been chosen to lead a group of people who were in dire need of a sincere pastor in a time in their church life as well as their personal lives is just phenomenal. There was suffering, but I could never have grown in faith if what I witnessed in the suffering at the Bethel Baptist Church in Westfield, New Jersey for fifteen years had not led to a deepening faith where I know, and everyone who personally observed and read in the media knew, that God was involved in that experience rescuing me at every turn where a trap had been laid out for me.

It was as though after receiving the training in the secular institutions of the highest caliber, I was now sent to receive the best training in the Christian Church, the Church of the Living God. An article printed in an international newspaper "The Religious News Service," explains all aspects of struggle.

Seeing that this treatise puts forth the next phase of the Life For Christ Foundation sponsored proposal based on the culmination of search for that power inherent in the Word of God that should have been made available to the young black boy in Florida, entitled, "Release to the Captives."

I chose to use an excerpt from my own son's, Miles J. Austin, Jr., letter sent to me at the height of the struggle to preach the Word of God. I am glad that Miles Jr. sent me this letter during this struggle. The principal at Manor Woods saw the article in local newspaper and commented, "Wherever there is controversy, there is hard work." From the letter Miles Jr. wrote, I quote, "Dad, I'm glad you're my father." It confirms that I practiced what I preached and that this struggle was for him, another young black boy. Miles Jr. had a rather turbulent high school experience in Westfield. He was very fortunate that I was involved in the criminal justice system in New Jersey at the time. Miles was selected, and accepted at a private school sponsored by the Federal Government, and the State of New Jersey, Manor Woods Academy in Manor Woods, New Jersey. It is my opinion that because of my visits and prayers with him during that time, Miles Jr. became a believer in Jesus Christ. Miles Jr. attended Buena Regional High School, played basketball, was elected "All County" and received a scholarship to Tarkio College in Tarkio, Missouri. He met and married Ann Appleby of O'Neill, Nebraska, and they now live happily in Garfield, New Jersey, and are the proud parents of Miles III and Jennifer, both excellent citizens of their respective communities, Miles III in Dallas, Texas, and Jennifer in Garfield, New Jersey. After graduating high school, Jennifer won a full scholarship to Rutgers University as a "world class" javelin thrower. She graduated with high honors in criminal justice, taking a masters degree in social work from Hunter College in New York. She now holds a position in the Guidance Department at Garfield High School in Garfield, New Jersey, from which she graduated. Miles III won a full football scholarship to Monmouth University in Long Branch, New Jersey, where he set records as a wide receiver. Miles III is now in the NFL with the Dallas Cowboys as a wide receiver and a member of Special Teams.

Along this same line of thinking, the *New York Times* sent a reporter to the services, Sunday morning. The article was dated January 9, 1978, Monday. I was quoted by that reporter as saying, "There's a time coming when Judge Ackerman is not going to be able to tell Reverend Austin to stop, not to preach anymore." There's no need for me to explain the link between my concern for that young black boy in Florida and the failure of the Church of Jesus Christ to be there to buttress his own efforts to maintain his self-esteem and dignity.

Chapter Eight

Jesus Christ Is the Embodiment of the
Perfection of the Law Given to Moses,
Necessary for the Perfection of His World
the Provisions for Our Salvation

When I attempted to bring together the great work of Dr. Martin Luther King Jr. of the civil rights movement of the 50's and 60's and the preaching of the word of God, the Gospel, I failed miserably.

THE PROBLEM: Because of the lack of spiritual enabling, the resulting powerlessness of the Church of Jesus Christ to solve the problems of our world, in our time, is summed up in a quote from G. K. Chesterton in his book, *What's Wrong with the World*. "The Christian ideal has not been tried and found wanting. It has been found difficult, and left untried."

Mrs. Leona Allen's charge, as it appeared to me then, as well as now, is memorably recorded in the timing of my search at Drew University beginning that same year in the fall of 1973. As she exited the door of the church where I greeted parishioners after the Brotherhood Week Services, she made this remark, "Reverend, I did not understand a word you said." I had referred in that sermon to some of the most provocative truths needed for change in our nation, and the world. My dissertation for the doctor of ministry degree is entitled, "To Increase the Congregation's Understanding of Christian Discipleship." This was the great crossroad in my ministry of the

Gospel, bringing together the Truth of God's will for the world. I felt that if, together we, the members and pastor, the spiritual leader, and the Christian Church universal, could not consolidate theologically, the union between the civil rights movement, and the liberation intended in God's work, the Gospel, then we were all blind to this great mystery needing to be revealed, or acknowledged in our world, in our own time.

THE MAGNIFICAT SETS THE SCENARIO FOR THIS CHAPTER: Luke 1:51-53: "He hath showed strength with his arm; he hath scattered the proud in the imagination of their hearts. He hath put down the mighty from their seats, and exalted them of low degree. He hath filled the hungry with good things; and the rich he hath sent away empty." (KJV) John 11.21, 24-26: Then saith Martha to Jesus, Lord, hadst thou been here, my brother had not died. Martha said unto him, I know that he shall rise in the resurrection at the last day. Jesus said unto her, I am the resurrection, and the life; he that believeth in me, though he were dead, yet shall he live; and whosoever liveth and believeth in me shall never die. Believeth thou this?"

This chapter answers the question of how to get help for two very different young men trying to find answers to a life gone wrong early on. The charge throughout the book is cast at the feet of the three citadels of authority—the church, the state, and the community, the governed; Vox Populi, the voice of the people. Also, it answers, on my part, the charge of Sister Leona Allen in reference to the provocative and highly moral oratory of Dr. Martin Luther King Jr. of the civil rights movement, and reiterated by me during Brotherhood Week in a sermon.

Jesus Christ is the embodiment of the perfection of the law given to Moses that is necessary for the perfection of human beings. Their salvation is of utmost concern, but also in order to coexist with God in his creation.

THE FOLLOWING STATEMENT IS CRITICAL JUSTIFICA-TION FOR THE ARGUMENTS FOR THE SUPERIOR AU-THORITY OF THE "CHURCH," CHRISTIAN, JEWISH, MOSLEM, BUDDHIST, HINDU, ETC.

The crux (a critical, pivotal and perplexing point where there is unresolved difficulty) of the 90 percent of Americans who say they believe in God must wrestle upon the horns of a dilemma if they are to be serious about these beliefs. I say that because of the subject chosen for the title of this book, "How Was I Supposed to Know that God Has Created a Perfect World/Universe?" I wrestled in the jungles of library book stacks at Howard University in the nation's capital, Washington D.C., during the civil rights movement of the sixties, and Drew University in Madison, New Jersey, during the seventies. The turbulent times of the sixties were revisited in the seventies as though the landscape of our "more perfect union" only then became visible once again. The nation was given another opportunity for the serious deliberations necessary to redefine the deeper meaning of the American Republic. This struggle involving the juxtapositions between the three citadels of authority, the church, the state, and the community for me went on for fifty years while ministering to congregations in two different Baptist Churches for twenty years, writing upwards of a thousand sermons on the subject. I am at this writing still getting revealed information from God of the depth, and breadth and height of His will for my life, as it relates to how deep I am to go into the inexhaustible well of an omniscient, omnipresent, and omnipotent God.

Dr. Martin Luther King, Jr., saw the struggles of the civil rights movement as representing not only the goals and objective of the Christian Church, but of all men of good will, referring to words from the Declaration of Independence by the framer Thomas Jefferson, "We hold these truths to be self evident that all men are created equal. That they are endowed by their Creator with certain inalienable rights, and that among these are life, liberty, and the pursuit of happiness." In many speeches following those words were those of Gloria Ward Howe from the "Battle Hymn of the Republic" — "Mine eyes have seen the Glory of the coming of the Lord, He is trampling out the vintage where the grapes of wrath are stored, He has loosed the fateful lighting of His terrible swift sword, His truth is marching on."

I knew that Dr. Martin Luther King Jr. was right, and that the ideas, and efforts that caused his death had the authentic ring, and call to every follower of Jesus Christ who say they believe in God. The gravitas and magnanimity bestowed on the movement by Dr. Martin Luther King Jr. and others made clear the sacrifices these times we lived in now demand.

The title of my dissertation for the doctorate degree is "To Increase the Congregation's Understanding of Christian Discipleship." The following statements from the "Prospectus" or blueprint for the completing of the professional project are as follows:

DESCRIPTION OF PROBLEM:

There is an apparent misunderstanding among church members as to their responsibilities as church members of a Christian congregation. I wish to determine the degree to which members of a Christian Church understand the meaning of membership as expressed in the New Testament.

PURPOSE:

It would be helpful to me in my ministry if I could measure the degree of understanding and locate the areas of misunderstanding.

Aspect of ministry such as preaching, teaching, and other special efforts would be adapted to correct this misunderstanding. Ten or twelve persons will be selected for special instructions along with the fifty or so that will be administered the questionnaire as explained under method. Also selected will be key officers of the church along with a cross-section of the membership, persons most amendable to this challenge to discipleship, and who also possess qualities of leadership for future implementation of the model of church membership as described in the Gospel of Luke, and in the book of Acts in the New Testament.

The subject of this chapter eight is "The critical justification for the arguments for the superior authority of the Church, Christian, Jewish, Moslem, etc., as stated in Chapter Seven." Before I complete this reference to the 90 percent of Americans who say they believe in God, I'd like to compare two references that I hope you agree with me that they are not only compatible, but indistinguishable in their call to be a follower of Jesus Christ. I should broach the possibility that it would be a problem of one's flawed perception of the truth of God's revealed Presence in three persons if he, or she, did not discern the Christian Church as being the embodiment of the presence of both God and Jesus Christ in the world presently, in the presence of the Holy Spirit of God, world without end. This is understood as the Trinity (see Chapter Nine and Ten).

The first reference is the civil rights movement as briefly discussed above by Dr. Martin Luther King Jr., a Baptist minister, and second reference, Matthew 25:31-46, where Jesus Christ will judge His followers as either having done this in His name, or He will say "depart from me, ye that work iniquity, I never knew you."

If I compared what the civil rights movement was about with leaders such as Dr. Martin Luther King Jr., Reverend Abanathy, Reverend Shuttlesworth, Hosea Williams, and others, the movement would compare unequivocally with the commitment and behavior Jesus Christ will apply in judging the Christian Church and its members when He returns. Matthew 25:31-46. (This discussion can be reviewed in Chapter Six, "Theological discussions leading to the description of the role of the church in the world.") It should have occurred even to the casual observer by now that the Spirit of God, the third Person of the Trinity, guides, and empowers the followers of Christ "into all Truth," thereby assuring the completion of the Kingdom of God in the finality of the end-time. We are now living in the universe/world that is totally consumed by the righteous Spirit of God, which Christ came to inaugurate the beginning having "led captivity captive," creating the condition of the Garden of Eden once again. After Jesus Christ has done this shall come to pass the totally spiritual medium of our existence, having put all principalities and powers under his feet (See Chapters Nine and Ten).

I will attempt to show with the conclusion of the dissertation presented to, and accepted by the faculty and the board of trustees of Drew University for the doctorate in ministry, that (1) It is possible to "Increase the Congregation's Understanding of Christian Discipleship," and (2) The questionnaire and responses by the member-participants involved in the professional project showed vague, and remote answers to questions-inquiry of their knowledge of Christian discipleship based on the books of Luke, and Acts in the New Testament.

THIS CHAPTER SPEAKS OF THE CRITICAL ARGUMENT FOR THE CHURCH TO PREVAIL, CONSIDERING BOTH CHURCH AND STATE'S CONCERN FOR THE FREEDOM AND THE WELFARE OF HUMAN BEINGS. OUR CASE INVOLVES THE NEED FOR THE CHURCH TO TAKE A MORE VIGOROUS STAND BY GOING A VERY SERIOUS STEP FURTHER TO SECURE THE PEACE OF MIND, AND THE SAVING OF THE SOUL OF THE HUMAN BEING.

Books are written every day, good books with indispensable information about things we need to know about life and living. However, few are written with practical solutions to very complicated and serious problems we face each day in life. The key here is that everyone believes these problems should be solved, nevertheless, they do not come up with serious thoughts about how they should be solved, and by whom. G. K. Chesterton had this to say, "The Christian ideal has not been tried and found wanting. It has been found difficult, and left untried."

I consider the answer to be found in this book with the title causing the casual observer to ask, "How Was I to Know that God has Created a Perfect World/Universe?" A clear understanding to this question can be grasped from two distinct sets of observations involving the linchpins to faith in God, seen in the life of Jesus Christ.

First: In order for human beings to live in God's perfect world/universe, they must have the yoke of bondage experienced by every man born of a woman broken. The first three chapters of the book are devoted to attempts made through the devices man has applied to the problem of breaking the yoke. There is nothing in the world planned more perfectly by an all wise and loving God than the body of Jesus Christ made available to each one of us by asking.

So we could say that this chapter, having stated earlier in chapter one through three, problems of mankind, seen in the light of which we speak, in this eighth chapter we supply the answers to them through the body of Jesus Christ, and the responsibility left to the Christian Church to effectuate why Jesus Christ had to leave. John 16:7-11, "Nevertheless I tell you the truth. It is expedient for you that I go away, for if I go not away, the Comforter will not come unto you. But if I depart, I will send him unto you. (8) And when he is come, he will reprove the world of sin, and of righteousness, and of judgment, of sin because they believe not on me. (10) Of righteousness because I go to my Father and ye see me no more. (11) Of judgment because the prince of this world is judged."

What is a yoke to the casual observer? A yoke is "A device for joining together a pair of draft animals, especially oxen. A yoke consists of a crosspiece with two bow shaped pieces, each enclosing the head of an animal. A yoke is an emblem or symbol of subjection and servitude. It is a bond. It is something that couples and binds together.

Second: "The Way" A method, plan, or means of attaining a goal. It is explained as a Passage or progress of a course. "Lead the way." Refer to Chapter Six, "Long Day's Journey into Light" Jesus' words, "I am the way," "Follow me" and "I never knew you." "Depart from me ye that work iniquity." Jesus command in Great Commissions, Matthew 28:18-20.

WHEN IT COMES TO DISCIPLESHIP AS I HAVE STATED ABOVE, IT TOOK ME SIXTY YEARS TO DISCOVER MY FAULT, WHICH COULD HAVE LEADTO MY SOUL'S SPIRITUAL DEATH.

1. I had to die as I existed as my old self, in order to enter the Kingdom of Heaven. I could have lost my spiritual soul, in fact and truth, while saving others. Jesus would not have recognized me, simply or from a Judgment's point of view. I would not have been like Him. I would not have seen Jesus in the people, the sinners He came to save. I would not have seen what He wanted me to see, because I would not have

seen it in myself, that I was just as sinful as they are, up to that point.

2. Emil Brunner, in *My Faith* comes to mind here: "To understand where God is at work in the world, to hasten to join Him, that is faith."

3. The first great commandment, thou shall love the Lord thy God, the second is like unto it, thy neighbor as thyself. On these two commandments hang all the Law and the Prophets.

4. This is Luke's correction of the Early Church in its misguided wait for the return of Jesus Christ in his two writings, Luke, and Acts of the Apostles. Luke recounted Paul's interpretation of the Ministry of Jesus Christ and considered him the quintessential missionary. Luke had Paul stand before Caesar in Rome, as God had intended for the church to do, then making the ultimate sacrifice, giving his life victoriously, that he might be raised with Jesus Christ. Philippians 2:5: "Let this mind be in you, which was also in Christ Jesus." Philippians 3:10: "That I might know Him, the power of His resurrection…" Romans 10:4, "Christ is the end of the Law for righteousness for those who believe."

THE THEME TO THIS SECTION IS (1) "BREAKING THE YOKE OF BONDAGE": Jer. 28:2, Is. 9:4, and 14:25, and MARY'S MAGNIFICENT CONFESSION in Luke 1:52 Luke, and (2) Consider that Christianity's saving message of suffering with Christ as stated above by Paul and as in Christ in the Garden of Gethsemane on His "Way" to stand-off before Pilate, representing the government of this world, went to suffer a death of crucifixion of Calvary with these words, "not my will, but thine be done." This standoff demonstrating the power of God to raise from the dead was greatly altered during the reign of King Constantine in the early Christian era. He took the side of the suffering Christian with the power of his office to prevent them from being set upon by the dominant culture.

Jeremiah 28:2: "Thus speaketh the Lord of hosts, the God of Israel, saying, I have broken the yoke of the king of Babylon."

Isaiah 9:4: "For thou hast broken the yoke of his burden, and the staff of his shoulder, the rod of his oppressor, as in the day of Midian."

Isaiah 14:25: "That I will break the Assyrian in my land, and upon my mountains tread him under foot; then shall his yoke depart from off them, and his burden depart from off their shoulders."

Matthew 11:28-30: "Come unto me all ye that labor, and are heavy laden, and I will give you rest. (29) Take my yoke upon you, and learn of me, for I am meek and lowly in heart; and ye shall find rest unto your souls. (30) For my yoke is easy, and my burden is light."

Luke 1:52: "He hath gained strength with His arm. He hath scattered the proud in imagination of their heart." "He hath put down the mighty from their seats, and exalted them of low degree, He hath filled the hungry with good things; and the rich he hath sent away empty."

Acts 9:2: "And desired of him letters to Damascus to the synagogues, that if he found any of this way, whether they were men or women, he might bring them bound unto Jerusalem."

Acts 19:9: "But when divers were hardened, and believed not, but spake evil of that way before the multitude, he departed from them, and separated his disciples, disputing daily in the school of one Tyrannus."

Acts 19:23: "And the same time there was no small stir about that way."

Acts 22:4: "And I persecuted this way unto the death, binding and delivering into prisons both men and women."

Acts 24:14: "But this I confess unto you, that after the way which they call heresy, so worship I the God of my fathers, believing all things which are written in the law and in the prophets."

Acts 24:22: "And when Felix heard these things, having more perfect knowledge of that way, he deferred them, and said, when Lysias the chief captain shall come down, I will know the uttermost of your matter."

If the *way*, as interpreted and understood in Acts was called into question as a correction of our use of Christians to explain the ministry of Jesus Christ there would be few members of the Christian Church in America left. Discipleship of Jesus Christ is quite another matter, proof being that it was not entered into the Library of Congress catalog, or in the seminary libraries in America.

Ninety percent of Americans say they believe in God. It is obvious from the Old Testament mentioned above that God intended that the yoke of oppression be lifted from the shoulders of human beings in His world (Mary's confession in Luke 1:52).

Many scholars have concluded that suffering, as in Christ's cross, was considered an honor in the early church until the time of King Constantine. He sided with the suffering of the people of the *way*, but without the intention of relieving the structures of oppression brought on by those in authority, which would be represented by people like him throughout history. Jesus Christ: "Follow me, I am the Way…. I never knew you, because you were never in my *way*."

Members of the Christian Church are inclined to want to be like Jesus Christ, rather than follow him. They would rather do things for Him, rather than what He said. They would rather be with people like themselves who say they know Him, rather than the people He came to *save* (Matthew 25:31-46). "Christians are baptized, but not unto the death and resurrection of Jesus Christ," (Philippians 2:5 and 3:10). THE YOKE OF DEATH AND SUFFERING HAS BEEN BROKEN, BUT MOST CHRISTIANS HAVE NOT BEEN FREED FROM THE FEAR OF BOTH SUFFERING AND DEATH. JOHN 8:31-32: "CONTINUE IN MY WORD, AND YOU SHALL KNOW THE TRUTH, AND THE TRUTH SHALL MAKE YOU FREE."

The presence and the reality of death is ever present in the existential, psychological, and emotional experience of man. The "Broken Yoke" if known, is either ignored or rejected. It is clear here that the threat of death, in the existential, ongoing awareness of man, saps him of the worth that God has made available through the "salvation experience" of Jesus Christ. Under this condition of "disgrace," it is impossible for man to have dominion over the creation, most decisively, his own flesh and blood, a part of that creation, which is the block to his own survival, life eternal.

KEY TO THE THREE PRONGS OF THE HORN OF THE DILEMMA MADE BY JESUS CHRIST TO SAVE US:
1. Follow me. He did not say follow where you think I am. We are like sheep that stray.
2. I am the *way*. Everything has a way in the world. I, am, *the way*.
3. If we spend most of our week, and most of our life making a *living*, what doth it profit a man to gain the whole world, and lose his soul? What will a man give in exchange for his soul? (Matthew 16:26)

Death must be overcome while life is still being experienced, or there is no life after death. Elizabeth Kublar Ross explains five stages in the death and dying experience. Jesus Christ after Lazarus's death, to his sisters, Mary and Martha in John 11:26 states, "I am the resurrection and the life, he that believeth in me, though he were dead, yet shall he live, and he that liveth and believeth in me shall never die." It becomes clear here how Jesus could have granted a convicted thief, hanging on the cross next to him, eternal life: "This day thou shall be with me in paradise," (Luke 23:43).

THE JUDGMENT OF JESUS CHRIST WILL BE INTERPRETED BY HIS VISIT TO JOHN ON THE ISLE OF PATMOS: Revelations 1:10-11

I was in the Spirit on the Lord's day, and heard behind me a great voice, as of a trumpet. (1) Saying, I am Alpha and Omega, the first and the last; and, What thou seest, write in a book, and send it unto the seven churches with are in Asia.

The Stelton Baptist Church, of which I have been a member for seven years, is on the weekend of the first week in September 2007, along with, I believe, five other Baptist churches which forms the Philadelphia Association, celebrating their 300th year. My only remarks to these five churches would be the same as those John was called to write to at Jesus Christ's command in Asia.

GENERAL SUMMARY
THE TURNING POINT
THERE ARE FIVE POINTS THAT STAND OUT HERE:

1. There was utter lack of support from the Christian Church for the condition of the boy in Florida preparing to be discharged back into the community after being incarcerated. We can say here that based on the philosophy, and program mission of the Life for Christ Foundation, he should never have had to leave his family and community in the first place. His condition leading to incarceration was brought on from the acknowledged oppression which we all face as black people, and minority citizens. But more than that, where are the black and minority Christians with a Biblical responsibility: Matthew 25:31-46.

2. God has allowed me to be continually involved in the criminal justice system; (a) Admission from the boys at East Jersey State Prison in New Jersey who admitted their wrongs and repented; (b) The admission of the staff at Talbot Hall that had repented after having their lives ruined from alcohol, and narcotic addiction, continuing to confess their shortcomings in recovery as they counsel the residents in cognitive behavioral therapy. Those brothers and sisters at Talbot Hall continued to be vigilant in their recovery by attending the 12 step programs of AA and NA.

3. There was an Attitude vs. Beatitude of the members of the Bethel Baptist Church in 1977. They filed charges against

me, their spiritual minister, in the Superior Court of Union County New Jersey for belittling them as sinners in my sermons as I preached the Gospel, of which I admitted being one among them.

4.   In late 2005, I was led to take time off to seek a "retreat mode" with pointed efforts to what I knew should be taking place in the Christian Church. I spent one year writing, and preparing my Spirit for what I found out approximately one year later, was preparation for my answer to "How Was I Supposed to Know that God has Created a Perfect Universe?" I completed the search for the true meaning and the "contact Point of Effort" for the Christian Church that God meant me to see.

5.   Approximately one year later, at the 2006 Thanksgiving service at the Tabernacle Baptist Church in New Brunswick, New Jersey, the Ministerial Alliance of New Brunswick and vicinity celebrated that occasion. Reverend William Riddick, the president, and former moderator of the Middlesex Central Baptist Association, congratulated all the preachers creating a spiritual atmosphere for praising and worshipping God at this Thanksgiving service. This is the dilemma that I struggled with after that service while experiencing a year-long retreat studying the meaning of the Holy Spirit having been given at Pentecost to bring about God's will for the Church of Jesus Christ in our world, in our time. Of all the ministers there at that service, none is more committed to the ministry Jesus speaks of in his Judgment in Matthew 25:31-46, which is to the community, than Reverend Riddick.

THIS WAS THE CHALLENGE I HEARD EXPRESSED AT THAT BEAUTIFUL WORSHIP SERVICE:

If the emotionally and spiritually charged service that we experienced there is not the expected result each time we gather in the name of Jesus Christ, something is missing.

Approximately a year later, as providential as it seems, Reverend Riddick called upon me to preach at his church in an emergency. What I said at Reverend Riddick's church on July 24, 2007 (See Chapter Six for this sermon and refer to the date it was preached.). This sermon was that challenge. This challenge was not only to "the pastors" that I worshipped with a year ago, but it was also the challenge I would have presented to those who heard me preach in Florida, and to the

Christian churches that I pastured for twenty years. It is there, this challenge, where there was refusal by the Church of the Living God to do what I knew then, and always will know, should happen. This same spiritual condition, actualized in the body, and presence of Jesus Christ was lacking as I preached to the people at the First Baptist Church of Mount Pleasant Plains in Washington, DC, while attending Howard University. This is the reason for my writings at Howard University, and my application to Drew University with the subject that I chose to find the Truth.

TRUTH: THE GUIDING PRINCIPLE

The power of the Holy Spirit directed by God through Jesus Christ His Son at Pentecost, and its significance, is the key to unlocking the *guiding principle* leading to God's establishment of His Kingdom on earth for the salvation of mankind.

Every government, either elected by the people, or a dictatorship, has violated God's intentions, and His will for humanity, His people seen in the *death and taxes* of King Solomon with all his wisdom. Any human whose life is not influenced by the Spirit of God is corrupt. Power corrupts and absolute power corrupts absolutely! Separation of church and state is but a thinly veiled obfuscation, knowingly or unknowingly, of the Truth.

"Description of the problem" doctoral dissertation: Drew University, October 8, 1976: Prospectus: "There is an apparent misunderstanding among church members of a Christian congregation. I wish to determine the degree to which members of a Christian Church understand the meaning of membership as expressed in the New Testament. It would be helpful to me in my ministry if I could measure the degree of understanding, and locate the areas of misunderstanding."

"Description of the problem after that Thanksgiving service in 2006," in *The Cost of Discipleship by* Dietrich Bonhoeffer, basis for my dissertation from Drew University, in the first chapter, there is no room left for a misunderstanding of my conclusion here:

"Cheap grace means grace as a doctrine, a principle, a system. It means forgiveness of sins proclaimed as a general truth, the love of God taught as the Christian "conception" of God. An intellectual assent to that idea is held to be of itself sufficient to secure remission of sins. The Church which holds this definition of faith by reason of knowledge only, violates the doctrine of grace as it is supposed, ipso facto (just as it is, by the fact itself) to be able to take part in that grace. In such a church, the world finds a cheap covering for its sin.

Cheap grace therefore amounts to a denial of the living word of God, in fact, a denial of the Incarnation of the Word of God."

In my dissertation presented and accepted for the doctor of ministry degree, on page 18, I make the following statements:

"LUKE'S IDEA OF THE WORK OF THE SPIRIT is one based on our ethic of God's plan of salvation, which is different from the mystery surrounding the performance of miracles. On the contrary Johnnine theology does not have a system of salvation as well defined as Lucan theology. In John 4:48, Meyer's comments in *Trajectories through Early Christianity* is proof of this as he states: "Jesus displeasure over the demand for a miracle as a guarantee of faith."

"The Gospel of John and the two volume work of Luke were written to address two very different issues. As Luke himself states in his introductory address to Theophilus in reference to 'the certainty of those things, wherein thou has been instructed.' He has gone beyond Mark in the understanding of suffering as being the paradigm for the 'story of salvation' as it relates to the birth, life, and ministry of Jesus Christ. Using the Gospel of John, notwithstanding that Mark's and John's theologies are very sound in that they dealt effectively with the problem of eschatology based on the audience they responded to. Luke goes beyond them both with the meaning of the church in the time as it relates to a delayed *Parousia*, and the work of the Holy Spirit. The fact that Luke wrote to interpret theologically the delay of the *Parousia* gave him the task of dealing with most important aspects of the will and plan of God—time."

"The Spirit is for the accomplishment of the plan of redemption of mankind. It is not without purpose that Luke points his theology from Israel, the original people of promise, to Jesus, the center of history in Jerusalem and thirdly to Paul, freely preaching the Gospel in Rome. This is all done as the power of God is in the Holy Spirit."

"If, in the understanding of Luke, we could construct the steps to discipleship for a new member coming into the church, it would begin with (1) proclamation or preaching, hearing the word leads to (2) repentance, and then one is (3) baptized. (4) Almost simultaneously with baptism the words, 'in the name of Jesus' introduces the person into the work of the Spirit as in apostolic succession. (6) Speaking in tongues represent a witnessing expression signifying the total commitment of the individual (not necessarily the will of God). (7) Prayer is the step to keep our will subservient to God's will, and (8) Missions is last but not least. When one understands Luke's 'story of salvation,' missions becomes the way of accomplishing the goal toward which God's plan and work in 'redemptive history' is moving. The Spirit is the power." The preceding excerpts were taken from the doctoral dissertation of Dr. Miles J. Austin: Drew University: Madison, New Jersey 1976.

Before I move on to extrapolating the *Truth, the Guiding Principle*, I repeat here that I must stop to thank my spiritual Father, God, for allowing me to be sequestered in His presence for more than a year, from late 2005 to late 2006. This time was taken off from all other activities of my daily life in order to study to show myself approved, and not to be ashamed, but be prepared to rightly divide the word of Truth.

If I had not been given this opportunity of sequestered time for a year in writing the basic material for this book I would not have been prepared to respond to the dilemma that I struggled with during this time. I knew that the exhilarating feeling of the Holy Spirit experienced there at that 2006 Thanksgiving service by all of us was to the glory of God, there was something missing. The final demonstration is to be understood in God's will for our salvation is the salvation of the entire world, inaugurating His presence totally, the Kingdom of God, in our time, world without end.

Any worship service to the Glory of God should be about what a disciple of Jesus Christ, His only begotten son, has been doing with his or her life as stated in Matthew 25:31-46. "When saw we thee a stranger?" "Notwithstanding in this rejoice not, that the spirits are subject unto you; but rather rejoice, because your names are written in heaven. See the sermon in Chapter Six preached by me at the Faith Hope Baptist Church June 24, 2007, at 11:00 A.M.

The continuing extrapolation of the *principle* is seen in how both church and state put all of their resources on rituals, ceremonies, and rules and regulations respectively, rather than on relieving structures of oppression which all of the cultural peoples of the world are faced with at the emergence of their people's established identity, and peace, as well as the successful maintenance of their civilization. The acknowledged goal of both, church and State is obscured, even as they struggle to make their enacted goals and intentions clear.

Since the fall of man in the Garden of Eden, man has been the servant of his flesh and blood, rather than the guardian of his soul. I continue to commend Dr. Bob, and Bill, pioneers of the Twelve Step philosophy of Alcohol and Narcotic Anonymous. These twelve steps acknowledge man's depraved nature, and his need to accept God's intelligent design provided in the body of Jesus Christ for the salvation of mankind.

EXTRAPOLATION: An analogy is seen in the final decisions when considering the directions in both the dissertation from Drew University, and the book, "How Was I Supposed to Know."

EXTRAPOLATION: After completing the outline of a Table of Content for "How Was I Supposed to Know," Charles Holt, a member of the Stelton Baptist Church, intuitively revealed a violation of the *principle*. By my leaving out what is now Chapter Two "Train Up A Child In The Way they Should Go," I had not spoken of anyone individually in the deeper sense of reality, not even myself, or Carol Lin.

EXTRAPOLATION: Because of the fallen nature of man Jesus' challenge to Nicodemus in John 3, and the need to press into the Kingdom of Heaven in Luke 16:16 leads to the book's title, "How Was I Supposed to Know?" I was supposed to search.

PRINCIPLE: Either we acknowledge "The God of the Oppressed," whose Judgment is rendered in Matthew 25:31-46, or we succumb to "cheap grace" of the 90 percent of Americans who say they believe in God. The critical judgment against them is understood as follows:

1. A soul cannot be saved unless it can exist in the presence of God's Holy Spirit. Sin is separation due to this inability of the human soul to coexist with God in His universe, the Kingdom of Heaven.

2. A person who faces death without the Spirit of God, and as Dr. Elisabeth Kublar Ross says, rejects the power of God to save them, and has not been forgiven of his, or her sins: And suppose a minister asks them do they believe in Jesus Christ, even at that late hour. They cannot be saved unless, as Paul says in I Corinthians 11:26, they discern the Body of Jesus Christ as the sole access to their salvation. John 14:6 "Jesus saith unto him, I am the way, the truth, and the life; no man cometh unto the Father, but by me." As I mentioned in the eight ways to becoming a disciple of Jesus, hearing a preacher precedes repentance. It is impossible to seek forgiveness for something you don't see as being wrong, flawed, or that you are guilty of.

3. SELF ADMISSION: I DO NOT ACT AS A JUDGE HERE. Ninety percent of those who say they believe in God may show no evidence of being either a disciple, or not being a disciple. Two statements from Jesus Christ will either validate or negate their salvation: (1) You cannot serve two masters, (Matthew 6:24), and (2) I am the way, (John 14:6).

Chapter Nine

**Whatever God Is Doing in this World to
Build Up His Kingdom, Jesus Christ Is the
Cornerstone, Nothing, and No Other Way Can
Be Used to Alter this Architectural Blueprint:
Key, the Law of Moses, the Decalogue**

Jesus Christ opens the seven seals of the Book of Revelations: This apocalyptic event inaugurates the final stages of God's revelation to man involving the end-time. This is the condition understood as grace that allows mankind to be returned to the conditions that existed in the Garden of Eden, the blood, and broken body of Jesus Christ atoning, or exonerating mankind from that death in the *fall*, Genesis 2 and 3. This condition justifies the book's title confirming the perfection of God's universe as it was in the beginning. And it refutes the title of Milton's novel, *Paradise Lost*.

THE PROBLEM: Because of the lack of spiritual enabling, the caricature of *Humpty Dumpty* being referred to generically as the human condition of man is judgmentally sound.

I refer here also to the Mary's *Magnificat* in Luke 1:46-55 to show that God has indeed restored man to the possibility of the sanctity of the Garden of Eden in Genesis 2 and 3, the death that He warned us of is graphically depicted by John in the Book of Revelations. Revelations 12:1-3: "And I saw a new heaven and a new earth; for the first heaven and the first earth had passed away; and there was no more sea. And I John saw the holy city, new Jerusalem, coming down from God out of heaven, prepared as a bride adorned for her husband. And I heard a great voice out of heaven, Behold, the tabernacle of God is with men, and he will dwell with them, and they shall be his people, and God himself shall be with them, and be their God," (KJV).

THE SEVEN SEAL SUMMARY

This summary begins with a preview from the Book of Revelations as stated in the twelve-volume *Interpreter Bibles* published by Abingdon Press. The ten-page document given to Charles and Tom also included this summary mentioned directly above.

The general thought was as follows: Leading up to the opening of the seven seals by Jesus Christ in Revelations, Jewish, Christian, and Mohammedan theologians, understood apocalypticism as representing the *last days* as they saw them. This was considered to be a period of time when the final judgment of God would be executed in His universe. If this was to be a final judgment, there would be no further opportunity for man's salvation. This represented the lack of understanding they had of God's will for man's salvation in these last days as they saw it. Acts 1:6 says, "When they therefore were come together, they asked him, saying, Lord wilt thou at this time restore again the Kingdom of Israel?"

THE SIGNIFICANCE OF THIS MISUNDERSTANDING, EVEN TODAY

The significance here is that although the final Judgment is not executed in the opening of the seven seals by Jesus Christ, the eschatological, and apocalyptical event of the *fall* of humanity in Genesis 3 shows us the following: It is clear that the Kingdom of God, heaven on earth, is again being revealed, with another opportunity for mankind to see the almost unexpected forgiveness by God with another chance for our salvation.

A key factor in the above statement is the judgment of death by God but now, after the opening of the seven seals by Jesus Christ, gives us another opportunity for salvation after the *fall* in Genesis 3. This is the challenge of discipleship or the challenge, and judgment of death and destruction of humanity if following Jesus Christ is not adhered to as He came to teach by precept and example, and died, was raised from the dead for proof and authority of His teachings, and God's unsearchable benevolence on our behalf.

REVIEW OF INFORMATION IN THE PREVIOUS DOCUMENT

The following information proves the understandable condition we face as human beings, and as a society, before a loving, all wise, forgiving, yet, a God that cannot lie, or change the laws on which His universe is established.

To continue the thought from the previous page, I refer to Luke's statement at the beginning of both Luke and Acts. I will quote only one statement, seeing that they are both almost identical. Luke 1:1-3, "FORASMUCH as much as many have taken in hand to set forth in order a declaration of these things which are most surely believed among us, Even as they delivered them unto us, which from the beginning were eyewitnesses, ministers of the word; It seemed to me also, having had perfect understanding of all things from the very first, to write unto thee in order, most excellent Theophilis, Most scholars understand Theophilis to be the generic name for the Gentiles that Paul spent his entire life trying to save, as Jesus intended in Acts 1:8, "That thou mightest know the certainty of those things, wherein thou hast been instructed."

THE ONLY WAY FOR MAN AND HIS SOCIETY TO SURVIVE THE JUDGMENT AND DEATH FROM VIOLATIONS OF GOD'S LAWS IS TO BE CLOSE ENOUGH TO HIM. THIS IS POSSIBLE BY MANKIND'S RELATIONSHIP THROUGH HIS HOLY SPIRIT, MADE POSSIBLE THROUGH THE PRECEPT, THE TECHNICAL OPERATION PERFORMED BY JESUS CHRIST, LEADING TO HIS RESURRECTION, OPENING THE SEVEN SEALS OF THE BOOK OF REVELATIONS AND ESTABLISHING THE KINGDOM OF GOD FOR ETERNITY. THE FOLLOWING ARE TWO SETS OF EXAMPLES OF THE PRECEPTS OR TWO SETS OF TECHNICAL OPERATIONS JUSTIFYING, AND VALIDATING THE PRECEPTS, OR TECHNICAL OPERATIONS THAT ISTHE BASIS OF THE SALVATION OF HUMANITY.
SET ONE

In the understanding of Luke, we could construct the steps to discipleship for a new member coming into church, it would begin with:

(1) proclamation or preaching, hears the word leads to,
(2) repentance, and then one is,
(3) baptized,

(4) Almost simultaneously with baptism the words, "in the name of Jesus" introduces the person into the work of the Spirit as in apostolic succession,

(5) laying on of hands,

(6) speaking in tongues represents a witness expression signifying the total commitment of the individual,

(7) prayer is the step to keep our will subservient to God's will, and

(8) mission is last, but not lest. Since a human being cannot serve two masters, Matthew 6:24, he or she is in God's Spirit and work, or as in Matthew 25:31-46 and Matthew 7:21-23, "Depart from me ye that work iniquity, I never knew you."

SET TWO

The following Scriptures confirm Luke's overriding significance of the Holy Spirit of God in the *last days*, or the apocalypticism of the times we live. Revelations 21:3 states, "And I heard a great voice out of Heaven saying, Behold, the tabernacle of God is with men, and he will dwell with them, and they shall be his people, and God himself shall be with them, and be their God."

(1) Ephesians 2:8: "By *grace* we are saved by faith."

(2) Philippians 1:6: "He that hath begun a good work in you will perform it until the day of Jesus Christ."

(3) Philippians 2:12: "Work out your soul salvation in fear and trembling."

(4) Luke 16:16: "The Law and the Prophets were until John, since that time the Kingdom of God is preached, and every man presseth into it."

(5) I Corinthians 1:18, "The preaching of the cross is to them that perish foolishness, but unto us that are saved it is the power of God."

THE SEVEN SEALS OF THE BOOK OF REVELATIONS

AND THEY SANG A NEW SONG, SAYING, THOU ARE WORTHY TO OPEN THE SEALS THEREOF: FOR THOU WAST SLAIN, AND HAST REDEEMED US TO GOD BY THY BLOOD OUT OF EVERY KINDRED, AND TONGUE, AND PEOPLE, AND NATIONS Revelations 5:9
THE BOOK OF REVELATIONS IS ABOUT THE APOCALYPSE
Its meaning of "Apocalypse"

It should always be noted that apocalypticism is always eschatological, is always concerned last things, with death and the end of this present age and with life in the age to come. This eschatological interest alone should be sufficient to differentiate apocalypticism from Old Testament prophecy, which is primarily, if not exclusively concerned with this life and this age of human history, rather than with the next life and the age to come. Accordingly, to avoid ambiguity the term "apocalypse" should never be used in connection with non-eschatological books like Joel, Amos, Ezekiel, Zechariah, and Isaiah (save for Isaiah 24-27), as is too frequently done. Likewise, this distinction should separate the concept of the Kingdom of God (an outgrowth of Old Testament prophecy) as taught by the pharisees and John the Baptist, as well as by Jesus, from apocalypticism; for the Kingdom of God was to be established in this age and in this time of human history, not in an entirely different age to be established by God. Authority reference: *The Interpreter's Bible* in twelve volumes: Abingdon Press,: New York and Nashville: Volume 12: Revelations, Page 347.

The eschatological book of Revelations reveals how the two worlds existing in judgmental juxtaposition: (1) The Kingdom of God that has come, and (2) The plagues and death that will result if humanity does not conform to the body of Christ in the World. First Peter 4:17, "For the time is come that judgment must begin at the house of God; and if it first begin at us, what shall the end be of them that obey not the gospel of God?"

The Gospel of Luke deals with the controversy around the imminent return of Jesus Christ. At the beginning of the book of Acts, he records "So when they came together they asked him, 'Lord, will you at this time restore the Kingdom of Israel?'" Conzelman points out that Luke's sole purpose for writing his Gospel, as I have mentioned in his introduction, was to correct this misunderstanding of the "story of salvation."

Luke's theology deals not only with a revised interpretation of the *eschaton*—the coming of Christ—but also with the description of what is to take place in the meantime. Luke's theology relates to the Holy Spirit and the Kingdom of God essential to the problem of faith in the delayed *Parousia,* or return, of Jesus Christ.

In Luke's theology, as it relates to the church, the Holy Spirit and the Kingdom of God play very important roles. In my opinion, Matthew's version of the great command of Jesus Christ: "All power is given unto me in heaven and in earth. Go ye therefore, and teach all nations, baptizing them in the name of the Father, and of the Son, and of the Holy Ghost: Teaching them to observe all things whatsoever I have commanded you: And lo, I am with you always, even to the end of the world," (Matthew 28:18b 20) KJV. AND Luke's recording of Acts 1:8 are to be taken in the same light of the story of salvation: "But ye shall receive power, after that the Holy Spirit is come upon you; And ye shall be witnesses unto me both in Jerusalem, and in all Judea, and in Samaria, and unto the uttermost parts of the earth," (Acts 1:8, KJV.)

Luke's idea of the work of the Spirit is one based on our ethic of God's plan of Salvation which is different from the mystery surrounding the performance of miracles. On the contrary Johannine theology does have a system of salvation as well defined as Lucan theology. In John 4:48, Meyer's comments in *Trajectories through Early Christianity* are proof of this as he states: "Jesus displeasure over the demand for a miracle as a guarantee of faith."

The Gospel of John and the two volume work of Luke were written to address two every different issues. As Luke himself states in his introductory address to Theophilis in reference to "the certainty of those things, wherein thou has been instructed." He has gone beyond Mark in the understanding of suffering as being the paradigm for the "story of salvation" as it relates to the birth, life, and ministry of Jesus Christ. Using the Gospel of John, notwithstanding that Mark's and John's theologies are very sound in that they deal effectively with the problem of eschatology based on the audience they responded to, Luke goes beyond them both with the meaning of the church in time as it relates to a delayed *Parousia* and the work of the Holy Spirit.

John's Gospel dealt with the *Gnostic Redeemer Myth*. This myth had to do with an assumption that Jesus was "Very God" but not "Very Man," that he was above all the suffering or, that our suffering is different. This *Gnostic Redeemer Myth* also has to do with the assumption that a believer in Jesus Christ had only to acquire knowledge of light as John chose to call it, in order to be saved. To understand was to be free of sin. John wrote to correct a misunderstanding of the nature of Christ work. The fact that Luke wrote to interpret theologically the delay of the *Parousia* gave him the task of dealing with the most significant aspect of the will of God, time.

Notwithstanding the particular emphasis on the church's mission, Luke is conscious of the individual needs and desires of the members of the Christian Church. When Jesus spoke, as in Luke 4:16-30, the Kingdom of God is indeed present. For Luke there is no need to consider any obstacle of any earthly nature as opposing the Kingdom, suffering notwithstanding. The Kingdom with its "everythingness" demands total sacrifice of self as a prerequisite to entering. "The Law and the Prophets were until John, since then the Kingdom of God is preached, and men press into it," (Luke 16:16). In Luke, the Passion of Jesus Christ is an appropriation of this total sacrifice.

Although the two volume work of Luke (also Acts) is accurately concerned with the Church, it is in relation to the work of the Church for the salvation of individuals that the Church is emphasized. The purpose of Luke's theology is to speak to the issue of this time, which is delayed *eschaton* and the need for a new way of life to cope with the dilemma.

The preceding excerpts were lifted from the doctoral dissertation of Dr. Miles J. Austin at Drew University, pages 16 through 20, October 8, 1976.

KEY TO OPENING THE SEVEN SEALS:
1. "By *grace*, we are saved through faith," (Ephesians 2:8).
2. "He that hath begun a good work in you will perform it until the day of Jesus Christ," (Philippians 1:6).
3. "Work out your soul salvation in fear and trembling," (Philippians 2:12).
4. "The Law and the prophets were until John, since that time the Kingdom of God is preached, and every man presseth into it, (Luke 16:16).
5. "The preaching of the cross is to them that perish foolishness, but unto us which are saved it is the power of God," (I Corinthians 1:18).

THE FOLLOWING INVOLVES UNDERSTANDING THE PRECEPT, OR THE TECHNICAL OPERATION INVOLVED IN SURVIVING OUR PHYSICAL LIFETIME IN "THIS WORLD," AND GAINING ETERNAL LIFE WITH GOD IN HIS HOLY SPIRIT, THE KINGDOM OF GOD.

Observe number 2 above under what Jesus Christ has done to open the seven seals where this statement is made: "He will perform it until the day of Jesus Christ." This gives understanding and credibility to the necessity of a precept, an operation being performed for man's salvation in God's perfect world/universe.

Sometime ago I was assigned as a substitute for a teacher at Edison High School, the subject being structural engineering. Plans left for me to follow included structural engineering demonstrating a monumentally technical operation. It involved actually stopping the North Atlantic Ocean; I think the country was Norway in which the operation took place. It occurred that each year, at a particular time, the ocean rose too high for imports to flow into the area, affecting the economy of the entire country. A massive gate-like structure of iron and steel on a massive ball joint that allowed the structure on hydraulic pistons, upon swinging out into the inlet, dropping deep into the seabed, the top rising high enough to hold back the millions of tons of water coming in from the ocean.

Ironic as it occurred, in that same classroom, during the afternoon, a class involving health had met that morning. In that class, that teacher had written on the board the effects of stress and pressure on the mind and emotions of a human being causing him or her to break under pressure and demonstrate behavior that he or she would be ashamed of after the stress and pressure is relieved.

The stress fractures and breaks prevented in the first technical operation above can also be prevented in the second observation. In the second case involving human beings, the ultimate violation of the Good News, the Gospel from God through Jesus Christ is suicide, is homicide, taking one's own life, or that life of another human being.

NOTE: Every human being must face death. Jesus Christ performed the first technical operation against death, which operation is necessary for any other human being that would also need to be raised from the dead to inherit eternal life. Follow me. I am the resurrection and the life. He that believeth in me, though he were dead, yet shall he live, and he that liveth and believeth in me, shall never die, (John 11:26).

Jesus Christ personally turned Apostle Paul around on the Damascus Road. Paul is the foremost exponent of the meaning of the Kingdom of God revealed in the birth, life, death, resurrection and continuing ministry of Jesus Christ, followed by the third person of the Trinity the Holy Spirit:

The following Scriptures are from *The Life Application Study Bible*
- Paul's letter to the churches in Rome: 12:1-3, "And so, dear brothers and sisters, I plead with you to give your bodies to God. Let them be a holy living sacrifice—the kind He will accept. When you think of what He has done for you, is it too much to ask? Don't copy the behavior and customs of this world, but let God transform you into a new person by changing the way you think. Then you will know what God wants you to do, and you will know how good and pleasing and perfect His will really is."

- Paul s letter to the churches at Philippians 2:5: "Your attitude should be the same that Christ Jesus had. Though He was God, he did not demand and cling to rights as God. He made himself nothing; he took the humble position of a slave and appeared in human form. And in the human form he obediently humbled himself even further by dying a criminal's death on a cross. Because of this God has raised him up to the heights of heaven and gave him a name that is above every other name, so that at the name of Jesus every knee must bow, in heaven and in earth and beneath the earth, and every tongue will confess that Jesus Christ is Lord, to the glory of God the Father.
- Philippians 3:7-10: "I once thought all these things were so very important, but now I consider them worthless because of what Christ has done. Yes, everything else is worthless when compared with the priceless gain of knowing Christ Jesus my Lord. I have discarded everything else, counting it all as garbage, so that I may have Christ, and become one with him. I no longer count my own goodness or my ability to obey God's law, but I trust Christ to save me For God's way of making us right with Himself depends on faith. As a result, I can really know Christ and experience the mighty power that raised him from the dead. I can learn to suffer with him, sharing in his death, so that, somehow, I can experience the resurrection from the dead!"
- Paul's first letter to the churches in Corinthians 15:56: "For sin is the sting that results in death, and the law gives sin its power. How we thank God, which gives us the victory over sin and death through Jesus Christ our Lord!"

THE CONCERN HERE IS THE POINT OF ENTERING THE KINGDOM OF GOD, WHICH IS HEAVEN ON EARTH, WORLD WITHOUT END. THIS IS BEST SEEN, UNDER-STOOD, AND OBTAINED WHEN ALL PHYSICAL, MATE-RIAL, AND MENTAL EFFORTS OF HUMAN BEINGS HAVE BEEN EXHAUSTED. THE LIFE FOR CHRIST FOUNDATION HAS CHOSEN TO INTERVENE IN THE CRIMINAL JUSTICE SYSTEM TO SALVAGE THE LIVES OF THE YOUTH IN OUR SOCIETY. WE ALSO CHOSE, AS PROVERBS STATES IN 22:6, "TRAIN UP A CHILD IN THE WAY HE SHOULD GO, WHEN HE IS OLD, HE WILL NOT DEPART FROM IT."

The statement that "Man's extremity is God's opportunity" makes sense and is justified by Luke 11:9, "And I say unto you, *ask*, and it shall be given you; seek, and ye shall find; knock, and it shall be opened unto you."

IN TERMS CALLED FIRST SUNDAY LORD'S DAY COM-MUNION, THERE IS BREAKING OF BREAD, AND DRINK-ING OF WINE. HOW DOES THIS RITUAL STACK UP WITH JESUS OPENING THE SEVEN SEALS, THE APOCALYPTI-CISM OF THE BOOK OF REVELATIONS?
KEY TO "OPENING THE SEVEN SEALS

1. The five Scriptures mentioned, under "Opening the Seven Seals" explicitly shows that God has sent Jesus Christ to make good his promise in Luke 11:9 immediately above.
2. Philippians 1:6: "He that hath begun a good work will 'perform it' until the day of Jesus Christ." The fact that God is "performing a work" means that it can be understood, obtained, and maintained.
3. For this reason, I am looking forward to discussing with Charles and Tom, two members of the Stelton Baptist Church Sunday School, the "technical operation" in God's "performing," and in relative similarities to high tech operation in computers models, etc.

It seems clear in my lifelong search for a clear understanding of this "performance of salvation" that God is involved through Jesus Christ, until the second coming of Jesus Christ is explicitly demonstrated in THE PURPOSE AND MISSION OF THE LIFE FOR CHRIST FOUNDATION INC.

Luke 5:30-32, "But the Scribes and Pharisees murmured against his disciples, saying, Why do ye eat and drink with Publicans and sinners? And Jesus answering said unto them, they that are whole need not a physician; but they that are sick. I came not to call the righteous, sinners to repentance."

Matthew 28:19-20: "Go ye therefore, and teach all nations, baptizing them in the name of the Father, and of the Son, and of the Holy Ghost; teaching them to observe all things whatsoever I have commended you; and, lo, I am with you always, even to the end of the world. Amen."

Matthew 25:31, 32, 37-40: "When the son of man shall come in his glory, and all the holy angels with him, then shall he sit upon the throne of his glory. And before him shall be gathered all nations; and he shall separate them one from another, as a shepherd divideth his sheep from the goats. And he shall set the sheep on his right hand, but the goats on the left. Then shall the King say unto them on his right hand, come, ye blessed of my Father, inherit the Kingdom prepared for you from the foundation of the world.

"For I was hungred, and ye gave me meat: I was thirsty, and ye gave me drink; I was a stranger, and ye took me in; Naked, and ye clothed me; I was sick, and ye visited me; I was in prison, and ye came unto me; Then shall the righteous answer him, saying, Lord, when saw we thee an hungred, and fed thee? Or thirsty, and gave thee drink? When saw we thee a stranger, and took thee in? Or naked, and clothed thee? Or when saw we thee sick, or in prison, and came unto thee?

"And the King shall answer and say unto them, verily I say unto you, Inasmuch as ye have done it unto one of the least of these my brethren, ye have done it unto me. Then shall he say to them on the left hand, Depart from me, ye cursed, into everlasting fire, prepared for the devil and his angels."

To understand current psychiatric practices, it is necessary to understand how and why the idea of mental illness arose and the way it now functions. In part, the concept of mental illness arose from the fact that it is possible for a person to act and appear as if they were sick without actually having a bodily disease. How should we react to such a person? Should we treat him as if he were not ill, or as if he were ill?

Until the second half of the nineteenth century, persons who imitated illness—that is, who claimed to be sick without being able to convince their physicians that they suffered from bona fide illnesses— were regarded as faking illness and were called malingerers; and those imitated medical practitioners—that is, who claims to heal the sick without being able to convince medical authorities that they were bona fide physicians—were regarded as imposters, and were call quacks (*The Myth of Mental Illness*, Dr. Thomas S. Szasz, M.D., Perennial-Harper Collins Publishers, NY, NY 10022, Page Preface-ix-x).

"The Church teaches dependence on one who adjusted himself to the purpose of God as he was given to understand it and who therefore is able to help others. Christ was a God-centered person who inspired confidence in others that he could and would deliver them from their moral defects and personality infirmities. He spoke with the voice of experience and authority, as one who was not a channel but a source of truth and the enrichment of life. The hopeless who came into contact with him were made hopeful; sinners sought and received forgiveness under his guidance; the mentally deranged were restored to normalcy. He gave zest to living."

(*The Church and Psychotherapy*, Dr. Karl R. Stolz, Abingdon-Cokesbury Press, New York - Nashville p. 83.)

Jesus Christ opened the seven seals which revealed the Kingdom of God for our admittance, even as our righteousness is as filthy rags. But, He also opened this great door of salvation, and he revealed the plagues of judgment and death as well necessary to motivate judgment, and our need to seek salvation.

There is a time, we know not when,
A place, we know not where
Which marks the destiny of men
To glory or despair.

There is a line, by us unseen,
Which crosses every path,
Which marks the boundary between
God's mercy and his wrath.
To pass that limit is to die,
To die as if by stealth;
It does not dim the beaming eye,
Nor pale the glow of health.

The conscience may be still at ease,
The spirit light and gay;
And that which pleases still may please,
And care be thrust away.

But on the forehead god hath set
Indelibly a mark
Unseen by man, for man as yet,
Is blind and in the dark.
He feels perchance that all is well
And every fear is calmed;
He lives, he dies, he walks in hell,
Not only doomed, but dammed!
Oh, where is that mysterious line
That may by men be crossed,
Beyond which God himself hath sworn,
That he who goes is lost?

An answer from the skies repeats,
"Ye who from God depart."
TODAY, Oh hear His voice,
TODAY repent and harden not your heart.
Author: Joseph Addison Alexander

I hope that those who feel that the statements above about Judgment are without substantiation will take time to realize that the reasoning, or the mental powers concerned with forming conclusions are clear here in understanding why having faith in God makes a lot of sense.

"Verily, verily, I say unto you, he that heareth my word, and believeth on Him that sent me, hath everlasting life, and shall not come into condemnation, but is passed from death into life," (John 5:24). "It is appointed unto man once to die, but after this the judgment," (Hebrews 9:27).

Dr. Elizabeth Kublar Ross, a medical physician, after studying patients in intensive care and in hospices (terminally ill housing units connected with hospitals) discovered and documented five stages of fear in the attitudes (versus a Beatitude, Matthew 5:1-12) of those about to die. The first stage is denial and isolation. The second stage is anger. The third stage is bargaining with God that should have been done in faith. The fourth stage is depression. (Having found a problem with God's perfect world/universe) Dr. Ross never tells a person in this stage not to be sad. They know already that they are going to lose everything in "this world." The fifth stage is acceptance. "The final rest before the long journey" is what one patient had to say. Dr. Ross: "This is the time when the family needs more help than the patient, or the dying."

PURPOSE OF THIS OCCASION

Several Sundays ago, I related a statement during the early Stelton Sunday classes as follows: "Now that the Kingdom of Heaven established by God, has come among mankind, any Christian, or nonbeliever for that matter, who finds something wrong with the perfectly established, and controlled universe by God, is in violation of His laws, and is thereby committing a sin, which is the fact of being separated spiritually from God."

Brother Tom Ng of the class made a statement during the following week that he had thought about the statement all week. I trust that he is still thinking more specifically about "principle of Salvation" that is applied in that statement.

The Ten Commandments, the great *Decalogue* of the Old Testament, sound like laws, but in fact they only point out defects in the nature of human beings after *the fall* mentioned in Genesis Chapter 3. In other words, the principle of salvation mentioned above to Tom Ng, only demands that Homo sapiens acknowledge that without Jesus Christ as Savior, there is no way under Heaven to keep from violating the laws required to prevail in God's presence, which is the Kingdom of Heaven. In other words, the presence of Jesus Christ in the world is Good News, the Gospel, commune with Him as He communes with God, His Father. Otherwise, the curses mentioned in the Book of Revelation will fall due on humanity. THIS IS WHERE THE PRECEPT, THE TECHNICAL OPERATION THAT GOD IS CONTINUALLY PERFORMING AMONG HUMAN BEINGS IS ESSENTIAL FOR THE SALVATION OF THE PHYSICAL WORLD. "NOT BY MIGHT, NOR BY POWER, BUT BY MY SPIRIT SAITH THE LORD," (Zechariah 4:6). "The wages of sin is death, but, the gift of God is eternal life," (Romans 6:23). Proverbs 14:34: "Righteousness exalteth a nation, sin is reproach to any people.

The Principle and precepts of salvation is necessary to live in the flesh, which is antagonistic to the Spirit of God. So we live in two distinct worlds at the same time, accepting the truth that never the two shall be at peace. "What shall we say then? Is the law sin? God forbid. Nay, I had not known sin, but by the law; for I had not known lust, except the law had said, Thou shalt not covet. But sin, taking occasion by the commandment, wrought in me all manner of concupiscence. For without the law, sin was dead," (Romans 7:7-8 KJV).

The principle of precept explained regarding Tom's reference requires a Beatitude. The only sermon Jesus preached as we know of is found in Matthew 5:1-12. Jesus Christ is saying in this sermon that this is how we must respond to the antagonistic flesh warring against the Spirit with our flesh if we want to bridge these two worlds diametrically opposed to each other. This is exactly what was said in the Sunday School Class on the occasion mentioned above. Any other behavior or attitude will be in violation to the Kingdom of God that results in heaven, salvation, and or being blessed.

A precept is referred in Isaiah 28:9, 16, and 17, referring to how Jesus was the knowledge of God for mankind. "Whom shall he teach knowledge? And whom shall he make to understand doctrine? Them that are weaned from the milk, and drawn from the breasts. For precept must be upon precept. Precept upon precept; line upon line.

Line upon line; here a little, and there a little: Therefore thus saith the Lord God, I lay in Zion for a foundation a stone, a tried stone, a precious corner stone, a sure foundation; he that believeth shall not make haste. Judgment will I lay to the line, and righteousness to the plummet; and the hail shall sweep away the refuge of lies, and the water shall overflow the hiding place."

WHY IS THERE A TERM LIKE PRECEPT TO TEACH THE SALVATION PRINCIPLE OF SALVATION?

A precept is a commandment of direction given as a rule of action or conduct. A precept is an injunction or judicial order as to moral conduct. A precept is a maxim. A precept is an Expression of a general truth or principle. A precept is directions for performing a technical operation.

Along with Charles and Tom, who perform exacting operations in their daily occupations, Albert Schweitzer comes to mind here. He was a physician, a musician, and a mathematician. My guess is that he dropped all of his gifts and energies to go to Africa and heal the sick because he saw the operation on disadvantaged human beings as the only way to be judged by God for his salvation, and admittance into eternal bliss and happiness, to be blessed, (Matthew 5:1-12).

Jesus Christ performed the principle of the ultimate technical operation on Calvary and called us to follow Him. "What doth it profit a man to gain the whole world, and then lose his own soul, and what will a man give in exchange for his soul. Take eat, this is my body given for you. I go to prepare a place for you. And if I go I will come again and receive you unto myself, that where I am, there you may be also. Let not your heart be troubled, in my Father's house are many mansions. Take my yoke upon you and learn of me, for my yoke is easy, and my burden is light, you shall find rest for your soul. I have come that you might have life, a more abundant life.

Chapter Ten

The Life of Jesus Christ Has Everything to Do with the Perfection with Which God Intends to Rule the Universe

God judges perfectly an eternal damnation and death to those who, in their lifetime in this perfectly designed universe, which is the precursor to the fullness of God's perfect kingdom, fail to experience what Jesus Christ experienced as he approached his death in the flesh. His resurrection established his eternal life spiritually inaugurating the Kingdom of God on earth. Death of the soul is real, and life in Jesus Christ is real for the salvation of the soul. Do not make the mistake of getting hung-up on the controversy of what Jesus Christ meant when he said, "Take eat, this is my body." John 14:6: "I am the way, the truth, and the life." John 21:19: "But he saith unto him, follow me." Luke 13:27: "Depart from me all ye workers of iniquity." Matthew 7:21-23: "Not everyone that saith unto me Lord, Lord, shall enter into the Kingdom of Heaven; but he that doeth the will of my father which is in heaven. Many will say unto me in that day, Lord, Lord, have we not prophesied in thy name? And in thy name have we cast out devils? And in thy name done many wonderful works? And then will I profess unto them, I never knew you, depart from me ye that work iniquity."

THE PROBLEM: Because of the lack of spiritual enabling, mankind, after thirty-five hundred years after the Law was given to Moses, and two thousand years after Jesus Christ passed the enabling

Spirit to mankind, is still living in the Dark Ages. The problem for anyone living on earth today is to be without the enabling spirit of the revolution that has taken place in our world, in our time, world without end, to save mankind from destruction.

SLEEPING THROUGH THE REVOLUTION
REVOLUTION IS A FUNDAMENTAL CHANGE!
The Key to Experiencing the Revolution
I would be remiss if I did not start this chapter with the story of *Rip Van Winkle*. He sought refuge from the hustle and bustle of life by being drawn up the quiet floral beauty of the Catskills Mountains of upstate New York. He slept for twenty years unmolested. Moreover, when he was awakened and returned to the village where he called home, the welcome sign that read King George IV of England, Governor, now read George Washington, President of the Thirteen Original Colonies of the United States of America. Rip Van Winkle had slept through a revolution.

"A paradigm shift is the way a person views and interacts with his or her world." According to years' worth of data collected by George Barna, the Church is undergoing the biggest revolution of our time.

For thousands of years, Christians have been inventing the Church, but neglecting to be the Church Christ commissioned. Droves of committed believers are foregoing Sunday mornings to live a 24/7 faith unfettered by the clutter and bureaucracy within church walls.

"In stark contrast to both the stuffy, formulaic religiosity sometimes found in the established church and the feel good, invent-your-own spirituality, the Revolution is casting off anything that hinders a full, vibrant life of discipleship in Christ." REVOLUTION, George Barna, 2005.

TO INCREASE THE CONGREGATION'S UNDERSTANDING OF CHRISTIAN DISCIPLESHIP: DREW UNIVERSITY: DISSERTATION BY DR. MILES J. AUSTIN: OCTOBER 8, 1976
The Doctrine of the Christian Church as a Prerequisite to Christian Discipleship
"Notwithstanding the particular emphasis on the church's mission, Luke is conscious of the individual needs and desires of the members of the Christian Church. When Jesus spoke, as in Luke 4:16-30, the Kingdom of God is indeed present. For Luke, there is no need to consider any obstacle of any earthly nature as opposing the

Kingdom, suffering notwithstanding. The Kingdom with its 'everythingness' demands total sacrifice of self as a prerequisite to entering. ("The Law and the Prophets were until John, since then the Kingdom of God is preached, and men press into it," (Luke 16:16.) In Luke, the Passion of Jesus Christ is an appropriation of this to total sacrifice."

Although the two volume work of Luke, including Acts, is accurately concerned with the church, it is in relation to the work of the church for the salvation of individuals that the church is emphasized. The purpose of Luke's theology is to speak to the issue of this time that is a delayed *eschaton* (the complete accomplishment of God in time through His Spirit) and the need for a new way of life to cope with the dilemma.

I would draw a picture of a story that has a somewhat humorous tint, but sheds light on the overpowering witness apparently hidden in the inauguration of the Kingdom of God, through his Son, Jesus Christ, explained immediately above.

If I sound as though I am casting blame on those in the pews, as might have been inclined by George Barna, in his book *Revolution*, let me show that we, the pastors, and teachers of the Word of God, share the lethargy of sleep as well. If not sleeping through the Revolution, we know it has happened and have not shared the "breaking new" with you sufficiently.

Soren Kirkegaard, a twentieth century existentialist, tells a story that puts us, pastors and teachers of God's Word, to being equally to blame for the "Light being put under a bushel." A circus had been planned for just outside of a large city in Europe. The circus caught fire and threatened to spread to inner city. A clown who had dressed for the day's activities hurriedly ran into the city to warn its citizens to flee for their lives. They laughed, clapped, and gave him rave reviews for a splendid masquerade as advertisement for the city's citizens to come out and enjoy the circus. The town burned to the ground. Perhaps Jonah and Nineveh would be a good example of this tragedy here, with the exception that Nineveh heard the warning from Jonah, and repented, and was spared the wrath of God.

"The real problems which are treated first and foremost are those which arise from the situation of the church in the continuing life of the world. Besides the regulation of everyday life, the main concern is with the Christian's behavior in persecution," (Dr. Austin's study at Drew University: Conzelman, theology of St. Luke, p. 232).

WHAT IS A BEATITUDE?

Webster's Universal College Dictionary: Supreme blessednes; exalted happiness. And this quote in *Webster* refers to Jesus' sermon in Luke on the plains (Luke 6:20 to 35: and Matthew 5:1-12).

Luke and Matthew point out Jesus' only recorded sermon as preaching. This Gospel, through this sermon that He has come into the world to have us live, as Conzelman states above, in a world of psychic stress, and pressure, and still be supremely blessed, and happy, is our instructions in the way of precept, and example.

In my *Life Application Bible*, Hosea 4:6 is very critical of priests, and teachers of God's Word. "My people are destroyed for lack of knowledge." If a soul does not live, behave, respond to life's tribulations and vicissitudes, while acknowledging that we are existing in the spirit and presence of the living God, existentially, which means to live, move, and have our being in that milieu, are going to die sooner or later, just as a fish would out of water (See below: Dr. Elizabeth Kublar Ross).

At the beginning of the book of Matthew, I see Jesus Christ interpreting the meaning of existentialism, or being in the "Now" of the Kingdom of God as we live, move, and have our being. The five wise, and the five foolish virgins. Oil in a lamp can be compared with knowledge of God's word in our Holy Spirit. The entire twenty-fifth chapter of Matthew speaks in words that will have to be deciphered by the believer who seeks the truth. Was not Paul doing this when in Corinthians 11:26, he mentions discerning the body of Jesus Christ in the communion elements of the blood and the wine? The reason why some are sick, and others die? Let a man examine himself, and so let him eat. If we eat and drink unworthily, we bring damnation upon ourselves, not discerning the Lord's body.

In Genesis, when Moses went up to get the *Ten Commandments* from God, *The Decalogue*, they made their own God, a small idol to serve them as a God. And later in Genesis, it says, "The people sat down to eat, and rose up to play."

"Luke sees the life of the individual Christian bound together in community, communion with the Holy Spirit. This community takes meaning from the 'idea of the Twelve.' Acts 1:8 gives credence to this, with the Holy Spirit giving power to the work of salvation that has been given to the church. In Luke's theology this community is necessary for the religious life to thrive because there is no life outside it. 'The church's one foundation is Jesus Christ her Lord.'"

"The steps or stages in the life of the new convert to the Christian Church are important in Luke's 'story of salvation.' In order to recall them to mind, briefly, they are: (1) Proclamation or preaching, (2) Repentance, (3) Baptism, (4) The words 'In the name of Jesus,' (5) 'Laying on of hands,' (6) Speaking in tongues, an in-depth communion of the worshipper with the Holy Spirit, (7) Prayer, and (8) Missions: The key to all the forgoing."

A new member who joins a Christian Church and does not grow to be able to discern the body of Jesus Christ in the elements of the Communion Sacrament does stand there, still, in time. "He, or she cannot serve two masters, he or she will hate one and love the other, or vice versa.

Backsliding is actually denying that we were baptized into the body of Christ at our baptism. Jesus explains that when we get the devil out of our heart and spirit, and then he returns, because we were not able to keep him out, we inherit seven devils rather than the one we admitted we removed originally.

Luke made it very clear where the church came from, what it is at this point in time, and where it is going. For the Christian who understood this, there is not only joy in knowing, there is joy in doing."

A "paradigm shift" can be explained as follows.

(1) The Holy Spirit is not given to Christians for their individual use, even if they understand it as their salvation.

(2) A Christian cannot live, existentially, that is, understanding the upcoming physical and spiritual death without the Holy Spirit of God at the center of their lives, day in and day out. "You cannot serve two masters." It is appointed unto man once to die, and then the judgment (Hebrews 9:27). The wages of sin is death, but the gift of God is eternal life, through Jesus Christ our Lord.

(3) In the mind/spirit - (reason: mental powers concerned with forming a conclusion) the Christian's world that he or she was born into should existentially—that is, the way they understand their life and living—be changing, or passing away with the passing years.

1. That by grace, he or she is passing from the death of the flesh, through faith, to eternal life. Corinthians 15:51, "Behold I show you a mystery, we shall not all sleep, but we shall all be changed."

Philippians 2:5, and 3:10, Only a Kingdom of God "paradigm shift" can supply the spiritual power necessary for humans to face death unafraid (Romans 12:1-4).

Dr. Elisabeth Kuebler Ross, a medical physician, after studying patients in intensive care and in a hospice (terminally ill housing unit connected with hospitals) discovered and documented five stages of fear in the attitudes. These five stages involved human beings about to die. The first stage, denial and isolation; (2) the second stage, anger; (3) the third stage, is bargaining with God, (which should have come earlier, and under much more reasonable, mental powers concerned with forming a conclusion) circumstances and opportunities; (4) the fourth stage, depression. Dr. Ross never tells a person in this stage that they would not be sad. They know already that they are going to lose everything in "this world;" (5) the fifth stage, is acceptance, or key: "The final rest before the long journey" is what one patient had to say. Dr. Ross, "This is the time when the family needs more help than the patient or the dying."

I think it is fitting to recall the words God gave Mary, His hand maiden, to speak, and understand. He has scattered the proud in the imagination of their heart, He has brought down the mighty from their seats, and exalted them of low degree, the rich he has sent away empty, the poor he has filled with great things.

The playing field was leveled when the Kingdom of God came in the Spirit of Jesus Christ. I can only wear one pair of shoes at a time, and it does not matter too much how they look. The slaves didn't have shoes, but it was their least worry, and they witnessed to the fact, I got shoes, you got shoes, all of God's children got shoes. I can only wear one dress of clothes. The slaves were probably wearing shabby garments, they became robes. I got a robe, you got a robe, all of God's children got robes. I have one life to make my peace with God, and keep it until the Day of Jesus Christ. Regardless how much money I acquire in my lifetime, the hearse will not stop by my bank to clean out my accounts on the way out to the final resting place.

I heard of a city called Heaven, I'm trying to make it my home. Soon I'll be done with the troubles of the world, going to home to live with God.

ROCK OF AGES, LET US STAND WITH MOSES IN CLEFT OF THE ROCK!

Like the preacher whose health was failing, after all he felt he had done, as he had been called to do, LEAD KINDLY LIGHT, I DO WISH TO SEE THE DISTANT SCENE, ONE STEP IS ENOUGH. BEAMS OF HEAVEN AS I GO, THROUGH THIS WILDERNESS BELOW, GUIDE MY FEET IN PEACEFUL WAYS, TURN MY MIDNIGHTS INTO DAY, I DO NOT KNOW HOW LONG IT WILL BE, NOR WHAT THE FUTURE HOLDS FOR ME, BUT THIS I KNOW, THAT IF JESUS GOES WITH ME, I SHALL GET HOME SOME DAY.

THE SLAVES HAD A PARADIGM SHIFT; THEY WERE CAUGHT UP INTO THE REVOLUTION; I LOOKED AT MY HANDS, THEY LOOKED NEW, LOOKED AT MY FEET, AND THEY DID TOO.

After a long row to hoe, I just need to get back to camp ground. DEEP RIVER, MY HOME IS OVER JORDAN.

BEEN IN THE SUN SO LONG, JUST GIVE ME A LITTLE TIME TO PRAY. THEY TALKED OF BEING "DUG UP, TRANSPLANTED, REGENERATED." THE ANGELS IN HEAVEN DONE CHANGED MY NAME!

THE MASSA GAVE ME HIS NAME, BUT THE ANGELS HAD OTHER IDEAS...

I'M GONNA LAY DOWN MY SWORD AND SHIELD...DOWN BY THE RIVERSIDE, AIN'T GONNA STUDY WAR NO MORE.

JESUS HAS GIVEN ME ANOTHER YOKE. LEARN OF ME, FOR MY YOKE IS EASY, MY BURDEN IS LIGHT. FIND PEACE FOR YOUR SOUL!

IF YOU MISS ME FROM PRAYING DOWN HERE, AND YOU CAN'T FIND ME NOWHERE, COME ON UP TO GOD'S KINGDOM, I'LL BE WAITING UP THERE.

SLEEPING THROUGH A REVOLUTION 2

THERE IS A PATH BEFORE EACH PERSON THAT SEEMS RIGHT, BUT IT ENDS IN DEATH Proverbs 14:12 (Life Application Study Bible).

TO IGNORE THE DECALOGUE, THE TEN COMMANDMENTS GOD GAVE TO MOSES, IS ALSO TO REJECT THE COGNITIVE SPIRITUAL UNDERSTANDING OF JESUS CHRIST'S BAPTISM, HIS DEATH AND RESURRECTION,

AND HIS LIVING PRESENCE IN OUR LIVES AT THIS PRESENT MOMENT IN TIME, WORLD-WIDE.

JESUS CHRIST HAS MADE IT IMPERATIVE THAT THOSE OF US WHO WOULD HAVE LIFE, MUST BECOME HIS DISCIPLE. THIS DISCIPLESHIP SERVES AS HIS LEGACY TO THE CONTINUING PRESENCE OF HIMSELF, HIS BODY, IN THE PHYSICAL WORLD AS WE KNOW IT. THIS IS IN FACT AND TRUTH, OUR ONLY HOPE. THIS IS HIS NEWTESTAMENT IN HIS BLOOD.

INCLUDED HERE IS HIS PURPOSE FOR COMING INTO THE WORLD IN THE FIRST PLACE. THIS CONTINUATION OF HIS SPIRITUAL PRESENCE IN OUR LIVES IS THE ONLY WAY TO HAVE LIFE EVERLASTING. THIS IS THE APOCALYPTIC REVOLUTION THAT WE ADDRESS HERE, AND WE EXPERIENCE THIS LIFE AS SPIRITUAL HUMAN BEINGS IN GOD'S PERFECT UNIVERSE.

I have a soul-searching need in my personal prayers for my fellow Christians at the Stelton Baptist Church. That need as I feel it is abated, or leads me to thank God for sending Charles Holt to Stelton. His selection of the study of the Trinity has led into the last phases of my year-long research and prayerful study to "Show thyself approved as a workman who needeth not to be ashamed, but to rightly divide the word of truth."

THE LORD'S SUPPER

Jesus taught both, by precept, and example. Paul explains both precept and example of Jesus' intentions of sharing with whosoever will take his broken body and spilled blood seriously as their own in order to transcend death, and become a part of God's Kingdom, Heaven at that moment of their cognitive understanding. This is explained in detail by Paul to those Christians in Corinth as they prepared to "Commune with God," "The Lord's Supper" in First Corinthians 11:26 forward.

PRECEPT AND EXAMPLE: I want to explain the mental and physical condition of all human beings so that Jesus' literal meaning to take "His" body does not just become a ritual or a ceremony on the first Sunday of each month.

It is a medical and psychiatric fact that a human being's limbic system of his brain, the autonomous nervous system of the brain controls all of his mental faculties to understand, and interpret what is taking place in his physical body at any given time, including his instinctive reactions resulting from that stimulation.

The following are examples, physically, establishing the brain as the interpreter of one's understanding of his existence:

- Socrates and Menos: Knowledge is more important than gold. What knowledge? To be brief, a conversation between Socrates and Menos led Menos to *believe*, with his reasoning abilities (power necessary to form a conclusion) that to have a lot of gold would, make his life good, or he would be well. If he, if you, the reader, considered the conversation here where having the body of Jesus Christ, His life as a precept and example, gold has absolutely nothing to do with the salvation of one's soul, as in His, Jesus' ability to be raised from the dead, after his physical death. Hosea 4:6: "My people are destroyed because of lack of knowledge."

- Up until a half century ago surgeons removed the frontal lobotomy of the brain from patients who suffered memories of past traumatic events.

- Anesthesia is used in medical surgery to relieve or block the brain's ability to send signals to other parts of the body thereby resulting in relief from pain.

- A stroke can affect parts of the brain in such a way that certain forms of aphasia results. We are unable to speak in one type of aphasia, and in another, not able to understand what is heard.

- Children have been born without the ability to feel pain. They must be cared for so that they do not injure themselves in such a way that causes death without ever feeling pain.

INSIGHT FOR UNDERSTANDING AND INTERPRETING JESUS' SPIRIT, AND HIS CONDITION, PHYSICALLY, AS A HUMAN BEING IN GOD'S KINGDOM HERE ON EARTH, AS HE WAS RESURRECTED TO PROVE THE NECESSITY OF "HIS WAY, HIS TRUTH, AND HIS LIFE."

The immediate facts above also prove that death without pain allows us to see that a painless death is still death of the soul if we have not the truth that Jesus implies in John 8:31-32, the inability to enter into the eternal presence of God. Jesus' words on the condition: "And fear not them which kill the body, but are not able to kill the soul; but rather fear him which is able to destroy both soul and body in hell," (Matthew 10:28 KJV).

The following excerpts are from Paul Tillich's work, entitled: THE COURAGE TO BE

"Being has non-being 'within' itself, as that which is eternally present and eternally overcome in the process of the divine life. 'Courage is usually described as the power of the mind to overcome fear.' 'Existential' (or existentialism) in this sentence means that it is not the abstract knowledge of non being that produces anxiety but the awareness that non being is a part of one's own being. It is not the realization of universal transitoriness, not even the experience of the death of others, but the impression of these events on the always latent awareness of our own having to die that produces anxiety. Anxiety is finitude, experienced as one's own finitude. This is the natural anxiety of man as man, and in some way all living beings. It is the anxiety of non being, the awareness of one's finitude as finitude," (pages 34 to 36).

THERE WILL BE BLOOD: This title comes from the 2008 Academy Award winning movie by that name. I saw the movie, and just as imagined the reference to blood typified the violence and animosity that existed between Cain and Abel that provoked Cain to kill his brother. The sin in human nature without intervention from God, through Jesus Christ's blood for the remission of that nature of our sins, put in practical terms for the correction of our behavior, there would be no hope for any peace at any time now or hereafter in the physical world. This is the significance of the second commandment to love thy neighbor as thyself. On these two commandments hang all the LAW and Prophets.

I CAN SAY WITHOUT FEAR OF EQUIVOCATION THAT I MOST LIKELY WOULD HAVE BEEN CAIN IN MY TIME, THERE BUT FOR THE GRACE OF GOD GO I.

TO PUT "THERE WILL BE BLOOD" INTO THE BIBLICAL PERSPECTIVE, I WILL SUMMARIZE THE BOOK OF HEBREWS CHAPTER 9:20-28.

Vs. 20: Then he said, "This blood confirms the covenant God has made with you." Vs. 21: "And in the same way, he sprinkled blood on the sacred tent, and on everything used for worship." Vs. 22: "In fact, we can say that according to the Law of Moses, nearly everything was purified by sprinkling with blood. Without the shedding of blood, there is no forgiveness of sins." Vs. 25, "Nor did he enter heaven to offer himself again and again, like the earthly high priest who enters the Most Holy Place year after year to offer the blood of an animal." Vs. 27:"And just as it is destined that each person dies only once, and after that comes judgment." Vs. 28: "So also Christ died only once as a sacrifice to take away the sins of many people. He will come again but not to deal with our sins again. This time he will bring salvation to all those who are eagerly waiting for him."

THE PROBLEM: THE DOCTRINE OF TRANSUBSTANTIATION

Christians broke away from England, the Church of England as Pilgrims looking to serve the True and Living God of the Holy Spirit in America based upon their individual relationship and consciousness of that presence.

Martin Luther, in the sixteenth century, broke from the Catholic Church, resulting in the Protestant Reformation for these very same reasons as did the Pilgrims. Charles Clayton Morris in his book *The Unfinished Reformation* CATALOGUES THE LITANY OF PROLIFERATION BECAUSE OF DIFFERENT UNDERSTANDINGS OF THE TRUE MEANING OF "THE" CHRISTIAN FAITH. NEVERTHELESS WE FAIL TO KEEP THE ONE REQUIREMENT JESUS CHRIST MADE IN THE EUCHARIST, ORTHE LORD'S SUPPER, "TAKE EAT, THIS IS MY BODY," (Mark 14:22).

The Gospel of John, Chapter 6:52-57, caused the "Transubstantiation Controversy" to become doctrine. This misunderstanding can be understood as the differences in Jesus' meaning as stated: Jesus used a metaphor, the application of a word or phrase to an object or concept it does not literally denote, suggesting comparison to that object or concept, as in, "A might fortress is our God."

The metaphor stands for dwelling in constant union with Christ, as the allegory represents spiritual relationship, moral, or other abstract meaning through the actions of fictional characters that serve as symbols such as the true vine. That which is symbolized in the Eucharist by the act of eating the bread and drinking the wine is that the believer in Christ, as he says, (vs. 56), abides in me, and I in him. This mystical union with Christ is not subject to the temporal chances and changes of this our mortality. BECAUSE, HERE JESUS CHRIST MAKES IT CLEAR: "Because I live, you will live also," (14:19; *The Interpreter's Bible: In Twelve Volumes*; vol. 8, Abingdon Press; NEW YORK, NASHIVLLE 1952 p. 575 center page).

DISCUSSION POINT:

These words of Christ were eschewed (to abstain, or keep away from, to shun, or avoid) from the very beginning with the Jews, and right through out time as explained above with the controversy, and Doctrine of Transubstantiation. If all Christendom bungled the clear meaning Christ used in our language, not Greek, or Hebrew, it is clear that based on what Jesus Christ actually did in making clear His meaning by going to Calvary, we would, as we have, accused Him of never meaning what, after two thousand years, we are still not adhering to in our lives.

WHEN WE OBSERVE THE CONFUSION IN OUR WORLD TODAY, THE REASON IS AS FOLLOWS:
HOSEA 4:6

My people are being destroyed because they don't know me. It is all your fault, you priest, for you yourselves refuse to know me. Now I refuse to recognize you as my priests. Since you have forgotten the laws of your God, I will forget to bless your children. The more priests there are, the more they sin against me. They have exchanged the glory of God for the disgrace of idols.

FOR DISCUSSION: One of the preachers of the Great Awakening Spiritual Movement in our country once said "Taking a child to church does no more to make them a Christian, than taking them to a garage makes them an automobile.

Taking children to church is like giving them food while they are growing up. They will be greatly impoverished as adults unless we teach them how to get their own food.

THE CHRISTIAN CHURCH SHOULD COME TO UNDERSTAND WHEN JESUS CHRIST WENT TO JAIL AND WHY, IN OTHER WORDS, OR IN OTHER ACTIONS, WE SHOULD BE WALKING THE WALK, AND NOT JUST TALKING THE TALK!

John 19:10-11: Jesus' response to the judge, Pilate: You have no power over me unless it be given to you from above. Therefore the one who brought me to you has the greater sin. Matthew 18:28, I have been given complete authority in heaven and on earth. Therefore, go and make disciples of all nations...

Jesus' words to Pilate were buttressed by Mary in Luke 1:51: "He hath shewed strength with his arm. He hath scattered the proud in the imagination of their hearts. He hath put down the mighty from their seats, and exalted them of low degree, he hath filled the hungry with good things; and the rich he hath sent empty away."

It ought to be clear here from the current miscalculation by the Christian Church, its ministries, that we cannot go to Heaven without being in the likeness, spiritually, of Jesus Christ in order to pass through death into eternal life.

When Jesus opened the seven seals in Revelations 5:9, He not only made the Kingdom of God an apocalyptic reality, it included death as well as life. There is a divine judgment that determines which conviction each of us has lived by, thereby determining our sentence.

Just as there is "Release to the Captives," there are outstanding judgments of conviction for those who, by the nature of their existence, as recorded by Paul Tillich, have not processed the integrity in order to *be* as *in* Christ. We will either be able to be like Him, or we will perish as non-beings.

A good example, which by the way is not out of the stretch of the imagination, is a prison inmate released to the community while charges are still leveled against him in the court of criminal justice. He is on probation. A document he signed in the presence of the criminal justice authorities states that if those conditions are violated, and found out, the outstanding laws on the books in his name become in force, they fall due immediately, a summons is issued for his arrest, and if not brought in he becomes a fugitive from Justice. IN THE UNITED STATES OF AMERICA, THESE ARE THE SAME LAWS GOD GAVE MOSES FROM MOUNT SINAI. WE CALL THEM JURISPRUDENCE.

The conditions an inmate violates are not too farfetched when we look at ours, as human beings before an all wise, all loving, and *just* God. Transubstantiation is confusion of the Lord's Body being necessary for us to escape violations, lacking spiritual identity with Christ, "Take eat, this is my body, given for you:"

As Paul explains in detail in 1 Corinthians 11:26, "For as often as ye eat this bread, and drink this cup, ye do show the Lord's death until He come. Wherefore, whosoever shall eat this bread, and drink this cup of the Lord, unworthily, shall be guilty of the body, and blood of the Lord."

Then, based on Mary's Magnificat, and Jesus denial that Pilate had power over Him unless it came from on High, we begin to understand faithful statements from Scripture such as:

1. God hath not given us the spirit of fear,...
2. Greater is He that is in you...
3. By grace, we are saved through faith, this not of ourselves, but the gift of God.
4. Philippians 1:6: "He that hath begun a good work in you will perform it until the day of Jesus Christ."
5. Philippians 2:12: "Work out our soul salvation in fear in fear and trembling."
6. Luke 16:16: "The Laws and Prophets were until John, since then the Kingdom of God is preached and men press into it."

7. I Corinthians 1:18: "The preaching of the Gospel is to them that perish foolishness, but to those of us who are saved, it is the power of God."

FAITH IS THE SUBSTANCE OF THINGS HOPED FOR AND THE EVIDENCE…

According to theologians of the Revolution-Apocalypticism, the violation of the condition stated in our contract at Baptism, is validated, or not validated each time we take communion. Means we are either in the Spirit of Jesus Christ in the World, doing what He would be doing if He were here in body, or we are in violation of that probation contract we signed. And we have breached our hope for life everlasting in the coming Kingdom in its fullness that is now seen partially as it unfolds before our hearts and minds.

In which case we deny our "Release to the Captives," surrendering to the lust of the carnal mind, and its coming destruction. "We cannot serve two masters."

Those outstanding detainers and judgments of convictions remain in our name until we come before the "Judgment Bar" of God, Christ Jesus. Hebrews 9:27, "It is appointed unto man once to die, and then the Judgment."

Job 14:14: "If a man dies, shall he live again?" Of all the days of my appointed time, I'll wait on my change.

THE WAGES OF SIN IS DEATH, AND THE GIFT OF GOD IS ETERNAL LIFE. THANKS BE TO GOD WHO GIVETH US THE VICTORY THROUGH OUR LORD JESUS CHRIST. WHEN THIS MORTAL SHALL HAVE TAKEN OFF MORTAL, AND PUT ON IMMORTALITY, THEN SHALL COME TO PASS THE SAYING, DEATH WHERE IS THY STING? THE STING OF DEATH IS SIN.

Jesus, to us, in reference to those last miserable feelings and fears that leads to our physical death, "Be of good cheer, I have overcome the world:" There are all kinds of "cheers," New Years, should all acquaintance be forgot, and never brought to mind. If you can walk the walk, instead of just talking the talk, you say in the words of our forefathers, walk together, children, and don't get weary, there's a great camp meeting in the Promised Land, they that wait upon shall run and not get weary, walk and not faint."

Trouble might endure for the night, but Joy comes in the morning. Do not grow weary in well-doing, for in "due time" we shall reap if we faint not. GOD IS AN ON-TIME GOD, HE MIGHT

NOT COME WHEN WE THINK HE SHOULD, BUT HE AIN'T NEVER BEEN LATE.

THE DANGERS OF SLEEPING THROUGH A REVOLUTION

The Scripture of the revolution is Revelations 5:9: "And they sang a new song. You are worthy to take the scroll and break its seals and open it. For thou was slain, and hast redeemed us to God by thy blood out of every kindred, and tongue, and people, and nation; And you have caused them to become God's kingdom and his priests. And they will reign on the earth."

The Gospel of Luke, Matthew, Mark, and John notwithstanding, explains the Holy Spirit given by Jesus at Pentecost, where He explains in Matthew 16:27-28, "For I, the Son of Man, will come in the Glory of my Father with His angels, and will judge all people according to their deeds. 28: And I assure you that some of you standing here right now will not die before you see me, the Son of Man coming in my Kingdom."

Revelations 21:3: confirming Jesus' significance as the Spirit representing His Kingdom as the "Last Days" of Apocalypticism as being now, says, "And I heard a great voice out of heaven saying, Behold, the tabernacle of God is with men, and He will dwell with them, and they shall be His people, and God Himself shall be with them, and be their God."

It is truly amazing the words God gave Mary to know to and speak. They were called the Magnificat, probably because they were too magnificent to leave as words alone. "He hath shown strength with His arm; He hath scattered the proud in the imagination of their hearts. He hath put down the mighty from their seats, and exalted them of low degree. He hath filled the hungry with good things; and the rich he sent empty away."

In Matthew 25:1: The Kingdom of Heaven can be illustrated by the story Jesus tells of the Ten Virgins which took their lamps and went forth to meet the bridegroom. And five of them were wise, and five were foolish because they took no oil for their lamps.

IN EVERY LIFE, MAN, WOMAN, BOY OR GIRL, THERE ARE TURNING POINTS: A RITE OF PASSAGE: IF A CHILD MISSES HIS OR HER TURNING POINT THEY CAN SPIN-OUT INTO A LIFE FILLED WITH MISERY, MELANCHOLIA, AND DEMENTIA, EYES ALWAYS FILLED WITH TEARS, FAILING TO MAKE THE TURN, FOCUSING OF THE INCI-DENTAL HIDDEN CROSSROAD, LATE AT NIGHT WHEN THEY ARE TIRED, WEARY, DISAPPOINTED, DROPPING

OFF A HILL INTO A DEEP VALLEY OF THE SHADOW OF DEATH, WHEN "LIFE COMES AT YOUR FAST," AS THEY SAY IN THE COMMERCIAL.

GOD GAVE THE CHILDREN OF ISRAEL THE BEST LIFE INSURANCE POSSIBLE, NO THRESHOLD, AND A RIDER WHICH VOIDS ANY ATTEMPT FOR MAN TO CANCEL THE GOAL OF ETERNAL LIFE.

TAKE A PERFECT LAMB, WITHOUT BLEMISH: In the New Testament, now we say the blood from the perfect Lamb must be placed on the door post of your heart. And God will say when He comes through each of our lives with the last plague which is death, He will ask did you understand that the blood you put on the doorpost came from the CROSS OF MY SON THAT I RAISED FROM THE DEAD. DID YOU DISCERN HIS LIFE AS YOUR OWN? ARE YOU PREPARED TO "CROSS OVER"?

If ever Satan has driven you into the "wilderness" of life, tell me how long you stayed, and how did you feel when you came out?

If you have been sick, and had work to do so your life would not fall apart, before you get to the end of the journey, tell me how you made it without giving up to Satan, and his "miserable comforters?"

Did your children get into so much trouble that you thought your weary heart would break? And feel the Spirit of the broken body of Jesus Christ rise up in you, and hear him say, "Take my yoked upon you, and learn of me, my yoke is easy, and my burden is light."

It seems that a year does not pass that a pastor of a mega church play the end-of-time game. What do they expect to happen? God has sent Jesus Christ as Savior to explain in detail what is to take place in the meantime. And if what is supposed to be happening is not happening, there is the "Last Judgment" Jesus promised in Matthew 25:31-46. In Matthew 16:1-4, "The Pharisees, also with the Saducees came, and tempting desired Him that He would show them a sign from Heaven. He answered and said unto them, when it is evening, ye say, it will be fair weather; for the sky is red. And in the morning, it will be foul weather today; for the sky is red and lowering. Oh ye hypocrites, ye can discern the face of the sky; but ye cannot discern the signs of the times? A wicked and adulterous generation seeketh after a sign; and there shall be no sign given unto it, but the sign of the prophet Jonah and He left them and departed." ARE WE IN ANY BETTER SPIRITUAL SHAPE THAN NINEVEH?

AFTER YOU CROSS OVER, YOU HAVE TO REMEMBER TO KEEP TURNING IT OVER TO JESUS. HE'S A WAY-MAKER, BATTLE-AX IN THE TIME OF A BATTLE. IT DOES

NOT MATTER WHO THE ENEMY IS, OR HOW MANY THERE ARE.

Story is told of a foreign missionary family, a long ways from America in Burma (Myanmar), trying to take the name of Jesus half way around the world to many who had never heard what God has done for broken hearts, and shattered lives, never taking the time to establish a family of their own. Deciding to have a child, the little beautiful girl, only a few years old contracted malaria and was near death. After praying, they asked God for healing power, thinking of all they had done for others. Tired, weary, and sad, they decided to give the little girl to God as a thanksgiving after all. WITH HUMILITY, AND THANKSGIVING, AS THEY RELEASED THE LITTLE GIRL FROM THEIR WOUNDED SPIRITS, THE FEVER BROKE ALMOST IMMEDIATELY. She then lived with them as a gift from an all-wise, all loving God, in a way they would never have loved, accepted, treated her, and considered her as a gift from God, which was their righteous obligation.

I have my own story. At Howard University in 1964, in the throes of the civil rights movement for Justice, equality, jobs, and freedom, I tried to give as much as I had to right these wrongs. Although I tried to blame a severe physical breakdown on a rigorous schedule, and a virus that put me in the Washington Medical Center for three weeks, it was my spirit that was taxed. One of my positions, among several others, was a community organizer among youth in a blighted area, Anacostia of Southwest Washington. I was determined to make a difference, based upon what I was searching for as outlined by Dr. Martin Luther King Jr., and those who sacrificed their lives in the name of Jesus Christ.

I was saved from any residual scars, physically or mentally and spiritually, it is my deep conviction that because my small suffering coincided with Jesus' Passion as He looked to Calvary 2000 years ago, I was overshadowed by his words to the thief next to Him on the cross. It was in April 1964 that I suffered in His footsteps, that led to the "Way of the Cross," "This day thou shall be with me in Paradise," with Him on the Via Dolorosa, the falls with His heavy cross, the fourteen times. A fever of 105, packed in ice by loving nurses, seeing evil crawling animals, and threatening figures in the paintings on the wall, it was when I retreated into the quiet of the beautiful chapel of worship that, looking at the beautifully colored stained glass pictures of His past suffering that My soul was relieved, and a warmth filled that place. It was either Good Friday, or the Monday after Easter that a student representing the faculty and students from Howard's

Divinity School brought over to my room a beautiful Easter lily, more beautiful than any you will ever see. The words might have come; "Jesus Savior, pilot me, over life's tempestuous, chart and compass come from thee, Jesus Savior pilot me."

II Corinthians 5:19: God was in Christ, reconciling the world to Himself. Because the five wise virgins had oil for their lamps, they could recognize Jesus as the bridegroom when He came. I'm fortunate, and blessed to have been given the call to go into the prisons of America during my entire professional career, where Jesus was. "I was in prison, and you did not visit me." Matthew 25:31-46: "I did not see you" because I was, and am still there, Jesus is with me in there, and on the streets. I would not have Jesus to say to me, "Depart from me ye that work iniquity, I never knew you."

Chapter Eleven

When God Delivered the Hebrew People from Pharaoh in Egypt, They Were the Chosen People for the Same Deliverance of the Other Oppressed People in God's Universe (II Corinthians 5:17)

GOOD WAS IN CHRIST, RECONCILING THE WORLD TO HIMSELF. TO THE "WORLD" HIS WILL IS "LET MY PEOPLE GO," (MATTHEW 25:31-46)

A discussion with a scenario towards relieving structures of oppression affecting human beings in God's perfect world/universe. This is a discussion on the original intent of the book, acknowledging the total perfection involving humanity in God's perfect universe.

THE PROBLEM: Because of the lack of spiritual enabling The Christian Church is suffering in despair, if we know mankind should be free as Jesus meant in John 8:31-32, and do nothing as in a worldwide concerted effort against violence, war. If we see that they are suffering in ignorance to their opportunity for freedom and we do nothing, we suffer with them because at least we know what it means to be free, and they do not. The Christian Church, the Moslem, Islamic faith, the Jewish faith, and other faiths should be acting together to bring civilization out of the Dark Ages of mankind into the glorious light of freedom in an enlightened reality. The final judgment will be experienced in Jesus' words in Matthew 25:31-46

The following statements preface the Carol Lin document, and are excerpted from the doctoral dissertation of Dr. Miles J. Austin. The title: "To Increase the Congregation's Understanding of Christian Discipleship," Drew University, October 8, 1976.

"In the first chapter of this paper, I have made a stand for ethical involvement on the part of every person who calls himself Christian based on the doctrine of the church. In this second chapter I will state my interest in (1)To be able to interpret the meaning of discipleship, which has been an intense concern of mine since entering the Christian Ministry over fifteen years ago; (2) What I consider to be set-backs to my diligent search for the true meaning to Christian Discipleship; and, (3) How Black theologians, expounding a theology based on social and cultural experiences of Black people, have aided me in correcting my approach to doing theology, aiding me in my ministry, which happens to be for black people.

The first time I stood up to preach a trial sermon for the ministry of Jesus Christ, I felt I should be as sincere about this profession as possible. As an assistant to the minister of the Greater First Baptist Church in Washington, DC, while attending the seminary at Howard University, I was called upon approximately once a month to deliver the sermon at the eleven A.M. service. I think that it is important to say here that the driving force in my life that led me to enter the ministry was the seeming helpless and fruitless effort put forward by those in authority to reach the necessary goals required.

Allow me to digress here to explain the situation in point that, as I think about my present involvement, has a direct bearing on this project. While a vice-principal at an institution in Florida for delinquent boys, I had authority to reform the minds of these less fortunate young men, but this authority had limits. On one occasion, a bright young black boy seized upon the challenge I had offered him to break out of the cycle of mental and psychological slavery by using his God-given abilities in a world that called for everything we've got. When plans were made for him to return to his home town, with a slightly different but improved setting, and including enrollment in public school, I found nothing but opposition. The young man said to me in clear language and with knowledge of the situation that left me embarrassed, "Sir, I could have told you what would happen."

As I stood there before the congregation time after time, I sought to relate the academic training with the preaching of the word of God, and somehow I saw a relationship between these and all those people who were seeking something too. I had no problem understanding what the word of God intended to mean for me and the people of

God. I had trouble finding effective structures in the Black or White community that were clear examples of the "ethical imperative" at work in relieving structures of oppression.

I am convinced today after reading J. Deotis Roberts' and James Cone's books on a Black theology that had this system of theology been taught to me at Howard in the early sixties during the "Strides toward Freedom" of the "people of God," it would have been easier for me to reconcile my preaching of the word of God based on His promise to Abraham and the burden of oppression and unmerited suffering experienced in America.

My own inner search, through intense concern for the suffering of Black people, had led me to want to hear what Jesus Christ has to say about the conditions of the oppressed Black people and what are viable solutions and alternatives.

As I look back to this "call to the ministry" I am convinced of the seriousness of this quest if the one who is called is willing to give all that he has. Bonhoeffer's statement in *The Cost of Discipleship* comes to mind here, "When Christ calls a man, he bids him come and die" (16) I am dealing with my search for authentic Christian witnessing here because I take Jesus Christ seriously when He compares the Kingdom of heaven with a pearl of great price. "Again, the Kingdom of heaven is like unto a merchant man, seeking goodly pearls; who when he had found one pearl of great price, went and sold all he had, and bough it," (Matthew 13:45-46 KJV).

"My search has led from the death to self that Bonhoeffer is talking about to the entrance to that Kingdom of heaven that Jesus Christ speaks of and for which a man will sell all he has to buy it," (To Increase the Congregation's Understanding of Christian Discipleship," Drew University, Madison, NJ October 8, 1976; Miles J. Austin. Page 32-34).

As I prepare to move into conclusive evidence, I must throw light on the circle of my academic search for Christian Discipleship being completed, using Ms. Lin's concern in the just mentioned title of my dissertation presented to Drew University. The following quotes are from Drs. James Cone and J. Deotis Roberts, excerpts from above reference work on file at Drew University.

Excerpt: "Then, black is not so much what a person is as much as what is happening to him or her in a social sense. The ethical and the eschatological are relevant here because God is doing something in history to relieve these structures that are inhibiting the oppressed from full humanity in life—this life.

The ethical demands in discipleship with God's deliverance of Israel from political bondage and seeing Israel's failure to be the people for further deliverance points to the judgmental consequences resulting from our actions or inactions in this life.

Again, James Cone in his monumental work, *God of the Oppressed* state:

Unfortunately this essential connection between liberation and reconciliation is virtually absent in the history of Christian thought. Theologians emphasized the objectivity of reconciliation, but they lost sight of the fact that reconciliation is grounded in history. This tendency is undoubtedly due partly to the influence of Greek thought and the church's political status after Constantine. The former led to rationalism and the latter produced a 'gospel' that was politically meaningless for the oppressed. Reconciliation was defined in timeless 'rational' grounds and was thus separated from God's liberating deed in history. The political status of the post Constantinian church, involving both alliance and competition with the state, led to definition of the atonement that favored the powerful and excluded the interest of the poor," (30; p. 55).

Excerpt: *A Black Political Theology,* J. Deotis Roberts:

"Roberts confirms Cone in this observation involving the inconsistencies in Western theology.

On the whole, German theology still dominates the thinking of American theologians. Someone has observed that the 'death of God' theologians were saying what we need is love, until the Germans said what we need is hope - and perhaps what we really need is faith. A noted American historian has remarked that German philosophies come to this country to die. Black theology is existential, but it is also political. It is a theology of survival, of meaning, of protest against injustice. It deals with the issues of life and death," (31; Drew University Dissertation - p. 55).

Pressing into the Kingdom of God is what Jesus Christ says must happen for a person to be "born again." Existentialism means to be able to extend one's conception of his spiritual existence, rather than his physical existence, and awareness at any given time to one's end in life, which goes beyond physical death. A paradigm, or what one considers the "world" to be, should be based on the above, and is, or should be, the result of one being involved in religious activity, going to church, and should have an expectation of moving towards the Kingdom of God, and for no other reason whatsoever.

Based upon what was just said, the following excerpt, or quote from a Muslim theologian is a presupposition for Ecumenical talks necessary to have the church defined with a capital "C," representing all faiths based on the *Ten Commandments* and uniting God with His created universe.

"The eschatology becomes intelligible only in terms of the nationalists' insistence that knowledge of one's own identity—one's self, nation, religion, and God—is indispensable to a creative life for the individual and for the group, and is the true meaning of heaven. Not having this knowledge is hell. The instructed individual acquires a new being and outlook on life; he enjoys heaven on earth. The individual gains a new, and better perspective on his past and present moral and material conditions and can initiate programs for his future and for that of his nation. New found self-respect and confidence inspires him to work hard and to make sacrifices for his nation's future. His sacrifices are justified by promises of the nation's final, ultimate grandeur," (47; Drew University 1976; pp. 86-87).

Excerpt: "My concern here is that the steps to this point in God's plan, which might be clearly focused in ministry, can be summed up in II Corinthians 5:19: 'God was in Christ reconciling the world to himself.' We should understand how the church fits into God's plan. We should understand how we as followers of Christ fit into God's plan. We should in coming to the third chapter, understand the program of the church in teaching, identity of the individual within his particular culture, and liberating the Black oppressed people of God from oppressor and self for union with the body of Christ in reconciling the world unto himself.

To hear his call, and in this call to hear where God will lead us, to have insight into God's plan for the world—that is faith," (51; p. 94).

"Systematic theologian that he is, Dr. Roberts has combined the most appropriate schools of thought to draw the following conclusion which sets the state for me to conclude the content of this project.

"Tucker has a tendency to write off the church because he sees the black community as issue oriented. To me, as a churchman and theologian, there is convincing evidence apparent to indicate that the black church remains the strongest tower of strength available for black liberation. What the black church needs is leadership, a political theology and a plan of action," (52; Drew Univ. dissertation, p. 94).

The Carol Lin discussion follows from where I started in Washington, DC, at the First Baptist Church of Mt. Pleasant Plains, down from Howard University, in the midst of the civil rights movement in 1960, in the United States of America. A brief background snap shot would be the Florida School for Boys in Okeechobee, Florida, where I was denied basic human, as well as Civil Rights. The Florida School for Boys was segregated and I was not allowed to have my family live in new homes built especially for the school's staff. Also, and most important, I was denied attempts to get a young man, incarcerated, but about to be released, who demonstrated acceptable standards of excellence, back into public school in order to bring him back into the mainstream of community citizenship and family responsibility.

It seems practical to the general observer to mention the pursuit engaged in by this writer to be led on, I say by Almighty God, towards the resolution of Carol Lin's mistakes in her flawed understanding of world or universal justice by an all-wise, all-caring and loving Creator, God. Before I state these calculated efforts by this writer, let me state that there was the same heavy weight on my cognitive responsibility and helplessness to do anything about the problem explained above while a student at Howard University, just as I felt in the tone and emotional embrace of the problem with Ms. Lin.

THE PIVOTAL AWARENESS FOR WHICH I HAD BEEN SEARCHING AND ON WHICH CAROL LIN'S FLAWED SENSE OF JUSTICE RESTS IS AS FOLLOWS: Where there is no fault, there can be no *correction*. Where there is no sickness, there can be no healing. "Those that are well need no physician," (St. Luke 5:31 KJV). Should I expect for Carol Lin to admit to her illness if she does not discern the perfect control of an all-wise and loving Creator and sustainer of our lives in His world and universe? If I challenged her I could be considered offensive, even abusive to the point of being charged and summoned before a civil magistrate in a court of law.

The cross purpose or dichotomy or even contradiction in the systems applied in these three citadels of authority the church, the state, and the community led to the confusion in Florida, with the young boy being released without either one of these three systems that should have been put in place to reintegrate him back into the community. A reference here would be St. Paul in the book of Philemon involving Onesimus in the New Testament, a young man who was in jail with Paul. Also, this closing "circle" of divine law appears to be moving in the direction of the Ecumenical Church with a capital "C" as with Charles Clayton Morrison, and George Barna.

Exposé on Ms. Carol Lin:

I see a watershed, *epiphany*, or paradigm shift, either we choose is appropriate to point out the same feeling for both myself, at the First Baptist Church in Washington, DC, preaching during the civil rights movement, and Ms. Lin. She was emotionally distraught upon the death of both Christopher Reeves and his wife, leaving a teenage son to be cared for. I sincerely wish I could pass on to her the insights from my relationship with God, revealed by my diligent search for an authentic personal relationship with Jesus Christ and the Spirit of God. Nevertheless, I will shed as much light as I can on that possibility as I shed light on my growth, thanks to Almighty God.

In America, 90 percent of the people believe in God, perhaps to the degree that I did fifty years ago, and wondered what I could do to bring justice to my community, during my commitment to the struggles of the civil rights movement in the 1960s. Why has nothing more significant happened in America that could be witnessed to, with this many people believing in God, with the ability to experience and act on God's Spirit available to save both them and society? Two words here would express the deficiency of their belief and faith, just as I admit during the first fifty years of my life, "Pressed Into" thereby ushering them into the Kingdom of God. Pick up today's newspaper and read the headlines any day and we all shudder at the misery and mayhem of false hopes and dashed dreams of *The Vox Populi*, the voice of the people.

Based upon my beliefs about the church failing at that time in the sixties, and the way Ms. Lin feels now, either God is slow to "act," or there is a conspiracy against His Will. There are three principles of thought that, if I had dealt with in the sixties, would be exactly what Ms. Lin would have to deal with now. We both are vicariously experiencing the essential necessity to throw ourselves into the problem as being the answer, or we become a part of the problem, "the conspiracy," or organized crime with a small case, that is being perpetrated by humanity against the ordained Will of God.

(1) The *fall*, (2) death: negates Life, and proves our lack of "knowledge," yet we believe in The God of life, and (3) Jesus Christ, God's perfect and intelligent design, that we reject by refusing to follow.

Treatment disciplines, for both mind and body for life in this medium of physical existence, are proof that the real answers have not been directed at the problem which is death. If I had the above theological Principles explained to me at the Howard University Divinity School during the civil rights movement, not only would I have known that the Christian Church was capable of accepting its challenge as it has been designed by Almighty God, but I, along with, I am sure, many other seminary students who looked to the church as I did, as in Florida, could have energized the entire Christian and religious community, to move beyond race to the endemic and systemic problems facing man as his predicament from the *fall*. These were the answers that I mentioned and sought in my thesis paper submitted to the Howard University Divinity School Faculty entitled, "The Implications of Black Nationalism for the Negro Church." Answers that I now know are to be exercised in ministry by applying the prescriptions for the Kingdom of God applied in the Power of God, expressed in detail in the ministry, death, resurrection, and the Spirit of God dispensed at Pentecost to give detail belief and power not only for each believer in Jesus Christ, but to bring about the Kingdom of God which Jesus Christ gave the Spirit for this accomplishment.

This is what people have done who could not bring an end to alcoholism, drugs, gambling, and any other addictions. They came into the Truth of their condition of the "fall" and realized that God was correct to warn Adam and Eve in the Garden. Had they never come to know evil, evil would have never had any power over their flesh and blood. This is what Ms. Carol Lin needs to *know*. Ms. Lin's only option is to devote as much time as an avocation will allow, to bring young Mr. Reeves into this knowledge for his salvation. "Seek first the kingdom of God and its righteousness, and all the other things will be added unto you."

Word to 90 percent of Americans: If they "knew" the power and Spirit of God over death, not only would they not fear it, they would not fear anything that might cause physical death, such as disasters, and suffering. The case of Mr. and Mrs. Christopher Reeves's son being left alone in "this" "world" is but a small problem when considered with the resources in any given community. In other words, seeking first the Kingdom of God and its righteousness and all these other things will be added unto you. So, like I was in Washington, DC, Ms. Lin is oblivious to the Truth and the conspiracy against it, which we both could have been, and may still be, "workers of iniquity" without it. And Jesus Christ would say when we get to meet Him in death, "I never knew you." Our efforts to live in this world would have become sounding brass, and tinkling cymbals.

Word to 90 percent of Americans: They see God's involvement in Katrina, and earthquakes, mass killings of large numbers of human beings, but they don't see God in every moment of their lives. They

have to see "God" both places, or they don't see him in either place, and they are like the man who never understood life at all. In Pirandello's play, *The Rules of the Game*, the following conversation takes place:
Leonne: Ah, Venanzi, it's a sad thing, when one has learnt every move in the game.
Guido: What game?
Leonne: Why…this one. The whole game—of life.
Guido: Have you learnt it?
Leonne: Yes, a long time ago.

Leonne's despair and resignation come from believing that there is such a thing as the game of life. Indeed, if mastery of the game of life were the problem of human existence, having achieved this task, what would there be left to do? But there is no game of life, in the singular. The games are infinite (Reference: *The Myth of Mental Illness, Foundations of a Theory of Personal Conduct*, Thomas S. Szasz, M.D., Revised Edition, Perennial press, 1974, p. 265).

Word to 90 percent of Americans: What game are you playing? Who thought it up? And are the people you are playing games with using the same games you are using, or playing with? (See also, *Games People Play*, by Dr. Eric Berne—A therapeutic treatment model referred to as *Transactional Analysis*.)

If Ms. Lin wanted to "live life righteously as in seeking God, the experience of being coexistent with Him in Spirit, which is the only form of life, in the process of everyday living," she would take young Mr. Reeves's welfare as her own. In the Kingdom of God, she would have no other priority. And if she did this, she would have put whatever that priority was, ahead of her own "life" with God in the Kingdom of God. She would be Judged and sentenced to death in any other medium to which she prescribed to for her existence. She would have recognized Jesus Christ in the life of young Mr. Reeves, and Jesus would have remembered her as He appeared in the spirit of young Mr. Reeves when she, Ms. Lin, came to assist him (Matthew 25:31-46).

I would like to give an illustration of what it means to "say" you believe in God, and the difference when it comes to acting on that shallow commitment. I would assume that in 1964 the statistics of those in America that believed in God were approximately 90 percent, or the same, or better than they are now. In 1964, Madeleine O'Hare petitioned the pipeline of the American judiciary all the way to the Supreme Court and had prayer taken out of the public schools in

America. If the 90 percent of Americans who believe in God believed in terms of what God is doing in the world, having sent Jesus Christ to lead the way as our savior, they would have simply let their municipal governments know how they felt, based on the knowledge of their faith in God, and this decision would have never gotten out of the thousands of municipal courts around the nation. Just as I said above, if a person who falls into that 90 percent of Americans who believe in God did nothing in 1964 when prayer was taken out of the public schools, whatever they were doing as they ignored this challenge, is their belief. And that belief had nothing to do with what God is doing in the world to establish the Kingdom of God. So those persons who did nothing to assist God in His Mission, in 1964, on God's behalf, Jesus Christ will say to them in that day, depart from me you that work iniquity, I never knew you.

AN ESSENTIAL INSIGHT: One of the most direct references to this rather chilling judgment by Jesus Christ, "Depart from me you that work iniquity, I never knew you" is directly related to two essential facts to develop a Righteous paradigm, or the way we make both casual, as well as critical decisions in life: (1) The Kingdom of God, and (2) Those who will be judged as worthy or righteous. Both of these insights come clearly to our cognitive awareness in this Scripture. Matthew 25:31-46

When the Son of man shall come in his glory, and all the holy angels with him, then shall he sit upon the throne of his glory. And before him shall be gathered all nations; and he shall separate them one from the other, as a shepherd divideth his sheep from the goats. And he shall set the sheep on his right hand, but the goats on the left. Then shall the King say to them on his right hand, Come ye blessed of my Father, inherit the kingdom prepared for you from the foundation of the world.

Jesus identifies with certain people so closely, that He becomes them in fact and Truth. Period. If I, or you, or any of the 90 percent of Americans who believe in God, don't see Jesus Christ representing the natural face of these people -those who are hungry, thirsty, a stranger, naked, sick, and in prison—we did not recognize Jesus Christ. And if we did not recognize Jesus Christ in these situations, He sees us in those situations as we fail to recognize Him, and ignore him. The key here is that when we see Jesus Christ in our Judgment, He saw us in these situations. And, listen to this, if we had not gotten to know and recognize Him then, He will say "Depart from me, you that work iniquity, I never knew you."

All human beings will be categorized here, I can't say which side of Jesus you were on, the side of the sheep, or the side of the goats. Most of us will accept the fact that we did not recognize Jesus in those particular situations, but what about this working iniquity? If you live three score and ten years, that's seventy years as the Bible acknowledges. If you did not recognize Jesus Christ in any of those situations mentioned above, you, or I, or anyone else for that matter, was doing a lot of things that, in this situation of the judgment of our souls to be worthy of the Kingdom of God, were indeed working a whole lot of nothing, iniquity. Mark 8:36-37: "What shall it profit a man if he shall gain the whole world, and lose his own soul? Or what shall a man give in exchange for his soul?"

I would like to ask Carol Lin what she would do if, hypothetically, she was regressed back to 1964 and heard about Madeleine O'Hare's efforts to have prayer taken out of the public schools? As a matter of fact, right now, a citizen of the country where ninety percent of its people believe in God, one individual in this country can petition the government and have any reference to God removed from any government building or other government related structure or legislation involving America's citizenry.

Let me ask Carol Lin a question to allow her to escape from the box she might be feeling encased in. If she is a member of the 90 percent of Americans who believe in God, my question to her would be, is she active in a Christian congregation? If she says yes, and I hope she does, what is her church and Ecclesiastical hierarchy doing to foster the Kingdom of God as detailed above, in spite of the separation of church and state? If she says I don't know, or that my question is out of order, she will be told by Jesus Christ at the Judgment bar of death, depart, I never knew you, as you never knew me.

I shall try not to refer to Scripture in this process with Ms. Lin as I explain the need for "Knowledge" that must be applied to the process of serving human beings. I have mentioned the three citadels of authority in this process, the Kingdom of God, the government of the state, and the people of humanity who make up the reason for the state and the church to exist. I feel this Scripture merits an exemption from my decision above: This is what Apostle Paul had to say to the Church at Rome, the tenth chapter verses as follows: Romans 10:1-4, "Brethren, my heart's desire and prayer to God for Israel is that they might be saved. For I bear them record that they have a zeal for God, but not according to knowledge. For they being ignorant of God's righteousness, and going about to establish their own righteousness, have not submitted themselves unto the righteousness of God." Verse 4: "For Christ is the end of the law for righteousness to everyone that believeth."

Failure to follow Jesus Christ, or another faith based on the *Ten Commandments* such as Islam, Judaism, will not only bring about disasters in the personal lives of human beings, but it mushrooms out to the decisions that are made in policies across the board from the family parenting models to corruption in government. This is where it seems, as I said before, God seems only to be blamed when disasters occur, never when things are going rosy. Whether it involves a death in a family where both parents are taken, or a massive Katrina-like disaster or like 9/11.

We live in a communication age. Hype and high visibility will get a smoothed over criminal elected to the highest office in the land. By the same flip-flop, a minister of the Gospel, or the following types of leaders are assassinated: Medgar Evers, Dr. Martin Luther King Jr., President Kennedy, Malcolm X, and all those murders in the South during slavery up through the civil rights movement.

Unless the Christian, and other faiths and denominations face the Truth of God, with all the "physical" death and suffering it will bring to those who follow in the steps of Jesus Christ in establishing the Kingdom of God on earth, we have only death and suffering as a judgment. Proverbs 14:34: "Righteousness exalteth a nation; but sin is a reproach to any people."

The Christian Church, as well as all other faiths, has not taken God the Father, or Jesus Christ our Lord and Savior of mankind seriously. As a result, all of the world religions have failed to take *spiritual death* seriously. Based on these Truths, no Law of God or man will prevent a terrible Judgment from the violations specifically outlined by God in the *Ten Commandments*.

Proof of the above statement, Carol Lin had a psychologist on *CNN* with her to explain the trauma involving the general viewer's concerns, relating to the psychological post traumatic stress following the death of both Christopher Reeves and his wife, leaving a young son without parental security. Ninety percent of Americans who believe in God, none called in to say how belief in God and His care for human beings exceeds any that can be contrived by man. It appears to me that separation of church and state can be interpreted as the state having divorced the Church from itself, and is demanding that the church pay alimony. The churches' weekly offerings that for the most part are immediately deposited in a local bank, in turn is funneled on to Wall Street to further the nation's bidding in the world.

A pittance of that offering which is stingily returned to the churches in what the state has come with as faith-based initiative.

If I were to take the role of an apologist for humanity, it would sound like this: God has never caused any harm to this world, including what we call "death." These two statements are prefaces to my apology. It is as clear to me as the five fingers on my right hand that there will never be any peace in God's universe unless we acknowledge Jesus Christ, which is not exclusive to other like faiths, as our Lord and Savior.

The apology is as follows: I was watching the late Tim Russert on *Face the Nation* Sunday, April 23, 2006. The occasion was the resignation of President Bush's press secretary, I think his name is Scott McClellan. The reason given was that he was out of the loop, and so, did not have the truth involving critical situations going on in the Oval Office. With the discussion concluding on the length of time press secretaries have served in the past, and some successful ones, Mr. Christian, Lyndon Johnson's press secretary came up, as having made a classical observation for serving in that capacity. "Tell the truth, but make sure you have a good sense of humor."

Before I make an apology for all humanity, here's my humor: A farmer once bought a mule for $500 for plowing his farm. However, the mule refused to plow. The farmer got on the phone, irate at possibly losing $500. The seller calmly reassured him there was nothing wrong with the mule, as a matter of fact he said, rather jauntily, as if knowing what the problem was, "I'll be right over." As he arrived he asked "Where is the mule?" "Around the back," the frustrated farmer quipped. On his way to the backyard the seller reached on the woodpile and secured a two by four piece of wood. Without any wasted moves physically, he went up side the mule's head with the two by four. The mule sprang up and began to plow as though nothing had happened. The seller dusted off his hands, and on the way back to his car, he turned to the farmer and said without any emotion, "There's nothing wrong with the mule, you just never got his attention."

There is one situation in the life of Jesus Christ that calls my attention to this story, from the apologist's side though. Jesus Christ came down through forty-two generations of God's deliberate love for Israel, the Jewish people we know today. St. Luke Chapter 19:41-46: "And when he came near, he beheld the city, and wept over it, saying, if thou hadst known, even thou, at least in this thy day, the things which belong unto thy peace! But now they are hid from thine eyes. For the days shall come upon thee, that thine enemies shall cast a trench about thee, and compass thee around, and keep thee in on every side, and shall lay thee even with the ground, and thy children within thee; and they shall not leave in thee one stone upon another; because thou knewest not the time of thy visitation. And he went into the temple, and began to cast out them that sold therein, and them that bought; saying unto them, it is written, My house is the house of prayer; but you have made it a den of thieves."

Historical record has it that the Roman General Titus carried out Jesus' predictions of the destruction of Jerusalem to the letter.

Ms. Lin's frustration represents that of millions—and billions—of anxious, stressed, and depressed human beings in God's creation. This is the verdict of the guilt and the sentence for breaking the laws of this perfect creation by an all wise beneficent "Father." Jesus Christ's words mean nothing until we have completely lost our "way." I have come that you might have life, Come unto me all ye that labor, and are heavy laden, and I will give you rest, take my yoke upon you and learn of me, for my yoke is easy, and my burden is light, and you shall find rest for your souls. I am the resurrection and the life, he that believeth in me, though he were dead yet shall he live, and he that liveth and believeth in me shall never die.

AN ESSENTIAL INSIGHT: BASED UPON THE ABOVE GIFT TO US BY GOD, THROUGH JESUS CHRIST OUR SAVIOR, ANY TIME A HUMAN BEING FINDS SOMETHING WRONG WITH GOD'S PERFECT CREATION, THEY HAVE ACKNOWLEDGED SELF-INFLICTED GUILT. THE WOUNDS OF WHICH RESULT IN STRESS AND ANXIETY, AND IS THEREBY A SENTENCE TO PUNISHMENT FOR THAT PARTICULAR VIOLATION. HOPEFULLY THEIR SINS WILL FIND THEM OUT, OR COME TO THEIR AWARENESS. WITHOUT ADMITTING THEIR ERRORS, AND BECOMING PENITENT AND CONFESSING THEIR SINS OR VIOLATIONS BEFORE GOD, THEIR ULTIMATE SENTENCE IS DEATH. BY MY OWN EXPERIENCE, I KNOW THAT IN MOST EXPERIENCES OF HUMAN BEINGS, WE MUST ALWAYS BE BROKEN IN OUR STUBBORNNESS, ARROGANCE, AND PRIDE OF SELF BEFORE COMING BEFORE GOD IN HUMILITY, WHICH IS OUR STRENGTH, WITH THAT ATTITUDE, RATHER THAN OUR PRIOR, NOW ADMITTED WEAKNESS.

What does it mean to be "good?" This is where the statement from the book by Dr. Szasz, *The Myth of Mental Illness*, speaks: The human being who thinks he knows all there is to know about life will become bored, if not frustrated and depressed with life as he or she knows it. A disciple of Jesus Christ who follows Jesus in causing trouble, as he did in bringing salvation to a lost world, will cause Ms. Lin to become disgusted by upsetting her example of goodness, which means to stay out of trouble as men considers trouble. Following all the rules of man's convention have brought us to the brink of extinction. That kind of staying out of trouble has caused young Mr. Reeves to be without a home, without a family, friends and comfort with provisions for his happiness. ONLY GOD IS GOOD, ALL THE TIME, IN ALL CONDITIONS AND SITUATIONS.

A TYPICAL FLAWED PARADIGM: Jesus Christ taught by precept and example that discipleship exempts no one from ministry and ministering. There will not be two areas in heaven, one for pastors, deacons, teachers, missionaries, and another area for regular church members. Based on Ms. Lin's belief in God, there are special people to do what is necessary to assist young Mr. Reeves, who seems to need a family of friends. When it comes to taking care of young Mr. Reeves, "Anybody could have done it." "After everybody wanted to do it." "Somebody started to do it." "But in the end nobody did it."

I'd like to mention a word that was used a lot during the sixties when civil rights and the Vietnam War threw the country, if not the world, into a question involving justice and truth. The word is "existentialism," Dr. Martin Luther King, Jr. gave the word a simple, but in depth understanding of it. "Unless a person has found something worth dying for, life is not worth living." Existential living requires that we understand everything involved in our expectation at the end of life. Jesus Christ could have been disappointed having to leave the world he came to save at thirty-three years of age. The key to existentialism in Jesus' case was his prayer in the Garden of Gethsemane. "Not my will, but thine be done." The key to the true existentialist is that his life depends on accomplishing the goal that is worthy of everything he is, and possesses and is thereby bigger and greater than he is. Any rewards that he might personally expect, must be forgone in order that the mission be accomplished. It is almost impossible to find this in the job or employment that we go to each day to make a "living." We all seem to know some older retired person who died shortly after wishing for, and becoming retired.

To live each moment with the end of life in mind, towards an end that is totally worth everything and anything that you can give to it, is truly humbling. This is the opposite paradigm of the world as that expressed by Ms. Carol Lin, and most of those included in that 90 percent of Americans who believe in God. When death comes they are at that terrible *end*, in a hospital or hospice. The five stages of those last days are (1) anger, (2) isolation, (3) argument, (4) bargaining, and finding no way out, (5) accepting their fate before God at the end of life for unbelievers expressed in *Death and Dying* authored by Elisabeth Kuebler Ross.

Understanding the word existentialism, a person faces death each time they have to make a decision, as simple as what they will do during their next rest break from their work schedule during the day. When these apparent small or little decisions are not made with the end of life in mind, or applying existentialism, facing a real or critical problem, fear sets in and life threatening emotional crises are experienced leading to anxiety and stress. And if not focused on with *spirituality* of the existentialism of the end of life, a person could have to be treated by a psychiatrist. Preferably, I would recommend a preacher of the Gospel of Jesus Christ. This is why Jesus could say to Pilate in the judgment hall, "you have no power over me." And this is why the rich young ruler came to Jesus and asked what he had to do to inherit the Kingdom of God. He knew, but he was looking for a way to take his wealth with him, which would have meant that the things of this world are equally important as the things of the Kingdom of God. And this undermines Dr. Martin Luther King Jr.'s genius, unless a person finds something worth dying for, life is not worth living. He is really saying you must choose, while looking death in the eyes that you will still choose to lose your life, as a preface to saving your soul. A line in a favorite hymn says, "Nothing in my hands I bring, simply to the cross I cling."

And again, I must propose an apology for Ms. Lin and the other 90 percent of Americans who believe in God. The Christian, as well as other churches, temples, mosques, etc. have not demonstrated any kind of close relationship to the Body of Christ, and their respective Patron Saints. There is a very close relationship between existentialism, Dr. Martin Luther King Jr.'s principle, and Jesus' words at the end of His ministry on earth, "I am he that was dead, and behold I am alive forever more, and have the keys to hell and death." Satan appears to have the upper hand in diverting the attention of human beings from a true belief in God, voice approval, yes, but when it comes to what is of utmost importance in our everyday decision making awareness when compared with death, not quite, not even close.

It is important for Carol Lin to see just how God has deferred judgment and death on violators of the Law given to Moses. There was a time in the Old Testament that the Judgment of God was instant. Death resulted immediately. Once that Law was adjudicated, it became in effect. An example would be Lot's wife being turned to a pillar of salt after being instructed by God to leave Sodom and Gomorra, and not to look back towards the city as it was on fire.

It is obvious in the Old Testament that God became impatient with the children of Israel, such terms as "God's wrath being kindled," "alienation from the Children of Israel," and "the estrangement of God from them." God sent Jesus Christ with an entire set of arrangements for our forgiveness. Many songs have the refrain, He has ransomed captive Israel: propitiation, expiation, and atonement. Christmas is a favorite time for these emotions to move throughout our universe. Soldiers in the thick of battle have been known in history to lay down their arms on the twenty-fifth of December, regardless of their particular faith.

"Rejoice. Rejoice, Emanuel has come to thee Oh captive Israel. Oh little town of Bethlehem, how still we see thee lie, amid thy deep and dreamless sleep, the silent stars go by. Yet in thy dark street shineth, the everlasting light, the hopes and fears of all the years are met in thee tonight."

THIS IS WHAT TOOK PLACE BETWEEN THE OLD AND THE NEW TESTAMENT TO RANSOM CAPTIVE ISRAEL, YOU AND I

Luke 16:16: "The law and the prophets were until John; since that time the Kingdom of God is preached, and every man presseth into it."

Ephesians 2:8: "By grace we are saved through faith, and this not of ourselves, it is the gift of God."

Philippians 1:3-6: "I thank God upon every remembrance of you, Always in every prayer of mine for you all making request with joy, For your fellowship in the gospel from the first day until now; Being confident of this very thing, that he which hath begun a good work in you will perform it until the day of Jesus Christ."

Philippians 2:12: "Wherefore, my beloved, as ye have always obeyed, not as in my presence only, but now much more in my absence, work out your own Soul Salvation with fear and trembling."

In other words God was always present everywhere, and was available for us to come into His presence, but we had to have a heart acceptable, or acknowledgeable of His Holiness. Grace is from God, faith and belief is from us. All things are possible if we believe, because God is always there.

Those who come to God must believe that he is, and that he is a rewarder of them who diligently seek him.

HEBREWS 11:6: "But without faith it is impossible to please him, for he that cometh to God must believe that he is, and that he is a rewarder of them that diligently seek him."

Chapter Twelve

Experiencing a Miracle in the
Process of Seeking Peace and Rest

This chapter outlines my miraculous sojourn with my wife, to the southernmost part of the State of New Jersey between 1992 and 1998. Early on in the book, I refer to this period as very challenging in a spiritual sense. As a matter of fact it is the most important time in my life as I came into the truth of my sin, or violation of God's Law which is to attempt to live without the continuing cognitive awareness of the need, or completeness through His Spirit.

THE PROBLEM: Because of the lack of spiritual enabling, mankind has failed to see the miracle of "life." God gave us Jesus Christ who is life in every sense of the imagination, even to the casual observer who shows interest. This is not a story-book fairy tale. This happened, in our world, in our time, the first century after Christ, not that long ago, comparatively speaking if we accept that the universe after the big bang is twelve billions years old, or whatever thousands, or millions of years you choose. Otherwise we remain in a general sense, Humpty Dumptys.

I had originally experienced with stress, and fatigue from the need to steal away from the hustle and bustle of metropolitan New York - New Jersey. As it turned out God had plans for my life, energy, and a future that had been put on hold in my life.

The casual observer reading this chapter will see that I have, if anything, understated the energetic activity, along with the involvement that I was allowed to demonstrate to be effective in the lives of people, and organizations during this short six-year stay. Most memorable would be the miracle of the healing of Mrs. Turman. She sustained a massive brain hemorrhage almost immediately after leaving the funeral of a deceased person known to the members of the First Baptist Church of which my wife and I were members.

The church was in the process of changing its pastor, or minister, the spiritual leader of the First Baptist Church of Woodbine, New Jersey. The challenging, intense and emotional, and volatile atmosphere threatened the constructive and continuing worship of God. It occurred as a fact that the overriding issue in the call to the new leader was respect for those who died in the membership, that the funeral director's race, or ethnic background should be paramount in this final decision.

To put oneself in the thickening plot of this excitement leading up to the miracle, one would have to at that time, be in the church's worship service the following Sunday after Mrs. Turman's very serious illness, and hospitalization at the Shore Medical Center in Somers Point, New Jersey, approximately the summer of 1998, the funeral was on the previous Saturday. She sustained a massive brain hemorrhage where the attending physicians informed her family that she was not likely to live through the night. The pastor-elect, Reverend Thomas Dawson, Jr., or members of the family, I'm not sure who suggested we visit with Mrs. Turman immediately after that worship service and have a prayer for her. I cannot be specific here in terms of time, however, the family was told to come and see her for the last time alive. Within the next day, or so, she was told that there was no evidence of her ever having been stricken with a massive brain hemorrhage, and she could go home.

I understand that the nurse who released Mrs. Turman to her family recorded on the medical chart of her treatment, "strange people." To that impression I would add, "Unto you therefore which believe he is precious; but unto them which be disobedient, the stone which the builders disallowed, the same is made the head of the corner. And a stone of stumbling, and a rock of offense, even to them which stumble at the word, being disobedient: whereunto also they were appointed. But ye are a chosen generation, a royal priesthood, a holy nation, a peculiar people, that ye should shew forth the praises of who hath called you out of darkness into his marvelous light," (I Peter 2:7-9 KJV).

I believe that this miracle was for those unbelieving Christians, not unlike Mary and Martha at Lazarus' death. Believing that the resurrection will come in a later life was bewildered at their loss of a brother. If you, or I, believe in God, as Jesus represents His love, the family that prays together does stay together. I believe God, in His infinite wisdom, and love is still saying to the beautiful Christians at the First Baptist Church, and all that community, John 11:26: Jesus says to his dear friends Mary and Martha at the mourning of their brother Lazarus, I am the resurrection and the life, he that believeth in me though he were dead, yet shall he live, and he that liveth and believeth in me shall never die." John 14:27: "My peace I leave with you, My peace I give unto you."

Romans 14:8: "For whether we live, we live unto the Lord; and whether we die, we die unto the Lord; whether we live therefore, or die, we are the Lord's. For to this end Christ both died, and rose, and revived, that He might be Lord both of the dead and living."

Epilogue

President Barack Obama, the forty-fourth president of the United States of American frames this epilogue with a philosophical, theological prophecy, that as well, naturally includes the body politic: "The arch of the moral universe is long, but it bends toward justice."

Before I lead into the substance of this epilogue it would enlighten the casual observer if I referenced my decision of the above quote with a few other observations in this regard. Reading from the Newark, *New Jersey Star Ledger* newspaper on Editorial Opinions, January 28, 2009, page 15, the article is entitled; "OMG! Smart may be the new cool." That article mentioned President Obama's favorite literary repertoire, including "Song of Solomon" by Toni Morrison, "Parting the Waters" by Taylor Branch; the Bible, and Lincoln's collected writings.

President Obama's reference to justice, as from that quote above, and his reading preferences listed immediately above, firmly sets the framework that composes the intentions that he has embraced to lead our nation, and the free world, toward the profound prophetic expectations of that above quotation. That being said, I continue to address the need for the world to pursue divine justice that I believe President Obama, observing the list of his readings listed above also believes. *CNN* is televising, at this writing, Robert Gibbs, the president's press secretary's press conference on the president's 850-billion dollar stimulus package. A question from the press corps inquired in reference to the president's response to Defense Secretary Gates' request, and search for additional U.S. Armed Forces for the war in Afghanistan. Press Secretary Gibbs responded that the countries in Europe are eager to assist the U.S. by supplying troops needed in the war in Afghanistan who were not so inclined under President Bush's administration. This support confirms the president's posture in the free world.

A critical progression in President Obama's strong belief in the prophetic movement of the "moral arch of justice in the universe" is religiously, socially, and politically grounded in the continuing momentum of the civil rights movement under the leadership of Dr. Martin Luther King Jr., and others during the sixties in America. The *dream* of this movement was unquestionably a very strong motivational drive on his part to seek the presidency of the United States of America.

I am convinced that the opposition against President Obama's 850-billion dollar stimulus package, and any other necessary and continuing progressive programs he proposes on a wide national, and world-wide human rights friendly basis, using general tax payer funds, or funds from wealthy, or those who can well afford to assist in these efforts will be opposed, requiring a struggle on the part of the *faithful*.

The substance of this epilogue is as follows: (1) The entire thrust involving Divine, theological justice in this book, *How Was I Supposed to Know That God Has Created A Perfect Universe?* is rooted in the quotation President Obama has set his presidency on, prophetically in the direction of divine justice, the Kingdom of God. I consider the most significant amendment to the United States constitution is the *Bill of Rights*. The *Bill of Rights* is the epitome of human rights-friendly legislation that is necessary to come from Washington, D.C., the agreed upon leader of the free world; (2) Matthew 25:31-46 is the epitome of divine justice as recorded by Jesus Christ in those verses of Scripture. A familiar reference to these verses of Scripture in Matthew are stated partially as follows: I was hungry and you did not feed me, I was in prison, and you did not visit me, I was sick, and you did not visit me.

Justice: The maintenance of administration of what is just according to law.

Truth: The true or actual state of a matter. Actuality or actual existence.

Democracy: A form of government in which the supreme power is vested in the people, and exercised directly by them, or by their elected agents under a free electoral system.

The Kingdom of God: The Kingdom of God is understood as the actual presence of God Spiritually. God is omnipresent or everywhere at the same time. He is Omnipotent or all powerful, and omniscient, or all wise. There is no presence or place where God is not. Jesus Christ, born of God Spiritually. In His obedience to the will of God he commands that we be obedient to God also. And in so doing we accomplish what Jesus Christ left the Church in the world to do, that is, set the condition for the absolute removal of any action, or human experience that is contrary or in opposition to the Spirit of God, which typifies, absolutely, His perfection as He has created His world. This Truth can be understood if one practices as nearly to perfection as humanly possible Islam, Judaism, or any of the world's seven major religions.

Americans should support as well as is necessary the administration and leadership of President Obama in both our nation and internationally, in order to offset the terrible judgment resulting from our failure to live up to the divine justice unfolding as the moral arch of the universe designed by God, based on His presence in His world, His Kingdom. If one reads this book thoroughly, and correctly, I have put no more authority, or burden on our president than he understands is there already, as a disciple, or follower, of Jesus Christ.

Failing in this, and resulting from the invisible shadows of the universal dim unknown, America will, from the examples of societies God allowed to be created, survive, and thrive in their existence in the Old Testament and throughout human history come to the Judgment He has set in time for His will to be done. Failure in obedience to His detailed instructions for our freedom, peace, and salvation, we will suffer after having spurned His blessing of the gift of a "promised land."

Chapter Thirteen

The Defense of a Truth That, to Many, Is Just an Assumption

SUBJECT: HOW WAS I SUPPOSED TO KNOW THAT GOD HAS CREATED A PERFECT WORLD/UNIVERSE?
THE CRITICAL INQUIRY IN THIS DEFENSE IS THE METHODS APPLIED TO REACH THE ANSWER TO THE BOOK'S QUESTION:
THE PHILOSOPHICAL METHOD
THE PSYCHOLOGICAL METHOD
THE GOVERNMENT OR STATE'S METHOD
THE THEOLOGICAL OR CHURCH'S METHOD

THE PROBLEM: Without the enabling Spirit of God, through Jesus Christ, the following explanations don't mean a thing. This includes the enabling Spirit in Islam, Judaism, and the other world faiths derived from the God of Abraham, Isaac, and Jacob.

Acceptance of the book's argument, and its defense, or apology involves the gradual coalescing of both philosophy, psychology, theology and church and state.

- Philosophy is the study of knowledge;
- Psychology is the science of the mind or of mental states and processes. It involves the science of human and animal behavior. (Psychoanalysis is a systematic structure of theories concerning the relation of conscious and unconscious

psychological processes involved in treating mental illnesses such as a psychopath, psychosis, schizophrenia, etc.);
- The government and the state might be explained as a democratic process involving a system" to respond to *Vox Populi*, or "Voice of the People;" and
- Theology is the study of God who has all knowledge, or who is all knowing, and is represented in accomplishing a *method* experienced in the body of Jesus Christ, Moses, or Muhammad in the Church: Christian-Catholic, Muslim-Islam, Jewish, or otherwise.

THE PHILOSOPHICAL METHOD

As I pull together a system of understanding, mindful of the need to relate to readers of a sixth grade capacity, I hope chapters nine and ten sum up what has been coming to make the system of truth in God's perfect world/universe not only understandable, but also the reader seeing the need to embrace totally, or existentially, as Jean-Paul Sartre explains in his *Search For A Method*.

Considering the monumental significance of the divine truths stated in this book as referred to above in bringing together what is mentioned throughout as the three citadels of authority in our civilization, the church, the state, and the community, having the undisputed Truth of God as all knowing, I choose to bring to the reader's awareness the impact of Jean-Paul Sartre in these efforts to the glory of God.

The writings of Jean Paul Sartre have probably been more influential in the West than those of any other thinker and literary figure since the war. M. Sartre's formal impact in the field of psychology and philosophy has come chiefly from his two studies, *Being and Nothingness* and the *Critique of Dialectic Reason*, both of which laid the theoretical foundation to his doctrine of *existentialism*. Sartre's concern, however, has been to relate this theory to human response and the practical demands of living. To this end, he has carried his philosophical concepts into his novels and plays, and there subjected them to the test of imagined experience. His uniqueness lies in the success with which he demonstrates the utility of existentialist doctrine while creating, at the same time, works of the highest literary merit. Thus M. Sartre has become the popularizer of his own philosophical thought.

Jean Paul Sartre was born in Paris in 1905; he graduated from the Ecole Normale Superieure in 1929 with a doctorate in philosophy. He then taught philosophy in Le Havre, Laon, and Paris. While teaching in Paris during World War II, Sartre played an active role in the French Resistance. His first play, *The Flies*, was produced in France, despite its message of defiance during the German occupation.

Jean Paul Sartre: *Search for a Method - The Sartrean Approach to the Sociology and Philosophy of History*

Page XV "Man's inhumanity to man" is not, for Sartre, a fact of human nature. There is no human nature if by this we mean an innate disposition to adopt certain attitudes and conduct rather than others. But against the background of need and scarcity man—every man—assumes for himself and for others a dimension which is non-human. The fact of scarcity forces upon humanity the realization that it is impossible for all human beings to coexist. Every man is a potential bringer of death to each other man. Sartre says:

Nothing—neither wild beasts nor microbes—can be more terrible for man than a cruel, intelligent, flesh-eating species which could understand and thwart human intelligence and whose aim would be precisely the destruction of man. This species is obviously our own…in a milieu of scarcity.

From the introduction by Hazel E. Barnes who translated the work into English from the French

"The methodological principle which holds that certitude begins with reflection in no way contradicts the anthropological which defines the concrete person by his materiality. This is the only position which allows us to get rid of all idealist illusion, the only one which shows the real man in the midst of the real world.

When knowing is made *apodeictic* (demonstrably, or necessarily true) and when it is constituted against all possible questioning without ever defining its scope or rights, then it is cut off from the world and becomes a formal system. But what are we to call this situated negativity, as a moment of *praxis* (action) and as a pure relation to things themselves, if not exactly "consciousness?"

But Marx's statement seems to me to point to a factual evidence which we cannot go beyond so long as the transformations of social relations and technical progress have not freed man from the yoke of scarcity.

As soon as there will exist for everyone a margin of real freedom beyond the production of life, Marxism will have lived out its span; a philosophy of freedom will take its place. But we have no means, no intellectual instrument, no concrete experience which allows us to conceive of this freedom or this philosophy.

Excerpts from pages 32, 33, and 34

SEARCH FOR A METHOD
JEAN PAUL SARTRE

I propose here to highlight the unfounded inconsistencies of those who see any measure of truth in Charles Darwin's *Origin of Species* dissolving all the physical, material, and spiritual Truth of the Bible. The argument here is between creation, by God, and evolution, by spontaneous creation, or evolution as explained by one human being, Homo sapiens, primate mammal, bi-pedal named Charles Darwin.

In the process of referring to Jean Paul Sartre in this regard, I also feel the need to extricate him from Karl Marx, who might raise some negativity as Sartre having been associated with the communist ideology. It is my sincere hope that the following statement will accomplish this effort.

Search for a Method: "It sets forth specifically those ways in which existentialism seeks to modify Marxism and to change its direction," (Page ix).

Anthropology: The science that deals with the origins, physical and cultural development, biological characteristics, and social customs and beliefs of humankind.

Sartre on Marxism: The movement can think itself only in Marxist terms and can comprehend itself only as an alienated existence, as a human-reality made into a thing. The moment which will surpass this opposition must reintegrate comprehension into Knowledge as its non-theoretical foundation.

In other words, the foundation of anthropology is man himself, not as the object of practical knowledge, but as a practical organism producing knowledge as a moment of *praxis* (action). And the reintegration of man as a concrete existence into the core of anthropology, as its constant support, appears necessarily as a stage in the process of philosophy's "becoming-the-world." In this sense the foundation of anthropology cannot precede it (neither historically nor logically). If existence, in its free comprehension of itself, preceded the awareness of alienation or of exploitation, it would be necessary to suppose that the free development of the practical organism historically preceded its present fall and captivity. (And if this were established, the historical precedence would scarcely advance us in our comprehension, since the retrospective study of vanished societies is made today with the enlightenment furnished by technique for reconstruction and by means of the alienations which enchain us.) Or, if one insisted on a logical priority, it would be necessary to suppose that the freedom of the project could be recovered in its full reality underneath the alienations of our society and one could move dialectically from the concrete existence which understands its freedom to the various alterations which distort it in present society. This hypothesis is absurd. To be sure, man can be enslaved only if he is free. But for the historical man who knows himself, and comprehends himself, this practical freedom is grasped only as the permanent, concrete condition of his servitude; that is, across that servitude and by means of it as that which makes it possible, as its foundation.

Biographical Encyclopedia of Philosophy by Henry Thomas, Ph.D.

"It was Bernard Shaw, I believe, who observed that the earth is an insane asylum for those who have gone mad on other planets. An unbiased study of history would seem to bear out the truth of this observation. Our so-called progress of ten thousand years has merely succeeded in perfecting the tools of our destruction, from the earliest slingshot to the latest weapons for murdering our fellow men.

Fortunately, however, history has produced a succession of wise men that have devoted themselves to the healing of our diseased minds. These dedicated "physicians" in our terrestrial lunatic asylum have been our teachers and our thinkers-prophets like Moses and Isaiah who have tried to scold us out of our madness, and philosophers like Socrates and Spinoza who have attempted to guide us to a saner life."

First two paragraphs of the introduction are by the author.

THE GOVERNMENT'S METHOD

- The Great Debaters: A movie/documentary from the Jim Crow South in 1935 growing rapidly in demand as a lost puzzle piece to the intense struggle leading to the national crisis for Civil Rights in the Jim Crow South in 1955.
- This movie/documentary involved Wiley College, a black college whose debating team drew national attention as they debated Tau Kappa Gamma, Harvard University's debating team and won with the subject being: "Is Civil Disobedience a moral weapon against injustice?"

The research material for Wiley College's debate came from Mahatma Gandhi's civil disobedience against apartheid in India at relatively the same time the problem existed here. The most potent point made by the Wiley debating team was that Henry David Thoreau is the original exponent of the principles of civil disobedience on which Gandhi has based his resistance, a graduate of Harvard University, who lived a few miles down the road from where the debates were taking place.

There are two points I wish to establish from this debate at Harvard that underlie the truth presented in this book:

1. God decides who wins, and not my opponent. Why? "My opponent does not exist. He is the dissenting voice of the truth I speak." This statement was drilled into the Wiley College debate team's conscience to energize, and create the paradigm for divine justice that was possible, and necessary there, even though further impacted by the harsh suffering experienced. The Harvard debating team chose as their opposition to civil disobedience, the rule of law and the fact that the lives of Americans lost in America's protecting the civil liberties during our involvement in First World War which basis for that war was the protecting of the rule of law. The Wiley College team's contention was that an unjust law is no law at all.

2. There is nothing about democracy that allows its adherents to truthfully determine what is right or wrong, but rather our conscience, and not the rule of law. The tyranny of the majority was exposed as the results at that time in the Jim Crow South. The criminals in Texas, who couched their evil in the unjust law with the approval of democracy while murdering, were the criminals and the violators of the law. There was no rule of law.

RESOLUTION

We resolve to implement the intentions of the Life for Christ Foundation, which is incorporated with the State of New Jersey, in the interest of its citizenry. We are also resolved to have granted 501(c)(3) status as a non profit tax exempt organization. Our target at risk population will be "First Time Offenders," primarily from the public schools of Middlesex County. The concern of our interest here will be to "broker" or act as an intercessor between the school administration and guidance department as they administer justice and discipline. The police department of any of the twenty-five municipalities in Middlesex County, actuating the diversion unit's program of "Station House Adjustment" will respond as needed to the specific school in the county as called upon. We are aware that approximately half of the twenty-five municipalities in Middlesex

County have police units to work in the diversion unit involving "Station House Adjustment," the other half or approximately twelve do not. In order for us to "broker" or intercede in the positive interest of all of the community in context with the "First Offender's" future wellbeing, any record of police involvement by these youth jeopardizes their future in the following ways, as it relates to having a State Bureau of Investigation (SBI) background check in any or all of the following: (1) getting a job, (2) joining the military, (3) working anywhere involving security clearance, (4) going to college or any other State of Federally funded program where money for a scholarship is offered, (5) being stopped for a minor traffic violation, (6) possibly airport clearance for air travel, (7) applying for driver's license, (8) receiving a contract or trying out for professional sports, (9) volunteering for any number of community interests where reputation, integrity, and character are essential, and these are just a few. We intend to intercede and "broker" with the parties mentioned above as an advocate, legally as we shall mention below, so no official report will be made of the provocation that would jeopardize the record of the "First Offender," and their responsibility for taking care of themselves in the future, and not become a tax burden in prison, or on welfare believing that life has dealt with him or her in an unjust manner. Blame society and its laws (The *Ten Commandments* corroborate them as being in violation for not obeying the Word of God.).

When we mention being a "broker," intermediary, intercessor, or an advocate for the accused, this is the crux of our program and objective as follows:

(1) The urgency of our mission is highlighted by the first offender's condition of vulnerability, being emotionally and mentally handicapped by flawed reasoning, and a misconception of the divine origin of justice, (2) Lack of parental education, discipline, responsibility, and supervision, (3) We ask, is the Word of God directly applicable to this most at risk group that will be lost with a lifetime of misery and failure, beginning at this very juncture in their lives that we plan to be involved with? We say yes. These are future leaders, mothers, fathers, hopefully taxpayers, lawmakers, teachers, preachers, Judges, and business persons.

Municipalities in Middlesex County have this particular diversion program operating. The lapse of time between the "informal diversion" program of the county and the next time the first offender gets into trouble, leading to the "Formal Juvenile Justice System Process" is very crucial to all the community and the government of Middlesex County.

EXTENT AND NATURE OF NEED:

We consider it a benefit to the first offender as a result of him, or her, not having their name entered into the "Formal Juvenile Justice System Process." Even so, this is only one side of the coin. There is a wide range of advantages and benefits accruing from informal diversion as we have recommended here such as, (1) Reducing community tension and disorder, (2) Reducing the extent of need, and the nature of need, (3) Release of policemen needed in several other areas of community unrest involving serious criminal activity, (4) Much sought after ways and means to reduce the frightening burden of taxes on our citizenry, and (5) Assisting in the overall lofty and worthy goals and objectives of the elected government officials of the great County of Middlesex.

MODUS OPERANDI

As clearly as it would seem acceptable to receive money from any level of government that taxes the general public, we would not be able to speak of the basic problem of these first offenders. We are convinced that they have violated the laws of the *Ten Commandments*, that are given to us from God, and because of separation of church and state violations, resulting in legislation and judgments handed down by the U. S. Supreme Court, any complaint from a taxpayer could result in the suspension of the advocate's efforts, which are specifically designed to bring true Justice between all parties involved, the violator, the violated, and the criminal justice system.

Any government that takes a youth first offender into custody, and declares no responsibility, either from a parent/guardian, or some other form of positive guiding authority, with a purpose of preventing the precise cause or reason for that violation, is a part of the problem, rather than the solution.

We imagine a contradictory scenario here: We'll use the prosecutor in any legal or legislative jurisdiction in Middlesex County. Based upon the punitive long lasting, possibly fatal results, many first offenders commit suicide experiencing the emotional trauma of being put in a cold dark cell block of steel bars and rough cement, sometimes with no windows or light to the outside, for what might seem like a much longer period of time than one who has their freedom would image, and feeling trapped, or worse entrapped. In their mind, to kill themselves gets even with "the system" that entrapped them, possibly including everyone in authority who made no effort to listen, or perhaps at least give them an opportunity to explain their mistake, this includes their parents, who under these desperate frightening circumstances, becomes a part of those in authority, "The System." That first contact a first offender has with "booking," without a trial or formal adjudication of guilt regardless how minor, or incorrect the charges or allegations might turn out to be, can result in a wasted life, seen only by the family of the youth. The community only sees this from shocking headlines like those of Omar Tindell (Front page, *Newark Star Ledger* - Friday, July 22, 2005: "A murder suspect's relentless record.")

This is an apparent contradiction, I say apparent or supposed contradiction, rather than contrived or conspired. I would never say that these results are intended, or even ever thought about in their resulting reality. But the truth is, they happen, over and over again in the everyday life of our community, involving minority youth from financially disadvantaged families who are feeling the same effects from "The System" that "Mary" or "Kevin" is feeling after being "booked" for an alleged offense in school.

We understand the very worthy efforts the diversion program funded by the Juvenile Justice Commission and the County Youth Commission is making in this area. The truth is there are far too many minority youth slipping through the cracks, which we might only see again in the headlines, such as Omar Tindell, (used several aliases) who slipped through "The System" after being arrested eight (8) times on different criminal charges. The ninth time it was for the shooting death of Newark Special Police Officer Dwayne Reeves on July 18, 2005.

Our position as *broker* or *advocate* seems frivolous, or even as an interference until we read the scary trail of violence and death as in the case of Omar Tindell. This apparent, or real wall of separation, if you get the facts correctly, is set between the first offender and the broker or advocate so that after the first offender is *booked* and in the process of being brought to justice, any real challenging support for due process or probable cause, or equal protection of the law, is in violation, if God is mentioned in any way by the broker or advocate or the organization they represent. Our facts tell us that there can be no real Justice if God is not mentioned, and if in fact the first offender is being brought to Justice based on the laws of God, the *Ten Commandments*.

THE THEOLOGICAL METHOD

"It may be seen that the church, which is the context for Christian nurture, is the bearer of redemptive activity which the members have experienced within it. This activity is the *Kerygma*, which forms the church and is formed by it. The *Kerygma* yields teaching, expressed in the words of the confessions and the activity of the sacraments, intellectualized in doctrine, and made relevant in the immediate situation in the terms of ethics. The *Kerygma* further yields teaching through fellowship—explaining the redemptive experience, nurturing children, and strengthening the community for witnessing in the world."

Robert C. Worley, *Preaching and Teaching in the Early Church*, excerpt: Drew University Dissertation: *To Increase the Congregation's Understanding of Christian Discipleship* by Dr. M. J. Austin—page 12.

It ought not to ever leave the reader's mind here that the story of salvation that Conzelman states very significantly in his book, *The Theology of St. Luke*, separates the "period of Israel," the ministry of Jesus Christ, and that of the *ecclesia pressa* or the church in time leading toward the *Parousia* or the of end time, the consummation of God's will in time. But in fact all these epochs, if they can be called this, are serving to accomplish the same end and so they represent a different period in time and a different method, rather than a change of direction or of purpose.

The call was to Abraham, he responded as the father of the faith, the beginning of a people of a covenant that carried with it a promise that would, in spite of their efforts, or the lack of same, reveal ultimately, the promise to Abraham in the covenant.
Conzelman puts it this way:

"The extent of this revelation is determined not by speculation but by soteriology. Plan and promise correspond (Acts 3:18) for the latter is made possible only by the former. This means that fulfillment is certain."

Hans Conzelman: *The Theology of St. Luke*, excerpt: Dissertation: Drew University: *To Increase the Congregation's Understanding of Christian Discipleship* by Dr. M. J. Austin—page 14

Although the two volume work of Luke (which includes Acts), is accurately concerned with the church, it is in relation to the work (method) of the church for the salvation of individuals that the church is emphasized. The purpose of Luke's theology is to speak to the issue of this time which is a delayed eschaton (a delay of the full blown Spirit of God actualizing His Kingdom in its intended perfection, in this world as we know it, and understand it, thus the title and subject of the book) and the need of a new way of life to cope with the dilemma. (Which every human being born of a woman, including Jesus Christ who overcame this world, must experience as He did in order to be saved from an eventual eternal spiritual death.)

Conzelman explains it this way:
    "The real problems which are treated first and foremost are those which arise from the situation of the church in the continuing life of the world. Besides the regulation of everyday life, the main concern is with the Christian's behavior in persecution."
    The above excerpt, including the quotation from Hans Conzelman, is taken from the doctoral dissertation of Dr. Austin—Page 21.

THE THEOLOGICAL POINT OF VIEW
THE FALLEN NATURE OF MANKIND
    It would be very helpful if laymen understood *the fall* of mankind. This explanation is found in Genesis of our Bible, the third chapter. Also, it would be helpful if laymen understood why God felt the need to state in the *Ten Commandments* what the result of *the fall* was on our nature, from what it has been, and was suppose to remain. The story of the *Ten Commandments*, or the laws are found in Exodus the twentieth chapter. Following on from those helpful observations, suppose we take the weight of responsibility for laymen understanding all this and putting it on the pastor or minister of all Christian Churches, Rabbis in synagogues, and Imams in mosques, and so on. Let's look at the Law that God gave in the *Ten Commandments*. Suppose each group of denominational leaders, Rabbis, Imams, and Christian pastors, went to the example in each faith and explained how Moses for the Rabbis, Muhammad for the Muslims, and Jesus Christ for the Christians, understood, and kept the Law of the *Ten Commandments*.
    Since I am a Christian, I will look at Jesus and see how He kept the Law, or the *Ten Commandments*. Before I do that, it is only fair to review why God threw Adam and Eve out of the Garden, resulting in the *fall* of human nature, or mankind, and why it was necessary for the Law, or The Ten commandments. When we look closely at Matthew the entire fifth chapter, considered to be Jesus' only sermon to us. If we obeyed His teachings we would behave as though we were still in the Garden of Eden with God's presence and blessings. Following from that conclusion, we might say that if we could see Jesus as our Savior, as God intended Him to be, and behaved like He did while He

was with us in body, we would bring the Kingdom of God back to earth as it was before the *fall* of our nature, our kind. Then the Spirit of God would move throughout the earth as it did in Creation, rather than with just some of us and just some times as we seek His presence.

There is one other obligation to keeping the Law, or the *Ten Commandments* necessary to bring the Kingdom of God back to earth. This Scripture and story from Jesus comes from Matthew, the entire twenty-fifth chapter with emphasis beginning with verse thirty-one. Jesus' parables here are not only self explanatory, but judgmental by our either having kept the Law or having violated it.

I am going to make another observation in conclusion regarding this matter. With all of the prophecies of Jesus' coming, the Messiah, after thirteen hundred years of waiting and wishing, why was He not recognized, except by the three wise men, kings of foreign lands, and a few local people, Simeon, a devout man, and believe Annah, a prophetess? What would the outcome be of Jesus coming back a second time and not being recognized any more than He was the first time? Judgment of God upon earth, His kingdom that has been mistaken for evil goings on.

A LETTER TO CHURCHES, SYNAGOGUES & MOSQUES FROM DR. MILES J. AUSTIN

The focal point at present is the interaction with the *first time offender* of the criminal justice system. This procedure involves contacting the parent or guardian, the defense attorney, the prosecutor, and the judge and court of jurisdiction. The initial process will be complete when the judge defers sentencing and agrees to allow time for counseling, hopefully, with the accused never committing another offense.

The urgency and significance of this program is based upon the widespread breakdown of the family structure from what we in America have come to know and appreciate. The segment of our population that we are targeting is perhaps the most acceptable to our efforts and the most collectively salvageable group in our society.

The symbolism is great with the potential thought of another "Great Awakening" for the start of the new millennium. The "Release to the Captives" counseling model that we will use has proven to be capable of awakening within those convicted persons, or in this case, those arrested for the first time, a definitive admission of a kind of repentance. We have found that this "repentance" that we speak of comes from their having underestimated the complexity of the workings of the criminal justice system to a degree that they never intended, and in many cases, if possible, they would alter their actions if given another chance to do so. This new found understanding that the counseled has acquired sounds like the repentance of a person who has listened to a sermon or the instructions of a Sunday Church School teacher. Nevertheless, in this case, although the Scriptures from the Bible were never mentioned directly, as in the case of "Alcoholics Anonymous," and "Narcotics Anonymous," reference is made to the "Creator of the universe." The information in the counseling booklet, *Release to the Captives*, is based upon the same phrases and terminology that the "first offender" has heard from birth, only now, he or she sees how their responses to critical events in their everyday lives, usually under stress, operating as a physical entity, in a physical world, was never explained as having a negative effect as now it has come to their attention, with drastic results.

The word of God says "train up a child in the way he should go, and when they are old they will not depart from it." Proverbs 22:6 I mention a watershed of symbolisms here in connection with the "Great Awakening" effect. These young people are being prepared to go before a judge to have explained to them their faults. No civil or criminal magistrate is capable of producing this needed correction. Jesus Christ stood before a criminal magistrate for all humankind for all time. In my "In-Depth Statement of Principle and Action," I state, "The State, in its effort, and in fact its legislative mandate, has no power to correct except it comes from God." Yes, there is and should be separation between church and state, but there can be no separation or difference between the Truth in God's efforts to "correct" and that of the state.

There is a Truth in God, or a reality in God, which every man born of woman must acknowledge if he or she is to be saved from the negative realities of the material and physical world we live in. The truth here in this case of the *first offender*, or the last offender for that matter, they must be able to establish in their mind that an offense against another human being, created by God, is an offense against God. To explain it, as we acknowledge with our carnal minds and physical senses, if we have been offended by another human being, our only right response is here explained by our Lord and Savior, Jesus Christ, "But I say unto you, that ye resist not evil; but whosoever shall smite thee on thy right cheek, turn to him the other also, et al." "But I say unto you love your enemies, bless them that curse you, do good to them that hate you, and pray for them that despitefully use you, that you be the children of your Father which is in Heaven," (Matthew 5:39, 44-45).

The offenses of which we speak are endemic to man. I John 1:10 says, "If we say we have not sinned, we make Him a liar, and His word is not in us." These young people who are preparing to go before a criminal magistrate, should not have to be subjected to this kind of worldly justice when there is the Truth of God to save to the utmost, which is much more acceptable and powerful. "For God has not given us the spirit of fear, but of power, and love, and of a sound mind. Be not thou therefore ashamed of the testimony of our Lord, nor of me his prisoner; but be thou partaker of the afflictions of the Gospel according to the power of God," (II Timothy 1:7-8). "For Christ is the end of the Law for righteousness to everyone that believeth," (Romans 10:4). "Ye are of God, little children, because greater is He that is in you, than he that is in the world," (I John 4:4).

I say this is the most optimistically salvageable group in our society because they are idealistic. They have the high hopes of the truly "Great Society." They have not yet given up hope. They have not yet completely made up their minds about what is right with the world and what is wrong with it. Perhaps this is why we say they think they are immortal, and that nothing in the world can happen to them.

In the Book of Philemon there is the great story, relevant here, of Onesimus being taken away to prison for having broken the criminal laws of his time, only to meet Apostle Paul there in chains. Paul had broken the laws that bind men, not those based upon God's laws that make men free. Based upon the same objective that the Life for Christ Foundation has set out to accomplish, Paul is confident that Philemon will accept his recommendation as stated in Chapter One, verse fifteen, "For perhaps he therefore departed for a season, that thou shouldest receive him forever. Not now as a servant, but above a servant, a brother beloved." There can be no greater parallel between our efforts than those of Paul here. What do we say to the judge on their behalf? "Let my people go, that they may hold a feast unto me in the wilderness," (Exodus 5:1).

This is just one of the "fronts" that Satan has chosen to wage his war for the souls of God's children, and which Jesus Christ, our Savior points out in Matthew 12:31 forward. If the Word of God is true, and we know it is, we failed this segment of our population when we did not train them up in the way they should go in the first place, so they would not have to depart for a season at this time. Let us not fail them a second time as we have been given this another great opportunity, filled with hope and optimism.

Chapter Fourteen

Several Excerpts from Books and Their Authors

The line of distinction between professing Christians and the ungodly is now hardly distinguishable. Church members love what the world loves, and are ready to join them; and Satan determines to unite them in one body and thus strengthen their cause by sweeping all into the ranks of spiritualism. Papists who boast of miracles as a certain mark of the true church will be readily deceived by this wonder-working power; and Protestants, having cast away the shield of truth, will also be deluded. Papists, Protestants, and wordlings will alike accept the form of Godliness without power, and they will see in this union a grand movement for the conversion of the world, and the ushering in the long-expected millennium.

The Great Controversy between Christ and Satan
E. G. White
The Second Edition
Pilgrim Books, Page 300
RELYING UPON A SUPER HELPER
"The Church teaches dependence on one who adjusted himself to the purposes of God as he was given to understand it and who therefore is able to help others. Christ was a God-centered person who inspired confidence in others that he could and would deliver them from their moral defects and personality infirmities. He spoke with the voice and experience of authority, as one who was not a

channel but as a source of truth and the enrichment of life. The hopeless who came into contact with him were made hopeful; sinners sought and received forgiveness under his guidance; the mentally deranged were returned to normalcy. He gave zest to living."

The Church and Psychotherapy
Karl R. Stolz
Abingdon-Cokesbury Press, Page 83
"Until the second half of the nineteenth century, persons who imitated illness - that is, who claimed to be sick without being able to convince their physician that they suffered from bona fide illnesses - were regarded as faking illness and were called malingerers; those who imitated medical practitioners - that is who claimed to heal the sick without being able to convince medical authorities that they were bona fide physicians - were regarded as impostors, and were called quacks."

The Myth of Mental Illness
Foundation of a Theory of Personal Conduct
Thomas S. Szasz, M.D.
Revised Edition
Perennial Publisher
An Imprint of Harper Collins Publishers, Pages IX, X

A REVOLUTION IS A FUNDAMENTAL CHANGE:

"A paradigm shift is the way a person views and interacts with his or her world. According to years' worth of data collected by George Barna, the Church is undergoing the biggest revolution of our time.

For thousands of years, Christians have been inventing church, but neglecting to be the Church Christ commissioned. Droves of committed believers are foregoing Sunday mornings to live a 24/7 faith unfettered by the clutter and bureaucracy within the church walls.

In stark contrast to the stuffy, formulaic religiosity sometimes found in the established church and the feel-good, invent-your-own spirituality, the Revolution is casting off anything that hinders a full, vibrant life of discipleship to Christ.

Get used to the fact that your life is lived in the context of warfare. Every breath you take is an act of war. To survive and thrive in the midst of the spiritual battle in which you live, seek a faith context and experience that will enhance your capacity to be Christ-like. This mission demands single-minded commitment and a disregard for the criticisms of those who lack the same dedication to the cause of Christ. You answer to only one Commander in Chief, and only you will give an explanation for your choices. Do whatever you have to do to prove that you fear God, you love Him, and you serve Him—yes, that you live only for Him."

That Is the Commitment of a Revolutionary Revolution
George Barna
TYNDALE HOUSE PUBLISHERS, INC.
CAROL STREAM, ILLINOIS 2005 - Page: Book cover panel, and pp. 26-27

"The rejection of intelligent design in the evolution debate is grounded in the claim that there is no God. Because they have no proof that there is no God their claims are merely assertions. The truth is that there is not a God who is a person like you and me. That may be. But there is significance and meaning and direction in our lives all the same. Perhaps that meaning is simply built into the hidden structure of the universe. But of course that may be what God is - the hidden unfolding of meaning in the universe. As a definition of God, that will do.

Can one have a personal relationship with the workings of history? That is a harder question. God in the Bible is not just destiny for an individual life or history for a people or humanity as a whole. God is a relationship to something like a person. In the New Testament, that person is Jesus. In the Old Testament as well, the moral process in history is not indifferent to human beings.

But this belief is not in the supernatural. It is not a belief in God who exists as a being. It is not an acceptance of either the Old or New Testament accounts of who God is.

This is a belief that the secular voter can accept, indeed accepts already. Perhaps in this way, the secular voter can participate in American religious democracy. The word God need not be a fairy tale when understood this way. Nor need the use of the word of God, in the sense used here, grant political power to certain religious and political groups."

THE GREATEST CHALLENGE TO RELIGIOUS DEMOCRACY WILL BE TO BRING ABOUT RELIGIOUS RENEWAL IN AMERICAN POLITICAL LIFE.

American Religious Democracy
Coming to Terms with the End of Secular Politics
Bruce Ledewitz,
Praeger, Westport, Connecticut, London Pages 195, 199, 200
"Support of unborn children has long been the cornerstone issue of the religious Right. But with the advance of technology and medicine, there are a host of new and novel life issues confronting our government. Technology is presenting moral and ethical questions that were not even contemplated when the Pro-Life movement began in the 1970s. But the heart of the matter remains unchanged: How do we as Bible-believing Christians uphold the sanctity of human life? What should be our policy objectives in 2008 and beyond? What are the personal steps we must take to truly build a life-honoring culture?

The challenge and mandate for us is to establish a consistent, principled pro-life position, that we can apply across the board to all issues. This will not only help us evaluate candidates for the nation's highest offices and to give them guidelines for future polices, BUT IT WILL ALSO EQUIP ALL OF US WITH A PRACTICAL GUIDE IN OUR QUEST TO ADVANCE A CULTURE OF LIFE.... If we don't define where we stand, we will find ourselves caught flat-footed by new technologies that effect how life is created, altered, and destroyed."

Personal Faith, Public Policy
Harry R. Jackson Jr., and Tony Perkins
Front Line, A Strang Company
600 Rinehart Road, Lake Mary, FL 32746 Pages 64-65
- Revelations 1:17: "Write the things which thou has seen, and the things which are, and the things that shall be hereafter."
- Albert Schweitzer: To be glad instruments of God's love in this imperfect world is the service to which men are called, and it forms a preparatory stage to this bliss that awaits them in the perfected world, the Kingdom of God.
- Classical utilitarians, Bentham and Mills: *Ethics and Morals.*

I) The good of society is the sum of the happiness of the individuals in that society.

II) The purpose of morality is promotion of the good of society.

III) A moral principle is ideal if and only if universal conformity to it would maximize the good of society.

IV) Universal conformity to the principle of utility ("Act always so as to maximize total net balance of pleasure and pains) would maximize the good of society.

Introduction Page VIII

God Is Back
How the Global Revival of Faith Is Changing the World
John Micklethwait and Adrian Wooldridge
The Battle for Modernity

"Ever since the Enlightenment, there has been a schism in Western thought over the relationship between religion and modernity. Europeans on the whole, have assumed that modernity would marginalize religion: Americans, in the main, have assumed that the two things can thrive together.

This schism goes back to the modern world's two founding revolutions. The French and American Revolutions were both the offspring of the Enlightenment, but with very different views of the role that religion should play in reason's glorious republic. In France, the revolutionaries despised religion as a tool of the ancient regime. By contrast, America's founding fathers took a more benign view of religion. They divided church from state not least to protect the former from the latter," (page 9).

"Almost everywhere you look, from the suburbs of Dallas, to the slums of Sao Paulo, to the back streets of Bradford, you can see religion returning to public life. Most dramatically, Americans and their allies would not be dying in Iraq and Afghanistan had nineteen young Muslims not attacked the United States on September 11, 2001. America's next war could be against the Islamic Republic of Iran—or it could it be dragged into a spat in Pakistan, where religious fanatics are determined to seize the country's nuclear weapons, or perhaps in West Africa, where there is a monumental clash between Evangelical Christianity surging northward and Fundamentalist Islam heading south. Indeed, there are potential battlegrounds all around Islam's southern perimeter, along the tenth parallel stretching through Sudan to the Philippines. Nor is it just a matter of Christians and Muslims. In Myanmar (Burma), Buddhist monks nearly brought down an evil regime; in Sri Lanka, they have prolonged a bloody conflict with Hindu Tamils," (page 13).

OUT OF THE CLOSET, INTO THE CHURCH

"The prospect of homosexual unions is unpopular with most religious people pretty much everywhere. Homosexuality, even between consenting adults, is illegal in most Muslim countries, including those that are generally tolerant of gays…. For instance, the biggest rally in Spain before the 2008 election was a 'Christian Family Day' that drew 150,000 people to Madrid and featured Spain's Catholic bishops tearing into the permissive policies of the socialist prime minister, Jose Luis Rodriguez Zapatero. The bishops failed to oust Zapatero, but it was an impressive display of power." Much of the fury against Gene Robinson's ordination came from Africa, where Anglicanism is a much more combative creed. The Archbishop of Kenya spoke of "a devil" entering the church; his counterpart in Nigeria describes gays "as lower than dogs." Some African churches broke their ties with the Episcopal Church as a whole; others have ruled out the American parishes that accepted gay marriage. Some two hundred African and Asian bishops refused to attend the 2008 synod, if only because some American bishops (though not Robinson) would be there. They have also gone on the offensive, offering shelter to disgruntled American parishes."

"All the same, there is something a little odd about well-heeled clergymen from suburban Virginia, where sports utility vehicles are standard issue, bowing the knee to bishops in Uganda, where people get by on a dollar a day." "There was a time when liberal Episcopalians were all for listening to the voices of the developing world, while their conservative brethren were not sure. Now, the reverse is true."

Matthew 25

NETWORK
ABOUT US

"Truly I tell you, whatever you do for the least of these brothers and sisters, you did it for me," verse 25:40.

Matthew 25 Network is a growing community of Christians who insist on a new kind of Christian engagement in our nation's political process. The core of our political passion rises from Matthew 25:40, in which Jesus tells his followers, "I tell you the truth, as you did it to one of the least of these my brothers, you did it to me." Out of this political passion, the Matthew 25 Network advocates for the public policies that stand for the least of these and to support the political leaders who will champion these policies.

Matthew 25 Network is committed to thoughtful dialogue and purposeful action. We reflect seriously on the words of Jesus and the implications of His teachings on our role as citizens in a diverse democracy. Matthew 25 org will serve as a new voice for Christian Thinkers—including pastors, theologians, seminarians, and other contributors—to explore how theological principles could inform public policy positions. As a forum of thinkers, we encourage lively debate. Our connecting common thread is our belief that we must engage the political process as citizens in support of public policy that supports the common good and justice for the least of these.

The Matthew 25 Network actively pursues an assertive engagement with our nation's political process. In line with this fundamental mission, the Matthew 25 Network will take stands on major policy debates and track progress on legislative priorities. We seek out political leaders who also stands for the "least of these" to endorse and will rally resources to get these leaders elected. We are proud that our first political endorsement was for Barack Obama for President.

The Matthew 25 Network is sensitive to the fact that Christianity has at time been used in our nation's politics as a weapon of division and fear. However, our Christianity is one of hope, compassion, and accepting community. We recognize and affirm the freedom of religion established in the same *Bill of Rights* that permits our participation in government. E Pluribus Unum, out of many, One: we work from our many beliefs towards one peaceful and just nation. "With malice toward none: with charity for all; with firmness in the right, as God gives us to see the right, [we strive] to finish the work we are in; to bind up the nation's wounds; to care for him who shall have borne the battle, and for his widow, and his orphan—to do all which may achieve and cherish a just and lasting peace, among ourselves, and with all nations"

Chapter Fifteen

The Basic Significance of The Main
Components of the Grant Applications

POSITIVE ACTIONS OFFSETTING THE NEGATIVE IMPACT
FACTORS:

The US Senate and House of Representative, on September 7, 1974, enacted the "Juvenile Justice and Delinquency Prevention Act of 1974" with an annual analysis and evaluation, submitted to the President and Congress. The U. S. Justice Department shall administer and implement the Federal legislation. (2) "The Justice Policy Institute" that has researched the conclusion that securely confining juveniles results in irreparable and irreversible psychological damage, and does not reduce recidivism rates. (3) Minority Concerns Committee of the New Jersey Administrative Offices of the Courts "Minority Concerns" and DMC, or Disproportionate Minority Confinement. (4) The Attorney General's Office of the State of New Jersey's "Station House Adjustment of Juvenile Delinquency Offenses" with special emphasis on "Disproportionate Minority Confinement" referenced in the laws of the 1974 Juvenile Justice Act of the U. S. Congress. (5) 2003-2004 Middlesex County Comprehensive Youth Services Planning Guide: Re: Disproportionate Minority Confinement.

If sought, the facts are available, these confirming the same hierarchy of legislated concerns from the Congress of the United States to the local County government focused on Human Resources, or the Welfare Departments, and the Boards of Education. Point being made, hopefully, we focus here of the impact of "No Child Left Behind" of the U.S. Department of Education.

The "Gap in the Delivery of Service" that we propose to fill is seen in the tension between the security departments of the local school districts, and the pressure of the administrators to adhere to the "No Child Left Behind" in order to both meet education requirements, and to improve discipline along with assuring acceptable behavior in the classroom. In other words, violators of the school's regulations for behavior lower the ranking of that district, resulting in the security department as being the culprit.

Presently, I am seeking legislation that I am pretty sure exist from discussions with school educators, to the effect that each school principal must refer a student suspended for a serious period of time to be involved in therapeutic counseling as has been initiated and implemented in Hackensack, New Jersey.

VERY IMPORTANT OR THERE WILL BE OBSTACLES PROBABLY TOO SEVERE TO OVERCOME!

We must draft this proposal/grant so that the implementation of the mandates enumerated therein become incumbent on those elected by the citizens of Middlesex County, the State of New Jersey, including the Administrative Offices of the Courts, and the U.S. Congress. In other words, Non Profit 501(c)(3) efforts more closely represent the confirmed answer to the problems verified by the U.S. Internal Revenue Service and is therefore required for Tax Exempt Status. These efforts more closely represent the saving of taxpayer dollars at this time of severe economic depression affecting everyone at all levels of society.

KEYNOTE: THE GROUNDWORK APPROACH AND THE SUCCESS THEREOF WILL REST WITH THE PROGRESSIVE PHILOSOPHICAL APPROACH TO GOVERNMENT EX-PRESSED IN THE LEADERSHIP OF PRESIDENT BARACK OBAMA.

Index

A

Alcohol & Narcotic Anonymous 17, 34, 36, 56, 58, 59, 85, 168, 172

Abington Press 200

Judge Ackerman 8, 158

Act of God 86

Acts 102, 466

Adolescent 15, 90

Joseph Addison Alexander 186

J. A. Alexander 4, 196

Leona Allen 24, 159, 160

American Red Cross 12, 156

Anesthesia 197

Anthropology 235

Apocalyptical 174, 175

Apocalypticism 54, 55, 174, 175

Thomas Aquinas 18

Ann Appleby 157, 158

Jennifer Austin 157, 158

Miles Austin, Jr. 157, 158

Miles Austin, III 157, 158

B

Backsliding 114
Baumgartner XIII
George Barna 190, 213, 247
George Bush 74, 220
Bayside State Prison XXII
Being and Nothingness 198
Bethel Baptist Church .... XXII, 8, 117, 150, 151, 157, 168
Bill of Rights 16, 82, 89, 230
Brown vs. Board of Education 148
Black Bourgeoisie 147
Black Muslims 143
Black People .... XX, 215
Black Theology 119, 140, 215
Bonhoeffer 17, 24, 93, 119, 170
Born Again 114, 120, 121
Taylor Branch 91
Brooks 30
Devon Brown 48

C

Carter 61
Cedar Knolls 140
Cheap Grace 170
Chesterton 98, 150, 159
Cho 27, 162, 167, 176, 189
Jesus Christ .... IX, X, XVI, XX, XXI, XXIII, XXIV, 3, 4, 10, 11, 13, 18, 25, 26, 50, 51, 53, 58, 68, 70, 71, 77, 80, 81, 86, 91, 93, 94, 102, 104, 108, 109, 115, 128, 137, 155, 158, 159
Christianity IX
Church .... X, 11, 24, 26, 50, 54, 58, 59, 68, 71, 77, 79, 84, 89, 96,

	103, 104, 112, 141, 154, 157, 160, 170
Church and State	XII, 24, 25, 54, 55, 82, 89, 90
Circus	191
Civil Disobedience	236
Civil Rights Act	97, 99, 236
Civil War	99
Cline	19, 79
CNN	12, 23, 219, 222
Conviction War	87
Concrete Existence	198
Corley	XIII
King Constantine	110, 211
Hanz Conzelman	70, 241, 242
Corinthians	XVI, 2, 66, 106, 109, 113, 116, 117, 121, 129, 134
Bill Cosby	11
Counter Culture	52, 53, 54, 58, 59, 83, 97, 104, 105
Steven R. Covey	22
Critique of Dialectic Reason	233, 234, 235
Jim Crow	236
Mario Cuomo	74, 83, 84, 89

D

Thomas Dawson, Jr.	227
Charles Darwin	85, 235
Decalogue	XV, 15, 104, 110
Declaration of Independence	73, 98, 99
Dice	XIII
Discipleship	70
Disproportionate Minority Confinement	253
Fredrick Douglas	99
Drew University	4, 24, 52, 76, 93, 94, 111, 119, 141, 142, 150, 161, 170, 172, 180, 190, 209, 210, 212, 241

E

East Jersey State Prison .... XXI, 37
Ecumenical Church Movement 84
Edison High School............................ 180
Egypt... 103
E. Franklin Frazier 143, 147
Emancipation Proclamation 146
NG XIII
England 76, 190
Ephesians...................................... XI, XVI, XXIII, 51,
68, 93, 95, 106
Eschatology 54, 146, 212
Essien-Udom 143, 149
Evangelical.................................... 23, 25
Existentialism................................. 92, 93, 105, 198,
223, 233
Exodus.. 103, 118, 120
Ezekiel 25

F

Fall... XVI, 2, 4, 60, 190,
115, 129, 174, 175,
187, 214, 215
Faith Hope Baptist Church 172
Jerry Falwell................................. 23, 25
First Baptist Church of Woodbine, NJ... 227
Florida A&M University..................... XX
Foundation of Anthropology 235
Founders' Library............................ 140
Sigmund Freud 17, 18, 35
Frontal Lobotomy............................ 197

G

Galatians 59, 72
Gandhi....................................... 90, 91, 94, 148,
236, 237
Gays... 58
Genesis .... XVI, 57, 60, 174
Great Controversy........................... 150, 246
Greater First Baptist Church................ 52, 146, 170, 209,
212, 214

H

Hailes XIII
Harvard University 236
Peter C. Harvey 73
Kyle Haselden 142, 144, 145
Hebrews 2, 7, 64, 66, 109,
110, 111, 129, 135
Charles Holt .... XIII, 188, 196
Hallman XIII
Hughes XIII
Homosexuals 58, 59
Hooper 44
Hosea 27, 60, 62, 201
Howard University 7, 51, 52, 140,
161, 170, 206, 212,
214
Gloria Ward Howe 74, 91, 115, 161
Hunter College 158

I

Isaiah 23, 56, 57, 73,
100, 103, 141, 165

J

Harry R. Jackson 249
Jeremiah 57, 165
Jim Crow South 236
Job 137
John .... XI, XIX, 2, 5, 12,
25, 50, 62, 63, 64,
65, 67, 69, 73, 93,
100, 101, 107, 120,
121, 128, 133, 160,
171
Lyndon Johnson 220
Joshua 153
July 4th 98

K

Kierkegaard 191
Kearney, NJ 9
John F. Kennedy 99, 219

Kerugma 241
Martin Luther King 24, 80, 91, 94, 99,
132, 143, 147, 148,
159, 160, 161, 206,
219, 222, 223, 230
King Constantine 110
Kingdom of God .... XI, XIX, XX, XXI,
3, 5, 6, 11, 12,
24, 25, 50, 51, 52,
58, 60, 62, 65, 69,
70, 76, 77, 79, 81,
88, 94, 104, 105,
108, 109, 113, 115,
117, 175, 189, 224
Kingdom of Israel 103, 112, 135
Rudyard Kipling 76, 92, 99, 115
Elisabeth Kuebler Ross .... X, 63, 106, 107,
167, 173, 186, 194,
223

L
Bruce Ledewitz 249
Lesbians 58
George Liele 144
C. Eric Lincoln 143
Life For Christ Foundation .... XVII, XXII, 8, 9,
16, 24, 26, 51, 54,
58, 61, 90, 117,
135, 151, 157
Luke .... XI, XXIII, 6, 11,
57, 62, 63, 94, 95,
99, 106, 112, 115,
129, 132, 160, 166,
171
Carol Lin 3, 4, 7, 9, 12, 23,
25, 209, 212, 213,
214, 215, 216, 218,
219, 221, 222, 223
Abraham Lincoln 74, 99, 146
Logan 38

M

Magna Carta 81
Malachi 79
Malcolm X 143, 219
Karl Marx.. 234, 235
Marxism... 234, 235
Matthew 25 Network........................... 251, 252
Matthew .... XI, XXI, 5, 6, 26,
53, 56, 62, 63, 64,
72, 76, 77, 79, 88,
91, 93, 94, 103,
108, 109, 111, 112,
113, 116, 117, 120,
150, 162, 166, 167,
169, 173
Benjamin E. Mays 142, 145, 146
Messenger of Allah............................... 147, 148
Metamorphosis 120
Micah... 86
John Micklethwait................................. 250
Middlesex County 123, 237, 238, 239
Milton.. 104
Miranda Ruling...................................... 61, 67, 73
Charles Clayton Morrison 53, 84, 213
Moses 103, 154, 155, 156,
223
Muhammad 110, 148, 212
Gunnar Myrdal 148
Myth of Mental Illness .... (see Dr. Szasz)

N

National Children's Rights.................... 253
Nationalist Movement........................... 148
NG .... XIII, 186, 187
New Convert 176
Newark Star Ledger.............................. X, 124, 229, 240
New York Times 156, 158
Joseph William Nicholson..................... 142, 145
Niebuhr 24, 91, 94

O

President Barack Obama	16, 229, 230, 231
Madeleine O'Hare	79, 82, 216
Onesimus	213, 245
Oppression	XIX, XXI, 55, 109, 113, 116, 118, 120, 147

P

Paradigm	7, 9, 18, 46, 47, 118, 193
Rosa Parks	148
Parousia	178
Pavlovian	19
Pentecost	XIX, 26, 56, 58, 71, 170
Peter	59, 105, 117
Philemon	213, 245
Philippians	XXIII, 6, 64, 70, 106, 126
Protestant Reformation	200
Pilgrims	74, 76, 91, 135
Colin Powell	125
Prerequisite to Discipleship	176
Proverbs	14, 15, 27, 90, 93, 105, 124, 126
Psalm	XI, 51, 69, 123, 134
Purcell	XIII

R

Christopher Reeves	3, 4, 7, 9, 10, 12, 23, 214, 215, 216, 219, 222
Dwayne Reeves	240
Revolutionary War	99
Revelations	104, 109, 112, 120, 168, 174
Rite of passage	14, 15, 16, 20, 21, 29, 49
Romans	XI, XXII, 2, 5, 25, 67, 70, 88, 106, 137, 153, 155, 165
Tim Russert	220

S

Jean Paul Sartre .... XVII, 233, 234, 235
Sartrean Approach .... XVII, 233, 234, 235
Seven Seals.. Chapter 9
Bernard Shaw.. 236
Slavery 58, 60, 110, 118
Socrates 197
Stelton Baptist Church .... XIII, 51, 56, 135,
168, 173, 196
Karl R. Stolz... 185, 247
Strict Construction............................... 92
Thomas S. Szasz.................................... 26, 34, 139, 184,
216, 221, 247

T

Tabernacle Baptist Church..................... 169
Talbot Hall... 36
Ten Commandments .... XVI, 29, 47, 54,
60, 62, 66, 72, 73,
74, 81, 82, 86, 89,
92, 95, 96, 103,
104, 124, 126
Tice... XIII
Thalamus 31
The Fall.. see "F" above
Transubstantiation................................. 200
Henry Thomas.. 236
Henry David Thoreau 148, 236
Paul Tillich... 119, 198
Timothy.. 10, 133
Mrs. Turman 226, 227, 228
Turpin... XIII

V

Rip Van Winkle...................................... 190
Velez XIII
Virginia Tech University 27
Van Houten XIII

W

Rick Warren.. 53
George Washington................................ 190

Gary Wasserman.................................. 83
Westfield, NJ..................................... XXI
E. G. White....................................... 150, 246
Adrian Wooldridge............................. 250
Woodbine, NJ.................................... XXII
Woodbridge, NJ................................. XXIII

Y
YMCA/YWCA..................................... 151

Z
Zechariah.. 24, 76

Miles J. Austin

P. O. Box 618
Edison, New Jersey 08817
Email lifeforChristfndn@yahoo.com

HOW WAS I SUPPOSED TO KNOW THAT GOD HAS CREATED A PERFECT WORLD/UNIVERSE?

MUST READ FOR:

1. Those who have said or believed that if God is loving, and has all power. There would not be so much evil in the world, such as wars, murder, poverty, and suffering.
2. Those who have said or believed that if God wanted a certain problem to be solved he would solve it Himself.
3. Those that have said or believe that if God wanted social problems such as are prevalent in our nation and were addressed during the civil rights movement to be settled He would not involve ministers or preachers of the Gospel to create violent demonstrations in the community and in the streets.
4. For politicians, lawyers, and all elected officials that have sworn to obey the laws of our nation that are based on the ten laws given to Moses by God, as they are known to repeat, "So help me God" at the end of that swearing on, with their right hand on the Bible.

5. Citizens: What is a citizen? A native, or naturalized member of a state or nation that owes allegiance to that government, and is entitled to that government's protection. For citizens who are not quite sure what kind of government to expect from those they have elected to serve them

6   Students in colleges and universities who, when asked if they might consider the possibility that there could possibly be some flaw in their human nature that could possibly be corrected through the Christian faith, or some other faith or religious training, say there is nothing wrong with them in any way, shape or form or fashion that can be changed or corrected.

7. The book explains, especially in the eleventh chapter, God's address to any problem mankind finds in his perfectly de-signed world/universe that might be summed up in title of a song: "Let there be peace on earth, and let it begin with me!"

One can never get an answer to a problem unless one knows what question to ask, and then where to look for the answer.

Miles Austin